The

Federalist Papers

Reader

The
Federalist
Papers
Reader

Frederick Quinn, Editor

preface by Warren E. Burger
foreword by A.E. Dick Howard

SEVEN LOCKS PRESS   WASHINGTON, D.C.

Library of Congress Cataloging-in-Publication Data

The Federalist papers reader / edited by Frederick Quinn ; preface by
  Warren E. Burger ; foreword by A.E. Dick Howard.
        p.   cm.
  Includes index.
  ISBN 0-929765-17-6
  1. Federalist.   I. Quinn, Frederick.
JK154.F44   1993
321.02'0973—dc20   92-36944
                                                                  CIP

Manufactured in the United States of America

Seven Locks Press
Washington, D.C.
1-800-354-5348

To Alison and Christopher

Table of Contents

Foreword

Democratization is in the air all over the world; from Albania and Brazil to Bulgaria and South Africa, fundamental questions about how to govern human society are being debated in parliament and press, among trade unionists and university students, entrepreneurs and constitutionalists.

The questions asked and the language of political discourse bear amazing similarities to those debated in America in 1787, when thirteen unruly, independent states took the radical step of uniting under an untried Constitution. Issues of separation of powers, checks and balances, the independence of the judiciary, and federalism were central to making this relatively short document both work in its immediate context and survive for over two centuries.

The Federalist Papers are both an explanation of why the Constitution emerged the way it did and, no less important, how the Founders understood human political behavior. Frederick Quinn has chosen carefully from among the original eighty-five essays, selecting twenty-three that reflect enduring wisdom about constitution writing in the contemporary world. His introductory essay, with admirable economy, frames the issues and describes the personalities, and his comments on key essays will be of value to students of the U.S. Constitution and the constitutional process in the United States or abroad.

Frederick Quinn brings unique skills to this task. As International Coordinator for the Bicentennial of the U.S. Constitution, he worked closely with former Chief Justice of the United States Warren E. Burger in advancing a global scholarly exchange among constitutionalists. As a foreign service officer and historian, he experienced firsthand the debate on basic issues of governance in embassies in Morocco, Burkina Faso, Haiti, Vietnam, Cameroon, and Czechoslovakia in times of political upheaval.

In particular, in Czechoslovakia, where he worked closely with the Charter '77 dissident community, questions of rule "by the one, the many, or the few" were active issues over which citizens died, were imprisoned, suffered deprivation of rights and property, and emerged ultimately with individual freedom and collective independence.

The Federalist Papers Reader is a timely and valuable guide for the modern reader on how James Madison, Alexander Hamilton, and John Jay interpreted the most basic issues of human politics and how, faced with perilous choices, they and the Founders established a Constitution that endures. They shaped a society that prospers, despite its imperfections, and a legal system that, flaws notwithstanding, contains the tumult of clashing factions that Madison witnessed and that have destroyed ordered government in countless states in recent history.

— **A.E. Dick Howard**
White Burkett Miller Professor
of Law and Public Affairs
University of Virginia Law School

Preface

Near the close of the Constitutional Convention of 1787, Benjamin Franklin, the elder statesman of the convention, commented to those sitting near him "that painters had found it difficult to distinguish in their art a rising sun from a setting sun." Then, while looking at the rising sun carved on the back of George Washington's chair, he stated, "I have . . . often and in the course of the session . . . looked at that behind the president without being able to tell whether it was rising or setting. But now at length I have the happiness to know that it is a rising sun and not a setting sun."

Benjamin Franklin's statement proved to be prophetic—in more ways than one. Two hundred years after the fact, it is tempting to look upon the convention and the events that followed and focus strictly on the remarkable document the delegates created—our Constitution. Having produced such a charter, the framers rightly departed from Philadelphia with the distinct impression that the sun was rising and not setting over America.

The delegates were realists, however. After having spent most of a sweltering Philadelphia summer debating behind the closed doors and sealed windows of Independence Hall, they were well aware the principles embodied in the Constitution would stimulate intense and extended debate in some of the states. Indeed, on September 17, 1787, only thirty-nine of the forty-two delegates in attendance were willing to sign the Constitution. Other respected statesmen had refused to attend the convention, perhaps the most noted being Patrick Henry, the freedom fighter from Virginia, who declined to become involved because he "smelled a rat"—a strong national government. In addition, the delegates had done more than just diverge from the "sole and express" mandate given by the Continental Congress, which had called only for a study of the existing commercial problems and possible amendments to the Articles of Confederation; no one in the Continental Congress had said anything about drafting a document constituting a new form of government.

So when the framers emerged from the convention with the Constitution, they knew the sun was also rising on a period of ratification that would be marked by significant controversy. Indeed, it was far from certain the Constitution would be ratified by the requisite number of states. When asked what the convention had created, Benjamin Franklin replied, "A republic, if you can keep it."

The Federalist Papers were written in this setting. They were drafted by three of the convention's most respected delegates—Alexander Hamilton and John Jay of New York, and James Madison of Virginia—during the ratification battle. The papers were written under the pseudonym "Publius," and the true identity of the authors was not known by the general public for decades. As was common for the era, the authors let their ideas rather than their identities do the talking.

Hamilton, Madison, and Jay wrote *The Federalist Papers* as briefs for those who were debating ratification of the Constitution. They directed their essays at the people of New York and, more specifically, at the delegates who were to attend the New York ratification convention. As such, *The Federalist Papers* were political papers. A New York newspaper published the first of *The Federalist Papers* on October 27, 1787. The authors, primarily Alexander Hamilton, subsequently made sure *The Federalist Papers* were distributed in virtually every state. Madison himself carried copies to the important ratification convention held in Richmond, Virginia.

However, Hamilton, Madison, and Jay undoubtedly wrote *The Federalist Papers* for future generations as well. Martin Diamond and others have observed that the authors of *The Federalist Papers* "looked beyond the immediate struggle and wrote with a view to influencing later generations by making their work the authoritative commentary on the meaning of the Constitution. . . . [*The Federalist*] spoke to thoughtful men then and now, with a view to permanence of its arguments."[1] Plainly the authors were writing on paper views they each had long entertained and wanted to pass on to yet unborn Americans.

Even if the extent to which *The Federalist Papers* contributed to the overall ratification process may be open to question, their subsequent impact in this and other countries is immeasurable. The Constitution sets forth the framework for the dynamic new form of government envisioned by the framers; but *The Federalist Papers* defend the framework, explain it, and fill many of the gaps left open by the charter. And even though the authors themselves certainly did not agree on all of the concepts contained in the eighty-five essays, *The Federalist Papers* elucidate the ideas and logic of three of the men who debated on the floor at Independence Hall; the essays are true constitutional commentaries and represent some of the most persuasive articles ever written about government. Logically, then, *The Federalist Papers* have become valuable tools for judges in interpreting the Constitution.

For example, beginning with the distinguished opinions of John Marshall, the Supreme Court has made clear that the Constitution serves not only as a limit on the powers of the federal government, but also as a guide to their use. When the text of the Constitution is silent or unclear on an issue, especially an issue dealing with the power of the federal government, the Supreme Court often cites *The Federalist Papers* as authority to support its decisions. Over eighty years ago Chief Justice Edward D. White wrote in *Pacific States Telephone and Telegraph Co. v. Oregon* that in ascertaining the meaning of the phrase "Republican Form of Government" found in Section 4 of Article IV of the Constitution, "The debates of the constitutional conventions and the *Federalist Papers* are of great importance, if not conclusive."[2] And, as in *Hines v. Davidowitz*, when analyzing the power of the federal government over areas such as foreign affairs, the Court looks not only at the text of the Constitution, but also to the "authors of the *Federalist Papers*."[3] In short, as Chief Justice William H. Rehnquist recognized in *Dames & Moore v. Regan*, whenever the Court is presented with a question that touches "fundamentally upon the manner in which our Republic is to be governed," it has "the benefit of commentators such as John Jay, Alexander Hamilton, and James Madison writing in the *Federalist Papers* at the Nation's very inception."[4] This is why, in the words of Justice Joseph Story, judges and historians alike view *The Federalist Papers* as "an incomparable commentary of three of the greatest statesmen of their age."[5]

After that long, hot summer in Philadelphia, Alexander Hamilton enlisted the efforts of James Madison and John Jay, and together they wrote *The Federalist Papers* in support of the Constitution. It seems only fitting that in the wake of this nation's celebration of the bicentennial of the Constitution we should read and learn more about these incomparable commentaries which support that great charter.

— **Warren E. Burger**
Chief Justice of the United States (Retired)

Editor's Preface

The origins of this study lie in the period of the Bicentennial of the U.S. Constitution, 1987–91. In a coincidence few could have anticipated, events and observances in honor of this historic document took place at a time of tremendous political upheaval in many parts of the world. Certain questions recurred in conversations with overseas jurists, constitution writers, teachers, and lawyers during that time: How do you govern a society? How do you create a constitution that works—and lasts? One era of dictators and military rulers is passing; but governments with broadly based citizen participation can be fragile institutions, prone, when challenged, to collapse into anarchy, and vulnerable to authoritarian takeovers followed by widespread citizen disenchantment with political life.

In discussions abroad, in meetings with civic leaders from other nations, and in talks in American classrooms, a frequent question was, Why has the American Constitution lasted more than two hundred years? What conceptual and structural features account for its longevity? During the bicentennial period, more than two hundred speakers went abroad to discuss constitutional subjects; the Constitution was distributed in thousands of copies and numerous languages; and law and history books, scholarly conferences, and interactive television programs involving several countries all contributed to the international traffic in constitutional ideas.

The former Chief Justice of the United States, Warren E. Burger, actively participated in these initiatives, often meeting with judges, lawyers, and students, and sharing the bicentennial commission's "history and civics lesson for America" with local and international audiences. Although each country has its unique historical, political, and legal traditions, a preoccupation with fundamental questions of governance is universal, and answering the question, What animated the framers of the Constitution? is useful for both overseas audiences, some of whom struggle with basic questions of political order, and domestic readers, who often venerate, but do not necessarily understand, the Constitution's dynamics.

The Federalist Papers, of course, provide much of the needed information, but not always in easily accessible form. Although of a high literary order and unparalleled as statements of political thought and explanations of the Constitution, they were initially works of advocacy journalism, turned out by skilled writers, often at three- or four-day intervals, to gain the important New York delegation's votes for the Constitution. James Madison wrote that "it frequently happened that whilst the printer was putting into type parts of a number, the following parts were under the pen and to be furnished in time for the press."

Nor do all of the essays written for that specific purpose in the autumn of 1787 and spring of 1788 have lasting relevance. The reasons for the failure of the Articles of Confederation are instructive to read, but are reworked and rewoven several times. Lengthy sections on the shortcomings of Greek and Roman models come close to law office history in places, and there are detailed commentaries on long-solved issues, such as the relationship of local militia to a national standing army. *The Federalist*'s case that a national government is advantageous because, among other things, it will be neither large nor costly, does not bear the test of time; nor does the argument that no Bill of Rights is needed because rights are protected adequately throughout the document and by state constitutions.

Nevertheless, the papers belong among the classics of global political thought, and modern readers will recognize the lasting appeal of the twenty-three included in this volume. A brief introduction to each of the papers collected here summarizes the content and clarifies the author's intent. The text of the papers is taken from the McLean edition of 1788, "printed and sold by J. and A. McLean, No. 41, Hanover-Square," with some modernization of spelling, punctuation, and typography. The division of authorship among Alexander Hamilton, John Jay, and James Madison is that established originally by the scholarly detective work of Professor Douglas Adair. A few paragraphs about the deficiencies of ancient republics have been deleted. Subheads have been added to more easily identify the subjects of individual papers. This accommodation for modern readers interrupts the symmetrical, meticulous structure and flow of *The Federalist*, but those who enjoy the original essays' worldview and elegant language can read them through unhindered.

Hamilton's finely honed enthusiasm, Madison's carefully wrought statements about the human condition, *The Federalist*'s hopeful vision for the new nation, and its clear arguments not only survive the test of time admirably but provide benchmarks against which future political theorists may measure the efforts of others. Even those with an aversion to hagiography will not contest Clinton Rossiter's statement that "*The Federalist* is the most important work in political science that has ever been written, or is likely to be written, in the United States. It is, indeed, the one product of the American mind that is rightly counted among the classics of political theory."[1]

"The essays were almost as important as the Constitution itself," the American historian Page Smith writes, adding, "In all arguments about the meaning or interpretation of that sometimes obscure document, they have been quoted by political scientists, judges, and lawyers as authoritative."[2] Though acknowledged as advocacy pieces, the U.S. Supreme Court has recognized *The Federalist Papers* to be an important explication of the Constitution, sufficient to impart the framers' objectives.

And so, at a time in world history when countries in Asia, Africa, Latin America, and parts of Europe are reconsidering both the ideas and structures of governance, they will find in Hamilton, Madison, and Jay thoughtful interlocutors. *The Federalist Papers'* authors were keen observers of humanity's destructive tendencies, its hopeful prospects, and the equally important task of translating ideas into practice in the enduring exercise of free people building self-government.

Acknowledgments

The Chief Justice of the United States (Retired), Warren E. Burger; Professor A.E. Dick Howard, White Burkett Miller Professor of Law and Public Affairs at the University of Virginia Law School; and Robert S. Peck, former Judicial Fellow and head of Public Education Programs for the American Bar Association, read and provided valuable comments on the manuscript. I am grateful to them and to Betty Southard Murphy of the Commission on the Bicentennial of the U.S. Constitution; Judge Charles J. Weiner of the Sixth Federal Circuit, Philadelphia, Pennsylvania; Robert A. Goldwin, former Director of Constitutional Studies of the American Enterprise Institute; and Professor John Norton Moore, Walter L. Brown Professor of Law at the University of Virginia for sharing their insights with me over several years. My thanks are due as well to Ann and Van Kirk Reeves of Paris, France; Fred G. Hilkert, M.D.; and Professor John N. Drobek of Washington University Law School, St. Louis, Missouri, for discussions of the law and its larger issues.

I want to thank Professor Eugen Weber, the Joan Palevsky Professor of Modern European History, University of California at Los Angeles, whose pioneering work, *The Western Tradition*, helped place *The Federalist Papers* in a global context; and Ambassador Thomas R. Byrne and Walter J. Shea, Chairman, Eastern Conference of Teamsters, for many interesting conversations on contemporary international political issues.

THE

FEDERALIST:

A COLLECTION

OF

ESSAYS,

WRITTEN IN FAVOUR OF THE

NEW CONSTITUTION,

AS AGREED UPON BY THE FEDERAL CONVENTION.
SEPTEMBER 17, 1787.

IN TWO VOLUMES.

VOL. I.

NEW-YORK:

PRINTED AND SOLD BY J. AND A. M'LEAN,
No. 41, HANOVER-SQUARE.
M,DCC,LXXXVIII.

Introduction

The long coastline was fair prey for foreign invaders. Roads were few, muddy when it rained, dusty otherwise. Transportation was slow and irregular, most dependable by water. The potentially prosperous, primarily agrarian economy was stagnant, owing to the recent eight-year war, and entrepreneurial people were not sure how it would improve. Scattered insurrections flared, and the prospect of angry mobs or unschooled peasants taking the law into their hands threatened whatever form of government the newly independent states selected. The central government was powerless, lacking authority to raise funds or an army, or to administer justice. Politicians debated at length whether the existing government should be patched up, or if there should be a strong president, a president and council with shared powers, or a legislature with most powers vested in it; but the discussions went nowhere.

The confederation's thirteen isolated states were in infrequent contact with one another, except for commerce along the main maritime arteries. Spanish, French, English, and other metallic coins still circulated long after the war; the Continental Congress's money was valueless. "Not worth a continental" was a popular expression. The wartime military leader, George Washington, wrote state governors in 1783 that he feared "the union cannot be of long duration, and everything must very rapidly tend to anarchy and confusion." Thomas Jefferson, then Minister to France, said, "We are the lowest and most obscure of the whole diplomatic tribe." A British cleric said Americans were "a disunited people till the end of time, suspicious and distrustful to each other, they will be divided and subdivided into little commonwealths, or principalities."

These conditions, which America faced two centuries ago, are applicable to many modern nations. *The Federalist Papers,* first published in 1787–88 in the middle of intense debates over what form the new government should take, explain how the authors of the U.S. Constitution arrived at that document. There is a congruence between basic issues of governance raised then in Philadelphia and now in Warsaw, Conakry, Brasilia, and Moscow. The questions are not rhetorical or theoretical, but are fundamental to the formation of a national government to which all citizens can subscribe, and that will endure.

If the American Revolution was a time of political upheaval, the writing and ratification of the U.S. Constitution was no less revolutionary. The Constitution's framers boldly exceeded their mandate to suggest ways of patching up the Articles of Confederation. The ratification debates required the people to decide whether they would adopt an untried form of government or hold on to an ineffectual one that was sure to result in the balkanization of the new nation. The temptation to maintain individual state sovereignty was strong, even though many conceded the necessity of regional defense treaties. If the Anti-Federalists had prevailed, the sketch in *Federalist* No. 2 of the potentially prosperous nation would have remained an exercise in mapmaking. Far from defending the status quo, *The Federalist Papers*, in measured argument, seek support for a revolutionary form of government, unknown in world history to that date.

Fortunately, the *Federalist* authors—Alexander Hamilton, John Jay, and James Madison—wrote their work at a propitious moment in American history. A few years earlier, in the shadow of the war and the British crown, a proposal for a strong central government would not have found acceptance.[1] Nor could such a concept have succeeded during the Age of Jackson, just around the corner. Its republican features, which kept the people somewhat distant from the reins of power, would have been voted down. *The Federalist Papers* thus explain a revolutionary document that faced a hotly contested ratification battle for the political soul of a nation at a critical turning point in its history.[2]

The Federalist Papers reflect the end of an era in America, a chapter that began with the Mayflower Compact of 1620 and the various covenants, declarations, and state constitutions that followed, and culminated in the Declaration of Independence and Constitution. During that period of more than a century and a half, American political thought was formulated and tried, and arguments were rehearsed and refined in press, pulpit, and legislative chamber, often to express opposition to the British crown, but also to give an expanding country a workable government. It was against such a background that *The Federalist Papers* emerged, combining the traits Robert A. Ferguson ascribes to the Constitution: "generic strength, manipulative brilliance, cunning restraint, and practical eloquence."[3]

Despite their length, the papers are remarkably concise—long enough to establish their argument and answer opponents, but free of invective, extraneous commentary, or florid embellishment. *The Federalist Papers'* grounding in eighteenth-century philosophy and economic theory is only tantalizingly suggested in brief sections seeded throughout the essays. We wish for an additional hour of tavern talk with Madison or Hamilton, or a public television interview program tying up loose ends on the origins of their ideas; but the information is not forthcoming. The authors were primarily practitioners rather than theorists, and *The Federalist Papers* were written for a specific purpose: to convince delegates to New York's ratification convention of the value of a particular course of action.

As such, the essays are a radical, revolutionary statement of well-reasoned political thought, carefully moving beyond the central ideas raised by theorists like Hume, Locke, or Montesquieu. Instead of dramatically overthrowing the old order of theory and practice, the Constitution writers, with careful study, took its best features and gave new meaning to them. As works of theory and guides for practice, the essays are more lasting than anything written by Marx, Lenin, Mao, Castro, or Metternich.

The Federalist Papers represent the most long-lived contributions of a golden age of pamphlet literature. It was a time when public service, most leaders believed, was a responsibility mandated by the Deity, and public documents often reflected a literary quality comparable to contemporary sermons or works of science, history, or political or moral thought.[4] Simultaneously there were improvements in the technology and availability of printing presses; the growth of a relatively affluent, lettered audience; and the emergence of urgent and revolutionary issues, like the coming of age of republican political thought and the question of assembling a machinery of government for the polities that had just defeated the British forces and now must govern themselves.

The Articles of Confederation

Had the Articles of Confederation not failed, there would have been no Constitution and no *Federalist Papers*. Two centuries later, it is difficult to imagine the chaotic state of America in the postrevolutionary period. A war had been won, but the eastern seaboard lay vulnerable to potential invaders. The economy was plagued by multiple currencies and tariffs; state governments were bankrupt and ineffectual; and the central government was central in name only. From 1776 to 1787 America was a loose alliance of states governed by the Articles, whose fatal flaw was that power remained with individual states. The central government could neither raise revenues nor enact legislation binding on individual states. The votes of nine of the thirteen states were required to pass laws, and a unanimous vote was necessary to effect any fundamental change in the Articles.

The central government's weakness was intentional; the American settlers had bitterly resented the British crown's power to control commerce and collect taxes. The legislative body created under the Articles was powerless, and there was no executive or judicial branch. Moreover, the thirteen states each had separate political and commercial interests, and the temporary unity forged from a decade of active hostility toward Great Britain failed to produce a national identity. Nine states had navies; seven printed their own currency; most had tariff and customs laws. New York charged duties on ships moving firewood or farm produce to and from neighboring New Jersey and Connecticut. When soldiers remarked, "New Jersey is our country," they echoed the widespread sentiment of other states.

Also contributing to political chaos in the 1780s were the insolvent state governments. Hamilton, in a stinging attack on the Articles, remarked in *Federalist* No. 9 that they encouraged "little, jealous, clashing, tumultuous commonwealths, the wretched nurseries of unceasing discord." Madison had the bankrupt state governments in mind in *Federalist* No.10 when he described the need to "secure the national councils against any danger from ... a rage for paper money, for an abolition of debts, for an equal division of property, or for any other improper or wicked project." Madison wrote on October 24, 1787, to Jefferson in France that the unstable state legislatures "contributed more to that uneasiness which produced the convention, and prepared the public mind for a general reform, than those which accrued to our national character and interest from the inadequacy of the confederation to its immediate objects."[5]

Toward Philadelphia

Trade disputes festered among the states in this disruptive setting. A commercial quarrel between Maryland and Virginia over an oyster fishery and navigation rights triggered the meeting that produced plans for a constitutional convention. The Maryland and Virginia delegates invited representatives from other states to meet "to take into consideration the trade of the United States." The issue was larger than informal negotiators could solve, and, at a meeting in Annapolis, Maryland, in the fall of 1786 to resolve commercial disputes, Hamilton and Madison urged delegates from the five states present to convoke all thirteen "to meet at Philadelphia on the second Monday in May next, to take into consideration the situation of the United States, to devise such further provisions as shall appear to them necessary to render the Constitution of the Federal Government adequate to the exigencies of the union." Congress endorsed the convention but gave it the limited mandate of recommending revision of the Articles.

A galvanic event that occurred shortly before the convention met was an agrarian debtors' uprising in western Massachusetts, Shays's Rebellion. Daniel Shays, an officer who had served in the Revolution, was an impoverished debtor by the winter of 1786. In an attempt to gain relief from unpaid debts, Shays and over a thousand destitute followers, armed with pitchforks and staves, tried to prevent county courts from sitting. They wanted tax relief, paper money, and the state capital moved westward from Boston. Their attempt to seize a federal arsenal was thwarted by the local militia. Funded by merchants' subscriptions, the rebels then hastily recruited Boston college students. The rebellion's leaders were hunted down in a snowstorm, sentenced to death, then pardoned or given short prison terms.

The event, which was replicated in several western Massachusetts towns, sent shock waves across the states because of who the participants were, how the crisis was handled, and the divisive issues it raised. The uprising influenced the states' decision to support a central government capable of enforcing public order. Many believed that creating a popular democracy with power vested in local authorities invited anarchy, tyranny, or dismemberment of the body politic.

The Constitutional Convention

The country's future form of government was shaped during four months' deliberations beginning in late May 1787. Twelve states named seventy-four delegates to the convention; only fifty-five came to Philadelphia, and some arrived well after a quorum assembled on May 25. The average age of the delegates was forty-two; five were less than thirty years of age. Madison was thirty-six, Hamilton thirty. Thirty-four representatives were trained as lawyers, many others were merchants and planters. About 60 percent had attended college; Princeton, Yale, Harvard, and Columbia were well represented. The delegates came mostly from their states' tidewater regions. They were professionals and property owners, although some ended their lives in penury. A stabilizing force during the deliberations was the presence of George Washington, convention president, war hero, and likely choice for first president of the United States. Another respected figure was eighty-one-year-old Benjamin Franklin, who contributed infrequently, but importantly, to discussions, and who entertained delegates often at his nearby lodgings during the hot Philadelphia summer.

In modern times, it would be unthinkable for more than fifty leaders to spend nearly four months in intense political deliberations without press coverage, media leaks, or detailed copies of speeches and votes made public. Yet the convention agreed to meet secretly and keep no record of votes, allowing issues to evolve and delegates to change positions. Madison's notes, which were not published until 1840, remain the principal source of subsequent information about the proceedings.

The four-month convention produced several compromises that made the Constitution possible. Shortly after the convention opened, the Virginia delegation tabled a proposal creating three distinct branches of government and a national legislature with power to negate and supersede state laws. A dispute flared over Virginia's proposal that membership in both branches of the legislature should be proportionate to a state's population. Fearing a loss of power, smaller states objected, and New Jersey's William Patterson offered a counterproposal, suggesting that states have an equal number of delegates regardless of size—one state, one vote. Alexander Hamilton observed correctly, "It is a contest for power, not for liberty." Roger Sherman of Connecticut then proposed a compromise, later adopted; membership in the Senate would be limited to two senators per state, and membership in the House of Representatives would be relative to population. Additionally, tax bills and revenue measures would originate in the House, where citizens would be represented by a greater number of members.

Once these compromises were reached, the remaining issues—many as potentially significant as the questions already decided—were soon sorted out. Powers to collect taxes, regulate commerce, and support a national army, which had been denied to the Continental Congress in the Articles of Confederation, were included in the Constitution with little opposition.

Although delegates differed on the new government's structural details, they accepted awarding the national government a more powerful role than anything previously contemplated in America. Basically, the government's powers were expanded, the new Constitution became the "supreme law of the land," and the national government was no longer subservient to state governments. It could reach the people directly through laws, courts, administrative agents, and the previously denied power to raise revenues and armies. "The federal and state governments are in fact but different agents and trustees of the people, with different powers and designed for different purposes," Madison wrote in No. 46. There were thus two distinct governments, state and national, derived from the people and responsible to them. The constitutional government was a democratic republic—democratic because the people were represented, republican because there were restraints on what people and government could do.

Madison and his colleagues engineered a solution to a problem plaguing American government at that time. Instead of depending on the states for its lifeblood of power and funds, the new national government reached down and around states directly to the citizenry, establishing both the central government's authority and creating possibilities for perennial tension as well. Individual rights, states' rights, and the intrusions of "big government" would later become substantive issues in American law and politics, especially with the exponential rise in population and the federal government's influence in the late twentieth century.

When mid-September arrived, some tempers were short, but the convention's principal work was done, and several delegates departed. Thirty-nine of the original fifty-five delegates signed the document. Only three delegates declined to endorse it, and four others who opposed it were absent.

Madison's final notes of the historic event state:

> Whilst the last members were signing it, Doctor Franklin, looking towards the President's chair [Washington was the presiding officer], at the back of which a rising sun happened to be painted, observed to a few members near him, that painters had found it difficult to distinguish in their art a rising from a setting sun. I have, said he, often and often in the course of the

session, and the vicissitudes of my hopes and fears as to its issue, looked at that behind the President without being able to tell whether it was rising or setting: but now at length I have the happiness to know that it is a rising and not a setting sun.[6]

With a deft turn of phrase, Gouverneur Morris made it appear consent was unanimous in the document's concluding lines, since at least one representative from each state in attendance signed: "Done in Convention, by unanimous consent of the States present the 17 September." Then, at 4 p.m. that same day, "The Members adjourned to the City Tavern, dined together, and took cordial leave of each other."

Although the prescient Franklin compared the proceedings to a rising sun, the Constitution's fate was uncertain. The slavery issue had been dealt with to the satisfaction of neither northerners nor southerners; inland farmers and pioneers feared the political and commercial power of tidewater planters; and landed interests, like New York's Governor George Clinton, were apprehensive of Congress's taxation powers. Creditable leaders of the revolutionary generation, like Patrick Henry and Samuel Adams, cast a cold eye on the new government's centralized powers, and there was growing sentiment throughout the states for a bill of rights.

In spite of the fact that their deliberations focused on immediate problems, the Constitution writers, in several instances, both showed a keen awareness of historical precedent and realized they were writing for posterity. Madison records Gouverneur Morris: "He came here as a representative of America; he flattered himself he came here in some degree as a Representative of the whole human race; for the whole human race will be affected by the proceedings of this Convention. He wished gentlemen to extend their views beyond the present moment of time; beyond the narrow limits of place."[7]

Hamilton reflected this larger perspective in *Federalist* No. 34:

> We must bear in mind that we are not to confine our view to the present period, but to look forward to remote futurity. Constitutions of civil governments are not to be framed upon a calculation of existing exigencies, but upon a combination of these with the probable exigencies of the ages, according to the natural and tried course of human affairs.

Still, in September 1787 the delegates were not certain their results would last more than a few years. Someone said all they had was a piece of paper and George Washington. They believed the summer's deliberations and compromises had resulted in a practical, workable frame of government, but many were pessimistic. Alexander Hamilton brooded that the Constitution represented "a weak and worthless fabric"; another delegate called it "the Continental Congress in two volumes instead of one."

The delegates' harmonious evening interlude of September 17, 1787, was a brief calm before a yearlong storm of argument over ratification.

An Uncertain Fate

The Constitution was forwarded to the Continental Congress on September 20, three days after being signed. Reaction was mixed; some members of Congress wanted to censure convention delegates for exceeding their mandate. Nevertheless, Congress moved on September 28 to ratify the document. A majority of nine states was required for the Constitution to become law. Convention delegates—skeptical of popular democratic power and of entrenched powerbrokers, who would oppose any centralization of power—had written into the new Constitution's Article 7 that special conventions, not state legislatures, were required for ratification. The Constitution's supporters eschewed popular referendums, believing that special conventions, whose members were thus "refined" or "filtered," in Madison's language, would produce enlightened delegates and assure the Constitution's passage.

But victory was far from certain. Considerable literature was directed against the Constitution, much of it of a high order.[8] Distinguished patriots opposed the document, including Virginia's George Mason, landowner and author of the Virginia Constitution and Bill of Rights, who called George Washington an "upstart surveyor"; and Thomas Paine, who echoed a widespread sentiment: "That government is best which governs least." The Constitution's opponents included well-known patriots, backcountry farmers, small landholders, artisans, and laborers. They resisted a strong presidency, which "squints toward monarchy," and a Congress with powers of taxation, which could "clutch the purse with one hand and wave the sword with the other," as Henry put it. Madison's opponents believed the ideas incorporated in the Constitution were elitist (*aristocratic* was the word used in the 1780s), favoring the ruling elements, owners of businesses and property, and ignoring small farmers, workers, and those at the margins of society.

The lack of a bill of rights was a major issue with opponents and the undecided, as it was with many of the new Constitution's supporters. Historians of a later generation called it "an *Iliad*, or Parthenon, or Fifth Symphony of statesmanship"; but New York's John Lansing said the Constitution was "a triple headed monster, as deep and wicked a conspiracy as ever was invented in the darkest ages against the liberties of a free people." It was against this backdrop that *The Federalist Papers* appeared.

The Name *Federalist*

Proponents of the American Constitution gained a tactical advantage over those who opposed it or had reservations by claiming the name *Federalist* for themselves and by calling opponents *Anti-Federalists*. In the 1780s, partisans of a strong national government were called *nationalists*. Federalists, in contrast, supported state sovereignty and opposed a dominant national government. By preempting the title *Federalist*, Hamilton and his coauthors gained an advantage for their position and avoided an all-out confrontation over the issue of state versus national power. They appeared as supporters of states' rights, a theme elucidated in *The Federalist Papers*, yet were clearly advocates as well of a strong national government.

Publius

The essays were signed "Publius." Classical pseudonyms and allusions to Greek and Roman history were popular with eighteenth-century American authors, and towns across the country were named Athens, Sparta, Rome, and Ithaca. Statues of heroes, like Washington or Jefferson, showed them clad in togas, with Roman features. Hamilton, originator of *The Federalist Papers*, made a shrewd choice in Publius. The name referred to Publius Valerius, the state builder who restored the Roman republic following the overthrow of Tarquin, Rome's last king. Plutarch compared Publius favorably to Solon, Greece's law giver. Now a modern Publius would help build the new American republic.

In selecting a name like Publius, the *Federalist* authors followed a practice common among eighteenth-century public document writers. They published a collaborative work under a pseudonym rather than a byline. If Hamilton, Madison, and Jay had publicized their authorship of

The Federalist Papers, they would have been identified as advocates of particular positions, and they, rather than their arguments, would have become part of the debate over the Constitution. Likewise, if Americans in 1787 had known it was Pennsylvania's aristocratic, conservative Gouverneur Morris who had taken the Constitution's penultimate drafts and composed the final document, it could have diminished chances for ratification. But Morris's anonymity was preserved until the 1830s, as was authorship of *The Federalist Papers* until the 1840s. Hamilton, Madison, and Jay thus upheld a practice common in that era, creating a veil of anonymity that forced readers to focus on arguments rather than authors. This allowed politicians to develop ideas free from public pressures, change their minds during deliberations, and explore differences until conclusions were reached.

Choosing anonymity was also a function of the rivalry between Hamilton and New York Governor George Clinton. Hamilton was the only New York delegate who signed the Constitution. Clinton was an Anti-Federalist leader in a state where those opposing the new Constitution held a commanding majority. Choosing Publius was, in part, an attempt to move the debate away from the strong personal animosity between Hamilton and Clinton.

The Federalist Papers Plan

A modern reader, interested in the papers' core arguments, will be drawn to approximately twenty essays that retain lasting appeal. Their broad categories were enumerated by Hamilton in *Federalist* No. 1, in which he proposes that his plea for union and republicanism be divided clearly into six "branches of inquiry": (1) the "utility of union," (2) "the insufficiency of the present Confederation," (3) the necessity of energetic government, (4) the Constitution's republican nature, (5) its compatibility with state constitutions, and (6) the security it provides both liberty and property.

The series has a careful unity, not always apparent to later readers. The first thirty-seven papers detail shortcomings in the Articles of Confederation. Numbers 2–14 advocate a federal union as opposed to independent states and argue that a large country supports democracy better than a small country, a much-debated issue in the 1780s.

Madison's No. 10, which in modern times has become the best-known single essay, contains his famous definition of faction and his observations on human nature. After an enumeration of the Articles' flaws in Nos. 15–22, Nos. 23–36 make the case for the new government.

The argument for the Constitution is then stated positively in Nos. 37–51. The House of Representatives is described in Nos. 52–61, the Senate in Nos. 62–66, the presidency in Nos. 67–77, and the judiciary, including the principle of judicial review, in Nos. 78–83. Number 84 contends a Bill of Rights is not necessary because rights are provided throughout the Constitution; in No. 85 Hamilton presents an upbeat finale, closing the series on the optimistic note with which it began.

Although the series has a clearly enunciated argument line and organization, certain papers and sections of papers—for example, Nos. 10, 37, 39, 47, 51, 78, and 84—move beyond skilled polemics to a place among the most profound commentaries ever published on human behavior in political society. These include some carefully shaped darker passages about the failure of the Articles of Confederation and humanity's propensity to greed and self-interest, and passages of controlled enthusiasm on future hopes for the young republic.

Even though the papers were turned out quickly and the principal authors represented different viewpoints, they were still the product of careful planning and execution. It was Hamilton's tactical brilliance that saw the need for this comprehensive project. He conceived the idea of writing *The Federalist Papers*, produced the outline, and recruited the writers, deciding against other potential contributors whose attempts at essays he regarded as mediocre. Hamilton and Madison were in close contact for over a year, lived under the failed Articles, and spent the summer of 1787 debating constitutional issues in Philadelphia. The careful reasoning and construction of some papers and sections of others, like Nos. 10 and 51, suggest their authors prepared some arguments in advance and reshaped them for use in the series. Madison could draw on several years' worth of carefully refined notes on earlier experiments in government, the results of long study and reflection.

The writers did not lack subject matter; the challenge was to order arguments convincingly. This took place against a barrage of pamphlets and newspaper commentaries from opponents like "Cato" and "Brutus" and the support of bombastic friends like "Caesar." Still, *The Federalist* authors seized the high ground with a thoughtful format and carefully crafted arguments, avoiding personal attacks and the ambushes and broadsides of traditional political journalism.

Publication: October 27, 1787 – August 15, 1788

The Federalist Papers were originally published to win New York's support for ratification of the Constitution. Ratification was to be decided at a special convention; thus, the essays aimed to influence the delegate selection process by building support for the Federalist candidates for election to the June 1788 convention.

The essays, part of a deluge of pamphlets and newspaper articles for and against the Constitution, first ran in New York's *Independent Journal* on October 27, 1787, and appeared on Wednesdays and Saturdays; on Tuesdays they were printed in another paper, and on Wednesdays and Thursdays in still another publication. When the *New York Journal* began circulating in 1788, it carried them as well. This outpouring extended until the following April, with the publication of No. 77, Hamilton's concluding essay on the presidency. The series resumed on June 17, with the important essays on the judiciary, and continued until August 15, 1788, when the last of the 85 works was published.

The Federalist Papers appeared in book form before the newspaper series ended; Hamilton dispatched them to Madison in Virginia to distribute to that state's delegation prior to its vote on the Constitution. Otherwise, their circulation was confined largely to New York, with scattered printings in Pennsylvania and some New England states. A French edition appeared in 1792, followed in the next two centuries by over a hundred editions or reprints in English and at least twenty foreign language editions. A Portuguese edition was published in Rio de Janeiro in 1840, a condensed German version in Bremen in 1864, and a Spanish edition in Buenos Aires in 1868.

Ironically, a French diplomat, writing in New York in 1788, found *The Federalist* not worth commenting on. It was "of no use to the well-informed, and . . . too learned and too long for the ignorant." A contemporary New York newspaper lamented "the dry trash of Publius in 150 numbers," and "Twenty-Seven Subscribers" protested the *Journal*'s "cramming us with the voluminous Publius," which "has become nauseous, having been served up to us no less than in two other papers on the same day."[9]

Alexander Hamilton arranged for the publication of *The Federalist Papers*. According to popular lore, he wrote *Federalist* No. 1 on board a ship bringing him down the Hudson River from Albany to New York City in early October 1787. He invited Madison to coauthor the series only after other choices either had declined or written unusable essays. Hamilton and Madison were both in New York in the fall of 1787 as congressional delegates and could confer with one another. Hamilton probably wrote Nos. 1, 6–9, 11–13, 15–17, 21–36, 59–61, and 65–85. Madison wrote the important Nos. 10 and 51, and 14, 37–58, and most likely 62–63. Madison and Hamilton may have jointly authored Nos. 18–20. Madison's contributions ended in March 1788 when he returned to Virginia for that state's ratification debates. John Jay, who was originally expected to have a more significant role in the project, became ill during the winter and wrote only five essays, Nos. 2–5 and 64. The authors, although drawn from the political and economic leadership of their time, represented both similarities and differences in viewpoints.

The Authors

Alexander Hamilton (1757–1804) was born on the island of Nevis in the West Indies of a Scottish merchant father and a mother of Huguenot descent. His family origins gave rise to romantic speculation; John Adams, his avowed opponent, called him the "bastard brat of a Scotch peddler." Hamilton entered Columbia University, then called King's College, at age sixteen. During the American Revolution he rose to officer rank and became George Washington's aide-de-camp and private secretary for four years. After the war, Hamilton studied law and practiced successfully in New York, entering Congress in 1782. In addition to originating *The Federalist Papers*, Hamilton was an energetic author on other subjects, having written in support of the Boston patriots and later founding a newspaper in New York. Handsome, intense, aggressive, and self-assured to the point of arrogance, Hamilton married the socially prominent daughter of a rich New York merchant. Hamilton was not an original thinker, but possessed a well-disciplined legal mind, skills in public debate, and an ability to lay issues before the public in a compelling manner. In Washington's cabinet, Hamilton served as secretary of the treasury until 1795, when he resigned to return to the practice of law, remaining a close advisor to Washington until the latter's death. Hamilton was a leader in the Federalist Party and in later years was often in conflict with his coauthor Madison. A proponent of nationalism but not direct democracy, Hamilton once said, "Men are reasoning rather than reasonable animals." This dashing figure, filled with promise, was killed in a duel with Aaron Burr in Weehawken, New Jersey, in 1804.

Hamilton and Madison (1751–1836) were a study in contrasts. Scion of an established Virginia family, Madison was a deliberate, rather than a dramatic, public figure, who counted on his careful preparation, an instinct for politics, and meticulously crafted arguments to carry the day. Ralph Ketchum, biographer of Madison, calls his subject "an ardent revolutionist, resourceful framer of government, clever political strategist, cautious, sometimes ineffectual leader."[10] Madison was raised on a four-thousand-acre tidewater plantation. He later studied at Princeton, where he stayed to tutor in political thought with John Witherspoon, the Scottish pastor, intellectual, and the university's president. Madison was well-read in classical and modern writers on politics and history, had thought long and carefully about the relationship of Protestant Christianity to the state, and knew Latin, Greek, Hebrew, and French. He served in the Continental Congress from 1779 to 1783 and in the House of Representatives from 1789 to 1797. He was Jefferson's secretary of state from 1801 to 1808, and president from 1808 to 1816, after which he retired to his Orange County, Virginia, estate, living there until his death in 1836. He is most remembered in history as principal drafter of the Constitution and the Bill of Rights, although he had argued originally a Bill of Rights was not needed, reasoning that the state and federal constitutions guaranteed individual rights sufficiently.

John Jay (1745–1829) was born into an established New York merchant family. His contribution to *The Federalist Papers* was minimal. Severe rheumatism limited him to writing essays Nos. 2 through 5, and No. 64 on the Senate. Like Hamilton, Jay was a successful lawyer and graduate of King's College. An author of the New York State Constitution, he served as president of the Continental Congress in 1778, as ambassador to Spain, and as secretary for foreign affairs from 1784 to 1789. In 1781 he participated in negotiating the treaty that ended hostilities with Great Britain. Jay became the first chief justice of the United States in 1789, and in 1795 he began the first of two terms as governor of New York. At age fifty-six, he retired from active political life to his Westchester County, New York, estate. Jay was a landowner who believed "the people who own the country ought to govern it."

National Security: The Preeminent Issue

There were several issues in the "great national discussion" of 1787 and 1788 to which *The Federalist Papers* spoke. But the authors began with the threat of external and internal danger, the "safety" of the young republic. With memories of the recent war with Britain fresh and the weakness of the Continental Congress apparent, no issue was more important to the Constitution writers than national security. The Federalists believed only a strong central government could defend the country's borders and promote commerce. Hamilton wrote in No. 34, "Let us recollect that peace or war will not always be left to our option; that however moderate or unambitious we may be, we cannot count upon the moderation, or hope to extinguish the ambition of others." Hamilton spoke in No. 34 of the "fiery and destructive passions of war," which are more prevalent than "the mild and beneficent sentiments of peace." He urged a strong national government to provide defenses the republic lacked, and observed, "To model our political systems upon speculations of lasting tranquility would be to calculate on the weaker springs of the human character."

Democratic Versus Republican Government

Certain key words recur in *The Federalist Papers*. Their use is deceptively simple. At first glance, they appear to be common adjectives and nouns; in reality, they carefully move republican political thought of the time decisively ahead, from episodic theoretical insights to a bold but yet untried plan for governing a new nation. Madison recognized the challenge. His explanation of the inadequacies of political language in No. 37 is more than a philosophical aside:

> Besides the obscurity arising from the complexity of objects, and the imperfection of the human faculties, the medium through which the conceptions of men are conveyed to each other adds a fresh embarrassment. The use of words is to express ideas. When the Almighty himself condescends to address mankind in their own language, his meaning, luminous as it may be, is rendered dim and doubtful by the cloudy medium through which it is communicated.

Here are the essential words. The authors wanted a *robust, energetic,* and *vigorous* government; they regarded *faction* as a great enemy of constitutional government; the dangers of uncontrolled popular government had to be *filtered* and *refined* through republicanism. This was done through "framing a government," Madison wrote in *Federalist* No. 51. *Framing* meant not only defining government's outer limits or parameters, but giving government internal form and cohesion as well.

In the worldview of *The Federalist Papers'* authors, the domains of politics, science, and religion were interwoven, and a graduate of one of the handful of eastern universities would be as conversant about the ideas of reformed Protestantism in politics as about developments in Newtonian physics. *Sphere, body,* and *orbit* are words lifted from eighteenth-century natural science; *The Federalist Papers'* writers move them directly into political literature, suggesting the order the new Constitution will provide.

There is a carefully planned use of political space in *The Federalist Papers.* The compact land described by Jay in No. 2, reminiscent of scenes depicted by early American landscape artists, extends gradually as the Confederation's limited confines are pushed back. By the time a defense of the new Constitution is introduced by Hamilton in No. 23, geographic and conceptual horizons are expanded. Hamilton, less the philosophe and more the power broker than Madison, wants *ample* authority, *ample* power, the *extension* of authority, and resists the idea that "we ought to contract our views." Amplitude as an idea in science, and with it the broadening of conceptual horizons, fit Hamilton's political goal of fashioning a political system to govern "so large an empire."

For the task of constructing a system of government, the Founders drew on Newton's understanding of a universe "moving according to mathematical laws in space and time, under the influence of definite and dependable forces." This concept was illustrated by David Rittenhouse, a Philadelphia scientist-politician and Pennsylvania's treasurer, whose orrery displays the motion of solar bodies through the rotation of metal balls moved by wheelworks.[11]

How can there be effective government that is truly representative of the people and that works in a "robust," "vigorous," "energetic" way? The focal point of the question was the clear division over republican government, with access to power separated and checked at various points in the political system, versus a broadly based popular democracy. Instead of votes under the village tree or in town meetings, with larger councils setting national policy, the Constitution writers were architects of an intricate machine whose structural components included such concepts as separation of powers, checks and balances, federalism, and an independent judiciary with the power of judicial review over the acts of legislative and executive bodies.

There were further barriers to a quick or sustained seizure of power: a bicameral legislature, indirect elections, the presidential veto, legislative control of the budget, and limitations on who was eligible to vote. It was

19

almost impossible for a zealous movement to sweep like wildfire through the structures of government and seize control. Likewise, because the safeguards engineered into the system were so elaborate, almost like mechanical safety devices, it was unlikely a tyrant could seize and hold the government for long. Madison used the words *refine* and *filter* to explain how the process differed from direct democracy. In *Federalist* No. 10 he said republican government would "refine and enlarge the public views by passing them through the medium of a chosen body of citizens whose wisdom may best discern the true interest of their country, and whose patriotism and love of justice will be least likely to sacrifice it to temporary or partial considerations." Here Madison deftly appropriated the word *republican* for a specific use, as had been the case with *Federalist*. Madison's republic was not a popular democracy; in it power was not left directly in the hands of the people but with elected officials, thus providing a protective barrier from impulsive or unwise mob governance.

Jay believed the filtering process produced more enlightened, able candidates for national than for state office. In *Federalist* No. 3 he argued that once an efficient national government was established, "the best men in the country . . . will generally be appointed to manage it." The national government "will have the widest field for choice, and never experience that want of proper persons which is not uncommon in some of the States." *Wisdom, regularity, coolness, temperate, reasonable,* and *deliberate* were words the three authors used to describe the leadership the national government would attract through its filtered and refined selection process. This protected the country against impulsive decisions by uninformed mobs who would put self-interest first, the sort of persons Pennsylvania's Gouverneur Morris described in 1774:

> I stood on the balcony and on my right hand were ranged all
> the people of property, with some few poor dependents, and on
> the other the tradesmen, etc., who thought it worth their while
> to leave daily labour for the good of the country. . . . The mob
> began to think and reason. Poor reptiles! It is with them a *vernal*
> morning: they are struggling to cast off their winter's slough. They
> bask in the sunshine, and ere noon they will bite, depend on it.[12]

Opponents like Patrick Henry and Richard Henry Lee rejected such views as elitist republican rhetoric. Lee wrote, "Every man of reflection must see that the change now proposed is a transfer of power from the many to the few."

The Anti-Federalists favored town meetings, public assemblies, frequent elections, and large legislative bodies—the larger the body, the more representative it was of the general will, an idea borrowed from Rousseau. In such a view, government mirrors, rather than filters, popular interest. Hamilton's opponent, Melancton Smith, articulated this position at the New York ratification convention. Smith believed officials were elected to defend the interests of their constituents; he pleaded for "a sameness . . . between the representative and his constituents." He feared "the middling class of life" would be barred from political participation in the system Madison, Hamilton, and Jay proposed. Madison was no supporter of frequent elections. He used the words *energy* and *stability* to describe government's ideal characteristics; and such government required wise, dispassionate leaders having both distance from constituencies and duration of appointment to represent a national, rather than a local, interest.

The *Federalist* writers, in short, were explicit about the difference between a pure democracy, in which liberty prevails and the people decide all questions, and a republican government, in which powers are carefully delineated and divided among the government's different parts. The shift from liberty to order reflected a transformation from ideas prevalent in America in 1776 to those current in 1787. The *Pennsylvania Packet* in September 1787 wrote, "The year 1776 is celebrated for a revolution in favor of liberty. The year 1787 it is expected will be celebrated with equal joy for a revolution in favor of government."[13] It reflected Alexander Hamilton's argument that in 1776 "zeal for liberty became predominant and excessive," and in 1787 the issue was "strength and stability in the organization of our government, and vigor in its operations."[14]

Hamilton, Madison, and Jay knew the national and state governments' weaknesses. States were debtors, so were individuals. Moreover, the revolutionary period's small circle of educated, purposeful national leaders had been replaced in state legislatures by less able figures. Madison in 1788 said the state governing bodies were filled with "men without reading, experience, or principle." Jay worried about states being governed by people whom "wisdom would have left in obscurity."

Although the Federalists won and the Constitution was accepted, the debate never completely ended; the issues remain two centuries later in appeals to populism or republicanism, state and local rights versus national responsibility.

Who Participates in the Political Process?

The analysis of political society Hamilton sketched favored "landholders, merchants, and men of the learned professions." In No. 35 he argued, "We must therefore consider merchants as the natural representatives of all these classes of the community." Mechanics and manufacturers "will always be inclined . . . to give their votes to merchants in preference to persons of their own professions or trades" because "they know that the merchant is their natural patron and friend." Learned professions "truly form no distinct interest in society." Hamilton acknowledged that his portrait of society was limited to a small circle of land-owning leaders. He deftly sidestepped the issue of popular democracy. "If it should be objected that we have seen other descriptions of men in the local legislatures," he wrote in No. 36, "I answer that it is admitted there are exceptions to the rule, but not in sufficient number to influence the general complexion or character of the government."

Still, the door to upward political, economic, and social mobility was not closed. Hamilton's words were autobiographical: "There are strong minds in every walk of life that will rise superior to the disadvantages of situation and will command the tribute due their merit, not only from the classes to which they particularly belong, but from the society in general."

He concluded, "for the credit of human nature . . . we should see examples of such vigorous plants flourishing in the soil of federal as well as of state legislation," but these will be exceptions.

American constitutional history can be charted by the continuing expansion of the voting franchise. The elimination of property requirements, the Fifteenth, Nineteenth, Twenty-third, Twenty-fourth, and Twenty-sixth amendments, and the Voting Rights Act are all aspects of the growth of suffrage rights.

Parenthetically, the Constitution was not ratified by plebiscite; property requirements for voting eliminated many small farmers and artisans who opposed the document. If the Constitution had been submitted directly to the people for a vote, it probably would not have passed. State constitutional convention delegates were elected on the same basis as delegates to state legislatures, which favored established tidewater interests. Nevertheless, in 1788 the voting franchise was broader than it had been when either the Declaration of Independence or the Articles of Confederation was adopted, and New York expanded its electoral rolls and recognized universal manhood suffrage for the election of delegates to its state ratification convention.

Faction

No question of governance received more of Madison's attention than how to have a vigorous, energetic, effective government without allowing a single majority or minority faction, or combination of interests, to seize control of it. Madison weighed both the aftermath of Shays's Rebellion in the north and the trouble hundreds of southern landowners, farmers, artisans, merchants, debtors, and failed property owners would make if allowed into the political arena as equals. He described the problem in *Federalist* No. 10:

> The most common and durable source of factions has been the various and unequal distribution of property. Those who hold and those who are without property have ever formed distinct interests in society.... creditors... debtors.... A landed interest, a manufacturing interest, a mercantile interest, a moneyed interest.... The regulation of these various and interfering interests forms the principal task of modern legislation.

Madison believed "all civilized societies" were "divided into different sects, fashions, and interests, as they happened to consist of rich and poor, debtors and creditors, the landed, the manufacturing, the commercial interests, the inhabitants of this district or that district." Enlarge the circle of political participants, he argued, while dividing the community into numerous interests and parties, and it will be increasingly difficult for a special interest group to consolidate power and dominate the country or ignore a minority within the nation.

In discussing faction, Madison foresaw not only a vociferous, intransigent minority, but the dangers a majority, bent on working its will, could wreak on society. It was the great mass of restless, propertyless people and small farmers that the Constitution writers both sought to include in a democracy and control in a republic.

Although *Federalist* No. 10 provides an encompassing statement of Madison's idea of faction, he elaborated on the concept elsewhere. In an October 24, 1787, letter to Jefferson he wrote, "*Divide et imperia,* the reprobated axiom of tyranny, is, under certain qualifications the only policy by which a republic can be administered on just principles."[15] Four months earlier, in a speech to the Constitutional Convention, he described his ideas in greater detail. The problem: to have a working republican government yet protect minority interests. This can only be done if government is

> to enlarge the sphere and thereby divide the community into so great a number of interests and parties, that in the first place a majority will not be likely at the same moment to have a common interest separate from that of the whole or of the minority; and in the second place, that in case they should have such an interest, they may not be apt to unite in pursuit of it. It was incumbent on us then to try this remedy, and with that view to frame a republican system on such a scale and in such a form as will control all the evils which have been experienced.[16]

Madison, in short, faced a balancing act; and a misformulation could tilt the new government, so full of hope and promise, into the hands of an authoritarian president, or worse, a tyrant, or an equally oppressive legislative body. In Madison's view, government was a framework, a mechanical structure to keep political currents within acceptable limits, as a carefully engineered watercourse contains raging streams. Madison was much like Locke in this regard and saw government as a neutral agent brokering competing interests, an umpire among contending forces, an agent to protect property rights, on which the well-being of the fragile new nation rested.

Separation of Powers

After the Revolution, Americans understandably opposed conferring political power on a strong ruler. The memory of George III was fresh, and a much more attractive prospect was a strong legislature. The Constitution failed to award such concentrated power to the legislature. Instead, it created a strong presidency, but power was shared among the executive, legislative, and judicial branches; within the legislative branch, it was further partitioned between two houses. Madison believed the new political system could be wrecked easily by an imbalance in the distribution of power or its concentration in one place, especially in the legislature. In *Federalist* No. 47 he wrote, "The accumulation of all powers, legislative, executive, and judiciary, in the same hands . . . may justly be pronounced the very definition of tyranny."

The only reason such a powerful presidency was approved was because everyone knew George Washington would be the first president and would set a clear precedent for how the office should be conducted. Congress, too, would be a strong institution, every bit as capable of despotic rule as the presidency. Madison wrote of the legislature's tendency to draw everything into its vortex; Jefferson earlier had said 173 legislators could be as dictatorial as 1. A strong counterweight in the presidency was important for that reason as well.

Thus the raw confrontation of power against power, ambition against ambition, was counteracted, not through any assumption of goodwill on the participants' part, but through a clear process of separation of powers, distinct checks and balances, and an independent judiciary with the power of judicial review (the right to initiate review of the constitutionality of any act undertaken by the legislative or executive branches, as well as state laws). Judges could face impeachment proceedings in Congress and, while appointed by the president, would be subject to confirmation hearings and sometimes rejection by the Congress.

Madison wrote, in one of the most often-quoted passages from the eighty-five essays, "What is government itself, but the greatest of all reflections on human nature? If men were angels no government would be necessary." Thus, "ambition must be made to counteract ambition"; the government must establish "a policy of supplying by opposite and rival interests, the defect of better motives." Madison's intent was clear: to create a governmental structure in which interests would vigorously contend but not obliterate one another. Elsewhere in No. 51 he stated, "Comprehending in the society so many separate distinctions of citizens . . . will render an unjust combination of a majority of the whole very improbable, if not impracticable."

The Presidency

It was in the presidency that the "energy" and "vigor" of the new republic fused. Hamilton devoted Nos. 67–77 to the presidency. In *Federalist* No. 70 he wrote, "Energy in the executive is a leading character in the definition of good government. . . . A feeble executive implies a feeble execution of the government. A feeble execution is but another phrase for a bad execution: and a government ill executed, whatever it may be in theory, must be, in practice, a bad government."

The president was given powers to veto laws made by Congress; a two-thirds vote of both houses was required to override the veto. The president was, likewise, commander in chief of the armed forces, but Congress declared war and financed the military. The chief executive could conduct foreign affairs, make treaties, and appoint federal judges with the "advice and consent" of the Senate, and pardon those who commit crimes against the nation. What emerged from the convention was a strong presidency, which opponents believed had "powers exceeding those of the most despotic monarch we know of in modern times."[17] Still, presidential power was both separate from legislative and judicial power, and checked and balanced in numerous ways carefully structured into the basic law by Madison and his contemporaries. For example, a president could be impeached for "treason, bribery, or other high crimes and misdemeanors."

Congress

The *Federalist* authors were careful to delineate the powers of Congress, bearing in mind the legislature was the principal governing body in the states. This would not be the case in the new national government. Still, many of the powers given Congress by the Articles were transferred wholesale to the Constitution, including the right to borrow money, declare war, maintain an army and navy, and establish a post office and post roads. In addition, Congress could "lay and collect taxes," regulate commerce with foreign nations and among the states, and invoke the so-called "elastic clause," expanding congressional powers "to make all laws which shall be necessary and proper for carrying into execution the foregoing powers."

The Judiciary

The Constitution and *The Federalist Papers* presented a radically new concept of an independent judiciary with, implicitly, the right to rule on the constitutionality of actions originated by the executive and legislative branches and by state governments. An independent judiciary would only work if judges were given long-term appointments "during good behavior." The judiciary was seen, in No. 78, as having "neither force nor will but merely judgment." Hamilton argued that an independent judiciary was essential to a creditable government because "no man can be sure that he may not be tomorrow the victim of a spirit of injustice, by which he may be a gainer today."

The judiciary's authority to nullify unconstitutional state laws did not come until this century. The Framers did not anticipate this, and the First

Congress rejected a Madison amendment that would have applied certain fundamental rights to state governments as part of the Bill of Rights. Once this power was vested in the judiciary, Justice Oliver Wendell Holmes was the first to note that it was probably more critical to the preservation of liberty than the authority to declare federal actions unconstitutional.

Ratification

When the first *Federalist* paper appeared in print in New York on October 27, 1787, the outcome of the ratification debates was still uncertain. There was widespread opposition, and the Constitution passed by only a narrow margin in several states. John Adams believed "the Constitution was extorted from a reluctant people by a grinding necessity."

Delaware was the first state to accept the Constitution by a unanimous vote on December 7, 1787, and Pennsylvania followed a week later by a margin of 46 to 23. In late December, New Jersey's convention ratified the document unanimously. Georgia ratified the document on January 2, 1788, as did Connecticut by a wide margin seven days later.

In early February the Constitution passed by a vote of 187 to 168 in Massachusetts, following a month of acrimonious debate. Twenty-nine of the 355 delegates meeting in Boston had fought with Captain Shays; many of them urged that the Constitution be sent to the towns for a vote. One of the Massachusetts delegates expressed opponents' fears of a strong central government:

> These lawyers and men of learning, and moneyed men, that talk so finely, and gloss over matters so smoothly, to make us poor illiterate people swallow down the pill, expect to get into Congress themselves; they expect to be managers of this Constitution, and get all the power and all the money into their own hands, and then they will swallow up all us little folks like the great *Leviathan*; yes, just as the whale swallowed up Jonah.[18]

Massachusetts ratified the Constitution, but proposed adding a bill of rights. The proposals were not binding, but they removed the Constitution's supporters from a nettlesome dilemma. The proposals secured votes needed for passage and preserved the flexibility to deal with rights issues reflectively in the drafting room rather than as an up-or-down vote in a public assembly. Many undecided or moderately Anti-Federalist voters were thus willing to give the document a chance.

Three states followed Massachusetts in quick succession with clear majority votes: Maryland in April, South Carolina in May, and New Hampshire in June. They gave the Constitution the needed votes for passage and authorized the formation of a new government.

Meanwhile, several important states, representing about 40 percent of the population, were not heard from, including Virginia, New York, North Carolina, and mercurial Rhode Island. The Virginia and New York votes were crucial if the Constitution was to gain national acceptance. In late June 1788, Virginia voted 89 to 79 to ratify the Constitution, ending a lengthy debate. Madison's presence at the Virginia deliberations was important in gaining the votes needed to support the Constitution. The Richmond contest pitted Madison against Patrick Henry, the colorful orator and patriot who spoke against the document for seven hours one day. Henry's effort, and that of the other Anti-Federalists, eventually resulted in a bill of rights—the first ten amendments to the Constitution— being added to the document. Henry, articulate in debate, was gracious in defeat. "I will be a peaceable citizen," he said. "My head, and my heart, shall be at liberty to retrieve the loss of liberty, and remove the defects of the system in a constitutional way."[19]

"One shudders to think what would have happened had Patrick Henry prevailed in Richmond," Warren E. Burger has written. "Earlier, there had been close votes in Massachusetts and New Hampshire in favor of ratification; Rhode Island had emphatically rejected it by popular referendum. With the Anti-Federalist views of Governor Clinton leading the opposition, sentiment in New York was sharply divided."[20]

New York was pivotal. The national capital and an important commercial center, it was also a geographic link between the nation's two halves. Governor Clinton, like other important New York landowners, opposed the Constitution, fearing both increased taxes and the loss of the state's profitable customs revenues to the national government. In a courthouse in Poughkeepsie during June and July 1788, delegates debated the issues raised in *The Federalist Papers* and at other ratification conventions. As had been the case with Madison in Virginia, Hamilton's spirited participation in the New York debate was crucial. News of the New Hampshire and Virginia votes endorsing the Constitution finally left New York's Anti-Federalists in disarray. On July 26, the New York convention approved the Constitution by a vote of 30 to 27.

That same month North Carolina rejected the proposed law but overturned the vote a year later. Rhode Island, which had not bothered to send a delegation to the Constitutional Convention, finally approved the document 34 to 32 in late May 1790, giving the United States a Constitution ratified by all the states.

It was time now to celebrate. There were parades and civic dinners in major cities; federal punch was a favorite drink, and federal hats were popular. Some parades included a horse-drawn replica of a ship; "The sloop of Anarchy has gone ashore on the rock of Union," read one banner.

Congress accepted the newly ratified Constitution. States sent presidential electors, senators, and representatives to New York, the temporary capital. The new House of Representatives and Senate both organized in March 1789, and George Washington was elected first president; but it took an additional week for the news from New York to reach Washington at his home in Virginia. After a triumphal carriage ride north, Washington took the oath of office on April 30 in New York, reciting the words spelled out in Article II, clause 7, that presidents have used for two centuries: "I do solemnly swear that I will faithfully execute the office of President of the United States and will, to the best of my ability, preserve, protect, and defend the Constitution of the United States."

The Bill of Rights was introduced by Madison in the House of Representatives on June 8, 1789, and approved by Congress on September 25. As approved, the Bill of Rights was part of a series of constitutional amendments Madison introduced. Not all were accepted by the House, and those that were passed were reformulated as an appendix to the Constitution rather than interlarded into the text. The Senate did not approve all of them either, sending twelve of the proposals to the states. Ratification took until December 15, 1791, when Virginia's favorable vote made ten of the twelve proposed amendments part of the Constitution.

The Commercial Republic

The new American experiment in government worked both because the Constitution was a practical, workable document, and because it was launched in an economically viable country. Hamilton, Madison, and Jay realized the importance of a strong commercial republic, although *The Federalist Papers* contain few expanded references to this subject. One of the most detailed was written by Hamilton in *Federalist* No. 12:

> The prosperity of commerce is now perceived and acknowledged by all enlightened statesmen to be the most useful as well as the most productive source of national wealth, and has

accordingly become a primary object of their political cares. By multiplying the means of gratification, by promoting the introduction and circulation of the precious metals, those darling objects of human avarice and enterprise, it serves to vivify and invigorate all the channels of industry and to make them flow with greater activity and copiousness.

"If we mean to be a commercial people," Hamilton argued in *Federalist* No. 24, the nation must have an army and navy. In No. 6, he described the darker side of commercial life in language not unlike that which Madison employed: "Are there not aversions, predilections, rivalships, and desires of unjust acquisitions that affect nations as well as kings? Are not popular assemblies frequently subject to the impulses of rage, resentment, jealousy, avarice, and of other irregular and violent propensities?"

In *Federalist* No. 11, Hamilton was lyrical about "what this country can become." Led by a "vigorous national government, the natural strength and the resources of the country, directed to a common interest, would baffle all the combinations of European jealousy to restrain our growth." Europe would cease being "mistress of the world," America would be the dominant political-economic presence. Hamilton disputed those who argued "that even dogs cease to bark after having breathed awhile in our atmosphere" and described "the adventurous spirit, which distinguishes the commercial character of America." He asserted in No. 12 that in such a republic "the assiduous merchant, the laborious husbandman, the active mechanic, and the industrious manufacturer . . . look forward with eager expectation and growing alacrity to this pleasing reward of their toils."

The Informing Vision

The Founders were in the direct tradition of David Hume and other figures of the Scottish Enlightenment as well as English republican theorists who opposed arbitrary rule and supported popular sovereignty.[21] The great question was one of balance—how to create a strong, acceptable, workable government while avoiding the pitfalls of mob rule or despotism. The Founders' dilemma was expressed by a New England clergyman, Jeremy Belknap: "Let it stand as a principle that government originates from the people: but let the people be taught . . . that they are not able to govern themselves."[22]

The Constitution writers knew Jean Calvin's views on the easy corruptibility of human nature. A seaport town trader or general practicing attorney was rarely a starry-eyed idealist, but was often a person with a clear idea of what was required for honest, workable government, even if such hopes were not always realized. Richard Hofstadter described the Founders' outlook: "Having seen human nature on display in the market place, the courtroom, the legislative chamber, and in every secret path and alleyway where wealth and power are courted, they felt they knew it in all its frailty."[23]

There is a distinctly moral, but not sectarian, cast to *The Federalist Papers*. The authors described "malignant passions" and the "disease," "defect," and "evil propensity" of human behavior in political society. Madison's moralism was evident in the somber analysis of human nature in *Federalist* No. 37. He depicted both "the obscurity arising from the complexity of objects" and "the imperfection of the human faculties." The world is a place with "dark and degraded pictures which display infirmities and depravities of the human character." "Discordant opinions" clash, as do "mutual jealousies... factions, contentions, and disappointments." On the positive side, he expressed "wonder" and "astonishment" at the constitutional convention's achievement and suggested only "a finger of that Almighty hand" could give mortals adequate understanding to produce a Constitution governing an unruly citizenry.

No influence on the Constitution writers was more important than the Scottish Common Sense school of philosophy. Authors like David Hume, James Harrington, and John Locke acknowledged both the theology of Calvin and the realities of human nature, especially as displayed in the ferment of mid-eighteenth-century Scottish religious, political, and economic councils. John Dickinson, representing Delaware, echoed this viewpoint: "Experience must be our only guide; reason may mislead us." By "reason" he meant the political theory of the Enlightenment. Madison, author of much of the Constitution, was taken with Montesquieu's idea of the separation of powers expressed in the French writer's *Esprit des Lois*; but what made the concept of checks and balances acceptable to the delegates was probably less political theory than economic practice, the desire, expressed in a modern idiom, "to play the game on a level playing field." The Founders' view of human nature was optimistic, but vigilant. "You trust your mother, but you cut the cards," in more recent language.

Madison was an Anglican who had studied with a Presbyterian tutor, John Witherspoon. The problem of morality in public life was central to the

Virginian's thought, more so than personal piety. Ketchum calls Madison's beliefs "eclectic, sensible, and reasonable, if not always wholly consistent," containing "realism about human nature, a comprehensive concept of political obligation, and an instinctive admiration for . . . moderation. From the Christian tradition he inherited a sense of the prime importance of conscience, a strict personal morality, an understanding of human dignity as well as depravity, and a conviction that vital religion could contribute importantly to the general welfare."[24]

The Summing Up

The contrast between the Articles of Confederation and the Constitution and the two ideas of government they represented is evident in the preambles to the two documents. The first was rambling: "To all to whom these presents shall come, we, the undersigned, delegates of the states affixed to our names, send greetings." The second was focused: "We the People of the United States, in Order to form a more perfect Union, establish Justice, insure domestic Tranquility, provide for the common defence, promote the general Welfare, and secure the Blessings of Liberty to ourselves and our Posterity, do ordain and establish this Constitution for the United States of America." In short, the difference was between a bankrupt, ineffectual effort at governance, built on some useful ideas but held together only with the dry sticks of rhetoric, and a bold new plan that balanced popular participation with numerous constraints on what forms that participation might take.

Instead of choosing to locate all political power and ideology in one place, the new idea of government balanced passion against passion, power against power, and harnessed them in an active political process. This is part of what was behind *The Federalist Papers'* studied description of "vigorous," "robust," "energetic" government.

Not often do political essays endure beyond their appointed moment; even more rarely does a lengthy collection of such works, fired off in the heat of polemical politics, claim any lasting place in literary tradition. *The Federalist Papers* endure because the debate is of an unusually high order, about fundamental questions of how society should be governed, by participants who were major actors in shaping the new government.

George Washington signaled the lasting quality of *The Federalist Papers* in a letter to Hamilton on August 28, 1788:

When the transient circumstances and fugitive performances which attended this Crisis shall have disappeared, That Work will merit the Notice of Posterity; because in it are candidly and ably discussed the principles of freedom and the topics of government, which will be always interesting to mankind so long as they shall be connected in Civil Society.[25]

The Federalist

*Addressed to the People
of the State of New York*

No. 1

Introduction

Alexander Hamilton describes the series. He asks the basic question, "whether societies of men are really capable or not of establishing good government from reflection and choice, or whether they are forever destined to depend for their political constitutions on accident and force." Next, he addresses the importance of containing political passion and protecting society from despots who emerge in the guise of proclaiming "zeal for the rights of the people." Hamilton makes a positive case for the new Constitution: "I am convinced that this is the safest course for your liberty, your dignity, and your happiness." He then states The Federalist Papers' *main arguments, which will unfold in eighty-five essays: the advantages of union to political prosperity, the present Confederation's weakness, how the Constitution will provide a structure where "the true principles of republican government" can flourish, its compatibility with state constitutions, and how the Constitution will contribute to the new country's security through safeguarding liberty and property.*

After an unequivocal experience of the inefficacy of the subsisting federal government, you are called upon to deliberate on a new Constitution for the United States of America. The subject speaks its own importance; comprehending in its consequences nothing less than the existence of the Union the safety and welfare of the parts of which it is composed, the fate of an empire in many respects the most interesting in the world. It has been frequently remarked that it seems to have been reserved to the people of this country, by their conduct and example, to decide the important question, whether societies of men are really capable or not of establishing good government from reflection and choice, or whether they are forever destined to depend for their political constitutions on accident and force. If there be any truth in the remark, the crisis at which we are arrived may with propriety be regarded as the era in which that decision is to be made; and a wrong election of the part we shall act may, in this view, deserve to be considered as the general misfortune of mankind.

This idea will add the inducements of philanthropy to those of patriotism, to heighten the solicitude which all considerate and good men must feel for the event. Happy will it be if our choice should be directed by a judicious estimate of our true interests, unperplexed and unbiased by considerations not connected with the public good. But this is a thing more ardently to be wished than seriously to be expected. The plan offered to our deliberations affects too many particular interests, innovates upon too many local institutions, not to involve in its discussion a variety of objects foreign to its merits, and of views, passions, and prejudices little favorable to the discovery of truth.

Among the most formidable of the obstacles which the new Constitution will have to encounter may readily be distinguished the obvious interest of a certain class of men in every State to resist all changes which may hazard a diminution of the power, emolument, and consequence of the offices they hold under the State establishments; and the perverted ambition of another class of men, who will either hope to aggrandize themselves by the confusions of their country, or will flatter themselves with fairer prospects of elevation from the subdivision of the empire into several partial confederacies than from its union under one government.

It is not, however, my design to dwell upon observations of this nature. I am well aware that it would be disingenuous to resolve indiscriminately the opposition of any set of men (merely because their situations might subject them to suspicion) into interested or ambitious views. Candor will oblige us to admit that even such men may be actuated by upright intentions; and it cannot be doubted that much of the opposition which has made its appearance, or may hereafter make its appearance, will spring from sources, blameless at least if not respectable—the honest errors of minds led astray by preconceived jealousies and fears. So numerous indeed and so powerful are the causes which serve to give a false bias to the judgment, that we, upon many occasions, see wise and good men on the wrong as well as on the right side of questions of the first magnitude to society. This circumstance, if duly attended to, would furnish a lesson of moderation to those who are ever so thoroughly persuaded of their being in the right in any controversy. And a further reason for caution, in this respect, might be drawn from the reflection that we are not always sure that those who advocate the truth are influenced by purer principles than their antagonists. Ambition, avarice, personal animosity, party opposition, and many other motives not more laudable than these, are apt to operate as well upon those who support as those who oppose the right side of a question. Were there not even these inducements to moderation, nothing could be more ill-judged than that intolerant spirit which has at all times character-ized political parties. For in politics, as in religion, it is equally absurd to aim at making proselytes by fire and sword. Heresies in either can rarely be cured by persecution.

Guarding Against Despots

And yet, however just these sentiments will be allowed to be, we have already sufficient indications that it will happen in this as in all former cases of great national discussion. A torrent of angry and malignant passions will be let loose. To judge from the conduct of the opposite parties, we shall be led to conclude that they will mutually hope to evince the justness of their opinions, and to increase the number of their converts by the loudness of their declamations and by the bitterness of their invectives. An enlightened zeal for the energy and efficiency of government will be stigmatized as the offspring of a temper fond of despotic power and hostile to the principles of liberty. An over-scrupulous jealousy of danger to the rights of the people, which is more commonly the fault of the head than of the heart, will be represented as mere pretense and artifice, the stale bait for popularity at the expense of public good. It will be forgotten, on the one hand, that jealousy is the usual concomitant of violent love, and that the noble enthusiasm of liberty is too apt to be infected with a spirit of narrow and illiberal distrust. On the other hand, it will be equally forgotten that the vigor of government is essential to the security of liberty; that, in the contemplation of a sound and well-informed judgment, their interests can never be separated; and that a dangerous ambition more often lurks behind the specious mask of zeal for the rights of the people than under the forbidding appearance of zeal for the firmness and efficiency of government. History will teach us that the former has been found a much more certain road to the introduc-tion of despotism than the latter, and that of those men who have overturned the liberties of republics, the greatest number have begun their career by paying an obsequious court to the people, commencing demagogues and ending tyrants.

In the course of the preceding observations, I have had an eye, my fellow-citizens, to putting you upon your guard against all attempts, from whatever quarter, to influence your decision in a matter of the utmost moment to your welfare by any impressions other than those which may result from the evidence of truth. You will, no doubt, at the same time have collected from the general scope of them that they proceed from a source not unfriendly to the new Constitution. Yes, my countrymen, I own to you that after having given it an attentive consideration, I am clearly of opinion it is your interest to adopt it. I am convinced that this is the safest course for your liberty, your dignity, and your happiness. I affect not reserves which I do not feel. I will not amuse you with an appearance of deliberation when I have decided. I frankly acknowledge to you my convictions, and I will freely lay before you the reasons on which they are founded. The consciousness of good intentions disdains ambiguity. I shall not, however, multiply professions on this head. My motives must remain in the depository of my own breast. My arguments will be open to all and may be judged of by all. They shall at least be offered in a spirit which will not disgrace the cause of truth.

The Proposal

I propose, in a series of papers, to discuss the following interesting particulars:—*The utility of the Union to your political prosperity—The insufficiency of the present Confederation to preserve that Union—The necessity of a government at least equally energetic with the one proposed to the attainment of this object—The conformity of the proposed Constitution to the true principles of republican government—Its analogy to your own State constitution*—and lastly, *The additional security which its adoption will afford to the preservation of that species of government, to liberty, and to property.*

In the progress of this discussion I shall endeavor to give a satisfactory answer to all the objections which shall have made their appearance, that may seem to have any claim to your attention.

It may perhaps be thought superfluous to offer arguments to prove the utility of the Union, a point, no doubt, deeply engraved on the hearts of the great body of the people in every State, and one which, it may be imagined, has no adversaries. But the fact is that we already hear it whispered in the private circles of those who oppose the new Constitution, that the thirteen States are of too great extent for any general system, and that we must of necessity resort to separate confederacies of distinct portions of the whole. This doctrine will, in all probability, be gradually propagated, till it has votaries enough to countenance an open avowal of it. For nothing can be more evident to those who are able to take an enlarged view of the subject than the alternative of an adoption of the new Constitution or a dismemberment of the Union. It will therefore be of use to begin by examining the advantages of that Union, the certain evils, and the probable dangers, to which every State will be exposed from its dissolution. This shall accordingly constitute the subject of my next address.

No. 2

Concerning Dangers from Foreign Force and Influence

John Jay states that whenever and however government is instituted, "the people must cede to it some of their natural rights, in order to vest it with requisite powers." America's geography favors union, he believes ("Providence has in a particular manner blessed it with a variety of soils and productions and watered it with innumerable streams for the delight and accommodation of inhabitants"), although the Articles of Confederation failed to achieve this union. Jay applauds the recently completed Philadelphia convention's work. The convention met "in the mild season of peace, with minds unoccupied by other subjects." The result is the Constitution, which delegates are now asked to ratify, for "the rejection of it would put the continuance of the Union in the utmost jeopardy." This sober theme is stated throughout The Federalist Papers: *the alternative to the system of government being proposed is weakness before other nations, anarchy within, and a political climate favoring self-interest and regional focus to the detriment of the whole society's security.*

When the people of America reflect that they are now called upon to decide a question, which in its consequences must prove one of the most important that ever engaged their attention, the propriety of their taking a very comprehensive, as well as a very serious, view of it will be evident.

Nothing is more certain than the indispensable necessity of government; and it is equally undeniable that whenever and however it is instituted, the people must cede to it some of their natural rights, in order to vest it with requisite powers. It is well worthy of consideration, therefore, whether it would conduce more to the interest of the people of America that they should, to all general purposes, be one nation, under one federal government, than that they should divide themselves into separate confederacies and give to the head of each the same kind of powers which they are advised to place in one national government.

It has until lately been a received and uncontradicted opinion that the prosperity of the people of America depended on their continuing firmly united, and the wishes, prayers, and efforts of our best and wisest citizens have been constantly directed to that object. But politicians now appear who insist that this opinion is erroneous, and that instead of looking for safety and happiness in union, we ought to seek it in a division of the States into distinct confederacies or sovereignties. However extraordinary this new doctrine may appear, it nevertheless has its advocates; and certain characters who were much opposed to it formerly are at present of the number. Whatever may be the arguments or inducements which have wrought this change in the sentiments and declarations of these gentlemen, it certainly would not be wise in the people at large to adopt these new political tenets without being fully convinced that they are founded in truth and sound policy.

Geography Favors Union

It has often given me pleasure to observe that independent America was not composed of detached and distant territories, but that one connected, fertile, widespreading country was the portion of our western sons of liberty. Providence has in a particular manner blessed it with a variety of soils and productions and watered it with innumerable streams for the delight and accommodation of its inhabitants. A succession of navigable waters forms a kind of chain round its borders, as if to bind it together; while the most noble rivers in the world, running at convenient distances, present them with highways for the easy communication of friendly aids and the mutual transportation and exchange of their various commodities.

With equal pleasure I have as often taken notice that Providence has been pleased to give this one connected country to one united people—a people descended from the same ancestors, speaking the same language, professing the same religion, attached to the same principles of government, very similar in their manners and customs, and who, by their joint counsels, arms, and efforts, fighting side by side throughout a long and bloody war, have nobly established their general liberty and independence.

This country and this people seem to have been made for each other, and it appears as if it was the design of Providence that an inheritance so proper and convenient for a band of brethren, united to each other by the strongest ties, should never be split into a number of unsocial, jealous, and alien sovereignties.

Similar sentiments have hitherto prevailed among all orders and denominations of men among us. To all general purposes we have uniformly been one people: each individual citizen everywhere enjoying the same national rights, privileges, and protection. As a nation we have made peace and war; as a nation we have vanquished our common enemies; as a nation we have formed alliances, and made treaties, and entered into various compacts and conventions with foreign states.

A strong sense of the value and blessings of union induced the people, at a very early period, to institute a federal government to preserve and perpetuate it. They formed it almost as soon as they had a political existence; nay, at a time when their habitations were in flames, when many of their citizens were bleeding, and when the progress of hostility and desolation left little room for those calm and mature inquiries and reflections which must ever precede the formation of a wise and well-balanced government for a free people. It is not to be wondered at that a government instituted in times so inauspicious should on experiment be found greatly deficient and inadequate to the purpose it was intended to answer.

Arguments for a Strong National Government

This intelligent people perceived and regretted these defects. Still continuing no less attached to union than enamored of liberty, they observed the danger which immediately threatened the former and more remotely the latter; and being persuaded that ample security for both could only be found in a national government more wisely framed, they, as with one voice, convened the late convention at Philadelphia to take that important subject under consideration.

This convention, composed of men who possessed the confidence of the people, and many of whom had become highly distinguished by their patriotism, virtue, and wisdom, in times which tried the minds and hearts of men, undertook the arduous task. In the mild season of peace, with minds unoccupied by other subjects, they passed many months in cool, uninterrupted, and daily consultation; and finally, without having been awed by power, or influenced by any passions except love for their country, they presented and recommended to the people the plan produced by their joint and very unanimous councils.

Admit, for so is the fact, that this plan is only *recommended*, not imposed, yet let it be remembered that it is neither recommended to *blind* approbation, nor to *blind* reprobation; but to that sedate and candid consideration which the magnitude and importance of the subject demand, and which it certainly ought to receive. But, as has been already remarked, it is more to be wished than expected that it may be so considered and examined. Experience on a former occasion teaches us not to be too sanguine in such hopes. It is not yet forgotten that well-grounded apprehensions of imminent danger induced the people of America to form the memorable Congress of 1774. That body recommended certain measures to their constituents, and the event proved their wisdom; yet it is fresh in our memories how soon the press began to teem with pamphlets and weekly papers against those very measures. Not only many of the officers of government, who obeyed the dictates of personal interest, but others, from a mistaken estimate of consequences, from the undue influence of ancient attachments or whose ambition aimed at objects which did not correspond with the public good, were indefatigable in their endeavors to persuade the people to reject the advice of that patriotic Congress. Many, indeed, were deceived and deluded, but the great majority of the people reasoned and decided judiciously; and happy they are in reflecting that they did so.

They considered that the Congress was composed of many wise and experienced men. That, being convened from different parts of the country, they brought with them and communicated to each other a variety of useful information. That, in the course of the time they passed together in inquiring into and discussing the true interests of their country, they must have acquired very accurate knowledge on that head. That they were individually interested in the public liberty and prosperity, and therefore that it was not less their inclination than their duty to recommend only such measures as, after the most mature deliberation, they really thought prudent and advisable.

These and similar considerations then induced the people to rely greatly on the judgment and integrity of the Congress; and they took their advice notwithstanding the various arts and endeavors used to deter and dissuade them from it. But if the people at large had reason to confide in the men of that Congress, few of whom had been fully tried or generally known, still greater reason have they now to respect the judgment and advice of the convention, for it is well known that some of the most distinguished members of that Congress, who have been since tried and justly approved for patriotism and abilities, and who have grown old in acquiring political information, were also members of this convention, and carried into it their accumulated knowledge and experience.

It is worthy of remark that not only the first, but every succeeding Congress, as well as the late convention, have invariably joined with the people in thinking that the prosperity of America depended on its Union. To preserve and perpetuate it was the great object of the people in forming that convention, and it is also the great object of the plan which the convention has advised them to adopt. With what propriety, therefore, or for what good purposes, are attempts at this particular period made by some men to depreciate the importance of the Union? Or why is it suggested that three or four confederacies would be better than one? I am persuaded in my own mind that the people have always thought right on this subject, and that their universal and uniform attachment to the cause of the Union rests on great and weighty reasons, which I shall endeavor to develop and explain in some ensuing papers. They who promote the idea of substituting a number of distinct confederacies in the room of the plan of the convention seem clearly to foresee that the rejection of it would put the continuance of the Union in the utmost jeopardy. That certainly would be the case, and I sincerely wish that it may be as clearly foreseen by every good citizen that whenever the dissolution of the Union arrives, America will have reason to exclaim, in the words of the poet: "Farewell! A long farewell to all my greatness."

No. 3

The Same Subject Continued

The national security of the new nation, which Jay calls its "safety," will be best assured by a united country, which will protect citizens against external threats and internal uprisings of "direct and unlawful violence." The national government will be "more temperate and cool" than the states in settling disputes because "the pride of states, as well as of men, naturally disposes them to justify all their actions, and opposes their acknowledging, correcting, or repairing their errors and offenses. The national government, in such cases, will not be affected by this pride, but will proceed with moderation and candor to consider and decide on the means most proper to extricate them from the difficulties which threaten them."

Also, a national government will attract talent, "it will have the widest field for choice, and never experience that want of proper persons" common to the smaller, more isolated state governments.

It is not a new observation that the people of any country (if, like the Americans, intelligent and well-informed) seldom adopt and steadily persevere for many years in an erroneous opinion respecting their interests. That consideration naturally tends to create great respect for the high opinion which the people of America have so long and uniformly entertained of the importance of their continuing firmly united under one federal government, vested with sufficient powers for all general and national purposes.

The more attentively I consider and investigate the reasons which appear to have given birth to this opinion, the more I become convinced that they are cogent and conclusive.

National Security

Among the many objects to which a wise and free people find it necessary to direct their attention, that of providing for their *safety* seems to be the first. The *safety* of the people doubtless has relation to a great variety of circumstances and considerations, and consequently affords great latitude to those who wish to define it precisely and comprehensively.

At present I mean only to consider it as it respects security for the preservation of peace and tranquillity, as well as against dangers from *foreign arms and influence*, as from dangers of the *like kind* arising from domestic causes. As the former of these comes first in order, it is proper it should be the first discussed. Let us therefore proceed to examine whether the people are not right in their opinion that a cordial Union, under an efficient national government, affords them the best security that can be devised against *hostilities* from abroad.

The number of wars which have happened or will happen in the world will always be found to be in proportion to the number and weight of the causes, whether *real* or *pretended*, which *provoke* or *invite* them. If this remark be just, it becomes useful to inquire whether so many *just* causes of war are likely to be given by *united America* as by *disunited* America; for if it should turn out that united America will probably give the fewest, then it will follow that in this respect the Union tends most to preserve the people in a state of peace with other nations.

The *just* causes of war, for the most part, arise either from violations of treaties or from direct violence. America has already formed treaties with no less than six foreign nations, and all of them, except Prussia, are maritime, and therefore able to annoy and injure us. She has also extensive commerce with Portugal, Spain, and Britain, and, with respect to the two latter, has, in addition, the circumstance of neighborhood to attend to.

It is of high importance to the peace of America that she observe the laws of nations towards all these powers, and to me it appears evident that this will be more perfectly and punctually done by one national government than it could be either by thirteen separate States or by three or four distinct confederacies. For this opinion various reasons may be assigned.

National Government Will "Never Experience That Want of Proper Persons"

When once an efficient national government is established, the best men in the country will not only consent to serve, but also will generally be appointed to manage it; for, although town or country, or other contracted influence, may place men in State assemblies, or senates, or courts of justice, or executive departments, yet more general and extensive reputation for talents and other qualifications will be necessary to recommend men to offices under the national government—especially as it will have the widest field for choice, and never experience that want of proper persons which is not uncommon in some of the States. Hence, it will result that the administration, the political counsels, and the judicial decisions of the national government will be more wise, systematical, and judicious than those of individual States, and consequently more satisfactory with respect to other nations, as well as more *safe* with respect to us.

Under the national government, treaties and articles of treaties, as well as the laws of nations, will always be expounded in one sense and executed in the same manner—whereas adjudications on the same points and questions in thirteen States, or in three or four confederacies, will not always accord or be consistent; and that, as well from the variety of independent courts and judges appointed by different and independent governments as from the different local laws and interests which may affect and influence them. The wisdom of the convention in committing such questions to the jurisdiction and judgment of courts appointed by and responsible only to one national government cannot be too much commended.

The prospect of present loss or advantage may often tempt the governing party in one or two States to swerve from good faith and justice; but those temptations, not reaching the other States, and consequently having little or no influence on the national government, the temptation will be fruitless, and good faith and justice be preserved. The case of the treaty of peace with Britain adds great weight to this reasoning.

If even the governing party in a State should be disposed to resist such temptations, yet, as such temptations may, and commonly do, result from circumstances peculiar to the State, and may affect a great number of the inhabitants, the governing party may not always be able, if willing, to prevent the injustice meditated, or to punish the aggressors. But the national government, not being affected by those local circumstances, will neither be induced to commit the wrong themselves, nor want power or inclination to prevent or punish its commission by others.

So far, therefore, as either designed or accidental violations of treaties and of the laws of nations afford *just* causes of war, they are less to be apprehended under one general government than under several lesser ones, and in that respect the former most favors the *safety* of the people.

As to those just causes of war which proceed from direct and unlawful violence, it appears equally clear to me that one good national government affords vastly more security against dangers of that sort than can be derived from any other quarter.

Such violences are more frequently occasioned by the passions and interests of a part than of the whole, of one or two States than of the Union. Not a single Indian war has yet been produced by aggressions of the present federal government, feeble as it is; but there are several instances of Indian hostilities having been provoked by the improper conduct of individual States, who, either unable or unwilling to restrain or punish offenses, have given occasion to the slaughter of many innocent inhabitants.

The neighborhood of Spanish and British territories, bordering on some States and not on others, naturally confines the causes of quarrel more immediately to the borderers. The bordering States, if any, will be those who, under the impulse of sudden irritation, and a quick sense of apparent interest or injury, will be most likely, by direct violence, to excite war with those nations; and nothing can so effectually obviate that danger as a national government, whose wisdom and prudence will not be diminished by the passions which actuate the parties immediately interested.

But not only fewer just causes of war will be given by the national government, but it will also be more in their power to accommodate and settle them amicably. They will be more temperate and cool, and in that respect, as well as in others, will be more in capacity to act with circumspection than the offending State. The pride of states, as well as of men, naturally disposes them to justify all their actions, and opposes their acknowledging, correcting, or repairing their errors and offenses. The national government, in such cases, will not be affected by this pride, but will proceed with moderation and candor to consider and decide on the means most proper to extricate them from the difficulties which threaten them.

Besides, it is well known that acknowledgements, explanations, and compensations are often accepted as satisfactory from a strong united nation, which would be rejected as unsatisfactory if offered by a State or confederacy of little consideration or power. . . .

HAMILTON

No. 6

Concerning Dangers from War
Between the States

Hamilton lays out both his views on political society and his support of the commercial republic, arguing that "the spirit of commerce has a tendency to soften the manners of men, and to extinguish those inflammable humors which have so often kindled into wars. Commercial republics, like ours, will never be disposed to waste themselves in ruinous contentions with each other. They will be governed by mutual interest, and will cultivate a spirit of mutual amity and concord." This is one of The Federalist Papers' *infrequent comments on the interplay of economics and politics. Possibly the authors believed the subject did not need much elaboration in these essays because most readers would agree that a stable, relatively prosperous economy was a prerequisite to a functioning republican government.*

Hamilton signals the dangers of "domestic factions and convulsions," which Madison will consider in greater detail in Federalist No. 10. *Hamilton believes humans live, not in a utopian society, but are "ambitious, vindictive, and rapacious"; political stability does not come naturally to a people. He sends a dark warning, comparable to any of Madison's more developed reflections on the human condition: "To look for a continuation of harmony between a number of independent, unconnected sovereignties situated in the same neighborhood would be to disregard the uniform course of human events, and to set at defiance the accumulated experience of ages."*

The three last numbers of this paper have been dedicated to an enumeration of the dangers to which we should be exposed, in a state of disunion, from the arms and arts of foreign nations. I shall now proceed to delineate dangers of a different and, perhaps, still more alarming kind—those which will in all probability flow from dissensions between the States themselves and from domestic factions and convulsions. These have been already in some instances slightly anticipated; but they deserve a more particular and more full investigation.

"Ambitious, Vindictive, and Rapacious" Humanity

A man must be far gone in Utopian speculations who can seriously doubt that if these States should either be wholly disunited, or only united in partial confederacies, the subdivisions into which they might be thrown would have frequent and violent contests with each other. To presume a want of motives for such contests as an argument against their existence would be to forget that men are ambitious, vindictive, and rapacious. To look for a continuation of harmony between a number of independent, unconnected sovereignties situated in the same neighborhood would be to disregard the uniform course of human events, and to set at defiance the accumulated experience of ages.

The causes of hostility among nations are innumerable. There are some which have a general and almost constant operation upon the collective bodies of society. Of this description are the love of power or the desire of pre-eminence and dominion—the jealousy of power, or the desire of equality and safety. There are others which have a more circumscribed though an equally operative influence within their spheres. Such are the rivalships and competitions of commerce between commercial nations. And there are others, not less numerous than either of the former, which take their origin entirely in private passions; in the attachments, enmities, interests, hopes, and fears of leading individuals in the communities of which they are members. Men of this class, whether the favorites of a king or of a people, have in too many instances abused the confidence they possessed; and assuming the pretext of some public motive, have not scrupled to sacrifice the national tranquillity to personal advantage or personal gratification. . . .

The Commercial Republic

But notwithstanding the concurring testimony of experience, in this particular, there are still to be found visionary or designing men, who stand ready to advocate the paradox of perpetual peace between the States, though dismembered and alienated from each other. The genius of republics (say they) is pacific; the spirit of commerce has a tendency to soften the manners of men, and to extinguish those inflammable humors which have so often kindled into wars. Commercial republics, like ours, will never be disposed to waste themselves in ruinous contentions with each other. They will be governed by mutual interest, and will cultivate a spirit of mutual amity and concord.

Is it not (we may ask these projectors in politics) the true interest of all nations to cultivate the same benevolent and philosophic spirit? If this be their true interest, have they in fact pursued it? Has it not, on the contrary, invariably been found that momentary passions, and immediate interests, have a more active and imperious control over human conduct than general or remote considerations of policy, utility, or justice? Have republics in practice been less addicted to war than monarchies? Are not the former administered by *men* as well as the latter? Are there not aversions, predilections, rivalships, and desires of unjust acquisitions that affect nations as well as kings? Are not popular assemblies frequently subject to the impulses of rage, resentment, jealousy, avarice, and of other irregular and violent propensities? Is it not well known that their determinations are often governed by a few individuals in whom they place confidence, and are, of course, liable to be tinctured by the passions and views of those individuals? Has commerce hitherto done any thing more than change the objects of war? Is not the love of wealth as domineering and enterprising a passion as that of power or glory? Have there not been as many wars founded upon commercial motives since that has become the prevailing system of nations, as were before occasioned by the cupidity of territory or dominion? Has not the spirit of commerce, in many instances, administered new incentives to the appetite, both for the one and for the other? Let experience, the least fallible guide of human opinions, be appealed to for an answer to these inquiries.

Sparta, Athens, Rome, and Carthage were all republics; two of them, Athens and Carthage, of the commercial kind. Yet were they as often engaged in wars, offensive and defensive, as the neighboring monarchies of the same times. Sparta was little better than a well-regulated camp; and Rome was never sated of carnage and conquest.

Carthage, though a commercial republic, was the aggressor in the very war that ended in her destruction. Hannibal had carried her arms into the heart of Italy and to the gates of Rome, before Scipio, in turn, gave him an overthrow in the territories of Carthage and made a conquest of the commonwealth.

Venice, in later times, figured more than once in wars of ambition, till, becoming an object to the other Italian states, Pope Julius the Second found means to accomplish that formidable league,[1] which gave a deadly blow to the power and pride of this haughty republic.

The provinces of Holland, till they were overwhelmed in debts and taxes, took a leading and conspicuous part in the wars of Europe. They had furious contests with England for the dominion of the sea, and were among the most persevering and most implacable of the opponents of Louis XIV.

In the government of Britain the representatives of the people compose one branch of the national legislature. Commerce has been for ages the predominant pursuit of that country. Few nations, nevertheless, have been more frequently engaged in war; and the wars in which that kingdom has been engaged have, in numerous instances, proceeded from the people.

There have been, if I may so express it, almost as many popular as royal wars. The cries of the nation and the importunities of their representatives have, upon various occasions, dragged their monarchs into war, or continued them in it, contrary to their inclinations, and sometimes contrary to the real interests of the state. In that memorable struggle for superiority between the rival houses of *Austria* and *Bourbon,* which so long kept Europe in a flame, it is well known that the antipathies of the English against the French, seconding the ambition, or rather the avarice, of a favorite leader,[2] protracted the war beyond the limits marked out by sound policy, and for a considerable time in opposition to the views of the court.

The wars of these two last-mentioned nations have in a great measure grown out of commercial considerations—the desire of supplanting and the fear of being supplanted, either in particular branches of traffic or in the general advantages of trade and navigation, and sometimes even the more culpable desire of sharing in the commerce of other nations without their consent.

The last war but two between Britain and Spain sprang from the attempts of the English merchants to prosecute an illicit trade with the Spanish main. These unjustifiable practices on their part produced severity on the part of the Spaniards towards the subjects of Great Britain which were not more justifiable, because they exceeded the bounds of a just retaliation and were chargeable with inhumanity and cruelty. Many of the English who were taken on the Spanish coast were sent to dig in the mines of Potosi; and by the usual progress of a spirit of resentment, the innocent were, after a while, confounded with the guilty in indiscriminate punishment. The complaints of the merchants kindled a violent flame throughout the nation, which soon after broke out in the House of Commons, and was communicated from that body to the ministry. Letters of reprisal were granted, and a war ensued, which in its consequences overthrew all the alliances that but twenty years before had been formed, with sanguine expectations of the most beneficial fruits.

Neighboring States: Natural Enemies Unless Held Together in a Republic

From this summary of what has taken place in other countries, whose situations have borne the nearest resemblance to our own, what reason can we have to confide in those reveries which would seduce us into an expectation of peace and cordiality between the members of the present confederacy, in a state of separation? Have we not already seen enough of the fallacy and extravagance of those idle theories which have amused us with promises of an exemption from the imperfections, the weaknesses, and the evils incident to society in every shape? Is it not time to awake from the deceitful dream of a golden age and to adopt as a practical maxim for the direction of our political conduct that we, as well as the other inhabitants of the globe, are yet remote from the happy empire of perfect wisdom and perfect virtue?

Let the point of extreme depression to which our national dignity and credit have sunk, let the inconveniences felt everywhere from a lax and ill administration of government, let the revolt of a part of the State of North Carolina, the late menacing disturbances in Pennsylvania, and the actual insurrections and rebellions in Massachusetts, declare—!

So far is the general sense of mankind from corresponding with the tenets of those who endeavor to lull asleep our apprehensions of discord and hostility between the States, in the event of disunion, that it has from long observation of the progress of society become a sort of axiom in politics that vicinity, or nearness of situation, constitutes nations natural enemies. An intelligent writer expresses himself on this subject to this effect:

"Neighboring nations [says he] are naturally enemies of each other, unless their common weakness forces them to league in a confederate republic and their constitution prevents the differences that neighborhood occasions, extinguishing that secret jealousy which disposes all states to aggrandize themselves at the expense of their neighbors."[3] This passage, at the same time, points out the evil and suggests the remedy.

No. 8

The Effects of Internal War in Producing Standing Armies and Other Institutions Unfriendly to Liberty

Hamilton makes the case for standing armies "and the correspondent appendages of military establishments." He states, "Safety from external danger is the most powerful director of national conduct." A standing army will discourage surprise invasions and suppress mobs and insurrections; without such a force "we should, in a little time, see established in every part of this country the same engines of despotism which have been the scourge of the old world." Hamilton favors a small army under civilian control. He tells readers, with the memory of a recent devastating war fresh in mind, "The laws are not accustomed to relaxation in favor of military exigencies; the civil state remains in full vigor." Warfare is to be avoided if possible; in Europe, "war . . . is no longer a history of nations subdued and empires overtaken, but of towns taken and retaken, of battles that decide nothing, of retreats more beneficial than victories, of much effort and little acquisition." In America war "would be desultory and predatory. Plunder and devastation ever march in the train of irregulars. The calamities of individuals would make the principal figure in the events which would characterize our military exploits."

Hamilton believes a commercially active, prosperous people will show little interest in war, because such people, "absorbed in the pursuits of gain and devoted to the improvements of agriculture and commerce, are incompatible with the condition of a nation of soldiers." He cautions, "It is in the nature of war to increase the executive at the expense of the legislative authority," which can lead toward authoritarian governments. He warns against the dangers of an overly strong military, especially because civil rights would be degraded and a military state created.

Assuming therefore as an established truth that the several States, in case of disunion, or such combinations of them as might happen to be formed out of the wreck of the general Confederacy, would be subject to those vicissitudes of peace and war, of friendship and enmity with each other, which have fallen to the lot of all neighboring nations not united under one government, let us enter into a concise detail of some of the consequences that would attend such a situation.

The Need for Standing Armies

War between the States, in the first period of their separate existence, would be accompanied with much greater distresses than it commonly is in those countries where regular military establishments have long obtained. The disciplined armies always kept on foot on the continent of Europe, though they bear a malignant aspect to liberty and economy, have, notwithstanding, been productive of the signal advantage of rendering sudden conquests impracticable, and of preventing that rapid desolation which used to mark the progress of war prior to their introduction. The art of fortification has contributed to the same ends. The nations of Europe are encircled with chains of fortified places, which mutually obstruct invasion. Campaigns are wasted in reducing two or three frontier garrisons to gain admittance into an enemy's country. Similar impediments occur at every step to exhaust the strength and delay the progress of an invader. Formerly an invading army would penetrate into the heart of a neighboring country almost as soon as intelligence of its approach could be received; but now a comparatively small force of disciplined troops, acting on the defensive, with the aid of posts, is able to impede, and finally to frustrate, the enterprises of one much more considerable. The history of war in that quarter of the globe is no longer a history of nations subdued and empires overturned, but of towns taken and retaken, of battles that decide nothing, of retreats more beneficial than victories, of much effort and little acquisition.

In this country the scene would be altogether reversed. The jealousy of military establishments would postpone them as long as possible. The want of fortifications, leaving the frontiers of one State open to another, would facilitate inroads. The populous States would, with little difficulty, overrun their less populous neighbors. Conquests would be as easy to be made as difficult to be retained. War, therefore, would be desultory and predatory. Plunder and devastation ever march in the train of irregulars. The calamities of individuals would make the principal figure in the events which would characterize our military exploits.

This picture is not too highly wrought; though, I confess, it would not long remain a just one. Safety from external danger is the most powerful director of national conduct. Even the ardent love of liberty will, after a time, give way to its dictates. The violent destruction of life and property incident to war, the continual effort and alarm attendant on a state of continual danger, will compel nations the most attached to liberty to resort for repose and security to institutions which have a tendency to destroy their civil and political rights. To be more safe, they at length become willing to run the risk of being less free.

Standing Armies

The institutions chiefly alluded to are standing armies and the correspondent appendages of military establishments. Standing armies, it is said, are not provided against in the new Constitution; and it is thence inferred that they may exist under it. This inference, from the very form of the proposition, is, at best, problematical and uncertain.[1] But standing armies, it may be replied, must inevitably result from a dissolution of the Confederacy. Frequent war and constant apprehension, which require a state of as constant preparation, will infallibly produce them. The weaker States, or confederacies, would first have recourse to them to put themselves upon an equality with their more potent neighbors. They would endeavor to supply the inferiority of population and resources by a more regular and effective system of defense, by disciplined troops, and by fortifications. They would, at the same time, be necessitated to strengthen the executive arm of government, in doing which their constitutions would acquire a progressive direction towards monarchy. It is of the nature of war to increase the executive at the expense of the legislative authority.

The expedients which have been mentioned would soon give the States, or confederacies, that made use of them a superiority over their neighbors.

Small states, or states of less natural strength, under vigorous governments, and with the assistance of disciplined armies, have often triumphed over large states, or states of greater natural strength, which have been destitute of these advantages. Neither the pride nor the safety of the more important States, or confederacies, would permit them long to submit to this mortifying and adventitious superiority. They would quickly resort to means similar to those by which it had been effected, to reinstate themselves in their lost pre-eminence. Thus we should, in a little time, see established in every part of this country the same engines of despotism which have been the scourge of the old world. This, at least, would be the natural course of things; and our reasonings will be the more likely to be just in proportion as they are accommodated to this standard.

These are not vague inferences drawn from supposed or speculative defects in a Constitution, the whole power of which is lodged in the hands of a people, or their representatives and delegates, but they are solid conclusions drawn from the natural and necessary progress of human affairs.

It may, perhaps, be asked, by way of objection to this, why did not standing armies spring up out of the contentions which so often distracted the ancient republics of Greece? Different answers, equally satisfactory, may be given to this question. The industrious habits of the people of the present day, absorbed in the pursuits of gain and devoted to the improvements of agriculture and commerce, are incompatible with the condition of a nation of soldiers, which was the true condition of the people of those republics. The means of revenue, which have been so greatly multiplied by the increase of gold and silver and of the arts of industry, and the science of finance, which is the offspring of modern times, concurring with the habits of nations, have produced an entire revolution in the system of war, and have rendered disciplined armies, distinct from the body of the citizens, the inseparable companion of frequent hostility.

Armies in Stable and Unstable Countries

There is a wide difference, also, between military establishments in a country seldom exposed by its situation to internal invasions, and in one which is often subject to them and always apprehensive of them. The rulers of the former can have no good pretext, if they are even so inclined, to keep on foot armies so numerous as must of necessity be maintained in the latter. These armies being, in the first case, rarely if at all called into activity for interior defense, the people are in no danger of being broken to military subordination. The laws are not accustomed to relaxation in favor of military exigencies; the civil state remains in full vigor, neither corrupted, nor confounded with the principles or propensities of the other state. The smallness of the army renders the natural strength of the community an overmatch for it; and the citizens, not habituated to look up to the military power for protection, or to submit to its oppressions, neither love nor fear the soldiery; they view them with a spirit of jealous acquiescence in a necessary evil and stand ready to resist a power which they suppose may be exerted to the prejudice of their rights.

The army under such circumstances may usefully aid the magistrate to suppress a small faction, or an occasional mob, or insurrection; but it will be unable to enforce encroachments against the united efforts of the great body of the people.

In a country in the predicament last described, the contrary of all this happens. The perpetual menacings of danger oblige the government to be always prepared to repel it; its armies must be numerous enough for instant defense. The continual necessity for their services enhances the importance of the soldier, and proportionably degrades the condition of the citizen. The military state becomes elevated above the civil. The inhabitants of territories, often the theater of war, are unavoidably subjected to frequent infringements of their rights, which serve to weaken their sense of those rights; and by degrees the people are brought to consider the soldiery not only as their protectors but as their superiors. The transition from this disposition to that of considering them masters is neither remote nor difficult; but it is very difficult to prevail upon a people under such impressions to make a bold or effectual resistance to usurpations supported by the military power.

The kingdom of Great Britain falls within the first description. An insular situation, and a powerful marine, guarding it in a great measure against the possibility of foreign invasion, supersede the necessity of a numerous army within the kingdom. A sufficient force to make head against a sudden descent, till the militia could have time to rally and embody, is all that has been deemed requisite. No motive of national policy has demanded, nor would public opinion have tolerated, a larger number of troops upon its domestic establishment. There has been, for a long time past, little room for the operation of the other causes, which have been enumerated as the consequences of internal war. This peculiar felicity of situation has, in a great degree, contributed to preserve the liberty which that country to this day enjoys, in spite of the prevalent venality and corruption. If, on the contrary, Britain had been situated on the continent, and had been compelled, as she would have been, by that situation, to make her military establishments at home coextensive with those of the other great powers of Europe, she, like them, would in all probability be, at this day, a victim to the absolute power of a single man. 'Tis possible, though not easy, that the people of that island may be enslaved from other causes; but it cannot be by the prowess of an army so inconsiderable as that which has been usually kept up within the kingdom.

"If We Are Wise Enough to Preserve the Union"

If we are wise enough to preserve the Union we may for ages enjoy an advantage similar to that of an insulated situation. Europe is at a great distance from us. Her colonies in our vicinity will be likely to continue too much disproportioned in strength to be able to give us any dangerous annoyance. Extensive military establishments cannot, in this position, be necessary to our security. But if we should be disunited, and the integral parts should either remain separated, or, which is most probable, should be thrown together into two or three confederacies, we should be, in a short course of time, in the predicament of the continental powers of Europe— our liberties would be a prey to the means of defending ourselves against the ambition and jealousy of each other.

This is an idea not superficial nor futile, but solid and weighty. It deserves the most serious and mature consideration of every prudent and honest man of whatever party. If such men will make a firm and solemn pause, and meditate dispassionately on the importance of this interesting idea; if they will contemplate it in all its attitudes, and trace it to all its consequences, they will not hesitate to part with trivial objections to a Constitution, the rejection of which would in all probability put a final period to the Union. The airy phantoms that flit before the distempered imaginations of some of its adversaries would quickly give place to the more substantial prospects of dangers, real, certain, and formidable.

The Utility of the Union as a Safeguard Against Domestic Faction and Insurrection

An attraction of the new union is its size, which means "the enlargement of the orbit within which . . . systems [of civil government] are to revolve." However, Hamilton believes even a large, stable government can only have popular support if political powers are separated through "the regular distribution of power into distinct departments." Additionally, there must be "legislative balances and checks." These are the "means, and powerful means, by which the excellencies of republican government may be retained and its imperfections lessened or avoided." Additional separation of powers includes courts "composed of judges holding their offices during good behavior," which means for long terms, and a legislature elected by the people. Hamilton cites Montesquieu's concept of a confederate republic, which represents "a luminous abridgment of the principal arguments in favor of the Union," in which several small states unite for the advantage of size and strength, while retaining their basic independence. "This fully corresponds, in every rational import of the terms, with the idea of a federal government."

A firm Union will be of the utmost moment to the peace and liberty of the States as a barrier against domestic faction and insurrection. It is impossible to read the history of the petty republics of Greece and Italy without feeling sensations of horror and disgust at the distractions with which they were continually agitated, and at the rapid succession of revolutions by which they were kept in a state of perpetual vibration between the extremes of tyranny and anarchy. If they exhibit occasional calms, these only serve as short-lived contrasts to the furious storms that are to succeed. If now and then intervals of felicity open themselves to view, we behold them with a mixture of regret, arising from the reflection that the pleasing scenes before us are soon to be overwhelmed by the tempestuous waves of sedition and party rage. If momentary rays of glory break forth from the gloom, while they dazzle us with a transient and fleeting brilliancy, they at the same time admonish us to lament that the vices of government should pervert the direction and tarnish the luster of those bright talents and exalted endowments for which the favored soils that produced them have been so justly celebrated.

Despotism Versus Liberty

From the disorders that disfigure the annals of those republics the advocates of despotism have drawn arguments, not only against the forms of republican government, but against the very principles of civil liberty. They have decried all free government as inconsistent with the order of society, and have indulged themselves in malicious exultation over its friends and partisans. Happily for mankind, stupendous fabrics reared on the basis of liberty, which have flourished for ages, have, in a few glorious instances, refuted their gloomy sophisms. And, I trust, America will be the broad and solid foundation of other edifices, not less magnificent, which will be equally permanent monuments of their errors.

But it is not to be denied that the portraits they have sketched of republican government were too just copies of the originals from which they were taken. If it had been found impracticable to have devised models of a more perfect structure, the enlightened friends to liberty would have been obliged to abandon the cause of that species of government as indefensible. The science of politics, however, like most other sciences, has received great improvement. The efficacy of various principles is now well understood, which were either not known at all, or imperfectly known to the ancients. The regular distribution of power into distinct departments; the introduction of legislative balances and checks; the institution of courts composed of judges holding their offices during good behavior; the representation of the people in the legislature by deputies of their own election: these are wholly new discoveries, or have made their principal progress towards perfection in modern times. They are means, and powerful means, by which the excellencies of republican government may be retained and its imperfections lessened or avoided. To this catalogue of circumstances that tend to the amelioration of popular systems of civil government, I shall venture, however novel it may appear to some, to add one more, on a principle which has been made the foundation of an objection to the new Constitution; I mean the enlargement of the orbit within which such systems are to revolve, either in respect to the dimensions of a single State, or to the consolidation of several smaller States into one great Confederacy. The latter is that which immediately concerns the object under consideration. It will, however, be of use to examine the principle in its application to a single State, which shall be attended to in another place.

The utility of a Confederacy, as well to suppress faction and to guard the internal tranquillity of States as to increase their external force and security, is in reality not a new idea. It has been practiced upon in different countries and ages, and has received the sanction of the most applauded writers on the subjects of politics. The opponents of the plan proposed have, with great assiduity, cited and circulated the observations of Montesquieu on the necessity of a contracted territory for a republican government. But they seem not to have been apprised of the sentiments of that great man expressed in another part of his work, nor to have adverted to the consequences of the principle to which they subscribe with such ready acquiescence.

Monarchy Versus Factious Commonwealths

When Montesquieu recommends a small extent for republics, the standards he had in view were of dimensions far short of the limits of almost every one of these States. Neither Virginia, Massachusetts, Pennsylvania, New York, North Carolina, nor Georgia can by any means be compared with the models from which he reasoned and to which the terms of his description apply. If we therefore take his ideas on this point as the criterion of truth, we shall be driven to the alternative either of taking refuge at once in the arms of monarchy, or of splitting ourselves into an infinity of little, jealous, clashing, tumultuous commonwealths, the wretched nurseries of unceasing discord and the miserable objects of universal pity or contempt. Some of the writers who have come forward on the other side of the question seem to have been aware of the dilemma; and have even been bold enough to hint at the division of the larger States as a desirable thing. Such an infatuated policy, such a desperate expedient, might, by the multiplication of petty offices, answer the views of men who possess not qualifications to extend their influence beyond the narrow circles of personal intrigue, but it could never promote the greatness or happiness of the people of America.

Referring the examination of the principle itself to another place, as has been already mentioned, it will be sufficient to remark here that, in the sense of the author who has been most emphatically quoted upon the occasion, it would only dictate a reduction of the size of the more considerable members of the Union, but would not militate against their being all comprehended in one confederate government. And this is the true question, in the discussion of which we are at present interested.

Montesquieu's Confederate Republic

So far are the suggestions of Montesquieu from standing in opposition to a general Union of the States that he explicitly treats of a confederate republic as the expedient for extending the sphere of popular government and reconciling the advantages of monarchy with those of republicanism.

"It is very probable" (says he[1]) "that mankind would have been obliged at length to live constantly under the government of a single person had they not contrived a kind of constitution that has all the internal advantages of a republican, together with the external force of a monarchical, government. I mean a confederate republic.

"This form of government is a convention by which several smaller *states* agree to become members of a larger *one*, which they intend to form. It is a kind of assemblage of societies that constitute a new one, capable of increasing, by means of new associations, till they arrive to such a degree of power as to be able to provide for the security of the united body.

"A republic of this kind, able to withstand an external force, may support itself without any internal corruptions. The form of this society prevents all manner of inconveniences.

"If a single member should attempt to usurp the supreme authority, he could not be supposed to have an equal authority and credit in all the confederate states. Were he to have too great influence over one, this would alarm the rest. Were he to subdue a part, that which would still remain free might oppose him with forces independent of those which he had usurped, and overpower him before he could be settled in his usurpation.

"Should a popular insurrection happen in one of the confederate states, the others are able to quell it. Should abuses creep into one part, they are reformed by those that remain sound. The state may be destroyed on one side, and not on the other; the confederacy may be dissolved, and the confederates preserve their sovereignty.

"As this government is composed of small republics, it enjoys the internal happiness of each; and with respect to its external situation, it is possessed, by means of the association, of all the advantages of large monarchies."

I have thought it proper to quote at length these interesting passages, because they contain a luminous abridgment of the principal arguments in favor of the Union, and must effectually remove the false impressions which a misapplication of other parts of the world was calculated to produce. They have, at the same time, an intimate connection with the more immediate design of this paper, which is to illustrate the tendency of the Union to repress domestic faction and insurrection.

A distinction, more subtle than accurate, has been raised between a *confederacy* and a *consolidation* of the States. The essential characteristic of the first is said to be the restriction of its authority to the members in their collective capacities, without reaching to the individuals of whom they are composed. It is contended that the national council ought to have no concern with any object of internal administration. An exact equality of suffrage between the members has also been insisted upon as a leading feature of a confederate government. These positions are, in the main, arbitrary; they are supported neither by principle nor precedent. It has indeed happened that governments of this kind have generally operated in the manner which the distinction, taken notice of, supposes to be inherent in their nature; but there have been in most of them extensive exceptions to the practice, which serve to prove, as far as example will go, that there is no absolute rule on the subject. And it will be clearly shown, in the course of this investigation, that as far as the principle contended for has prevailed, it has been the cause of incurable disorder and imbecility in the government.

The definition of a *confederate republic* seems simply to be "an assemblage of societies," or an association of two or more states into one state. The extent, modifications, and objects of the federal authority are mere matters of discretion. So long as the separate organization of the members be not abolished; so long as it exists, by a constitutional necessity, for local purposes; though it should be in perfect subordination to the general authority of the union, it would still be, in fact and in theory, an association of states, or a confederacy. The proposed Constitution, so far from implying an abolition of the State governments, makes them constituent parts of the national sovereignty, by allowing them a direct representation in the Senate, and leaves in their possession certain exclusive and very important portions of sovereign power. This fully corresponds, in every rational import of the terms, with the idea of a federal government. . . .

No. 10

The Same Subject Continued

In this concise analysis of political behavior, Madison defines political faction and how it may be contained. This essay's carefully crafted language and analytical depth draw on Madison's earlier studies of this issue. Faction introduces "instability, injustice, and confusion" into public life. Madison regards "the superior force of an interested and overbearing majority" as the most dangerous form of faction. A faction is a majority or minority of citizens bound "by some common impulse of passion, or of interest, adverse to the rights of other citizens" or to the community's "permanent and aggregate interests." Zeal for differing religious and political beliefs and the personal ambitions of political leaders represent some of the "latent causes of faction." The other great causes of faction are the division between property owners and those without property, and between creditors and debtors. Additionally, there are landed, manufacturing, mercantile, and monied interests dividing into different classes. "The regulation of these various and interfering interests forms the principal task of modern legislation and involves the spirit of party and faction in the necessary and ordinary operations of government."

Madison believes the causes of faction cannot be removed or suppressed, but their effects can be contained in a republic, where citizens elect a small number of leaders to represent them. A factious leader or political factions may spring up in a particular state, but "will be unable to spread a general conflagration" across the union. The Madisonian imagery is of a fiery, passionate, difficult to control force that cannot be removed or avoided, but can be checked and contained in political life. "Liberty is to faction what air is to fire, an aliment without which it instantly expires," he writes, adding, "It could not be a less folly to abolish liberty, which is essential to political life, because it nourishes faction than it would be to wish the annihilation of air, which is essential to animal life, because it imparts to fire its destructive agency."

Finally, a republic's size contributes to containing faction. Here Madison turns accepted political theory on its ear. Conventional wisdom had it that republican government was best suited to small states; larger polities required centralized, more tightly controlled leadership. Just the opposite is true, Madison argues. Republican government is best suited to large territories because "extend the sphere and you take in a greater variety of parties and interests; you make it less probable that a majority of the whole will have a common motive to invade the rights of other citizens; or if such a common motive exists, it will be more difficult to all who feel it to discover their own strength and to act in unison with each other."

Among the numerous advantages promised by a well-constructed Union, none deserves to be more accurately developed than its tendency to break and control the violence of faction. The friend of popular governments never finds himself so much alarmed for their character and fate as when he contemplates their propensity to this dangerous vice. He will not fail, therefore, to set a due value on any plan which, without violating the principles to which he is attached, provides a proper cure for it. The instability, injustice, and confusion introduced into the public councils have, in truth, been the mortal diseases under which popular governments have everywhere perished, as they continue to be the favorite and fruitful topics from which the adversaries to liberty derive their most specious declamations. The valuable improvements made by the American constitutions on the popular models, both ancient and modern, cannot certainly be too much admired; but it would be an unwarrantable partiality to contend that they have as effectually obviated the danger on this side, as was wished and expected. Complaints are everywhere heard from our most considerate and virtuous citizens, equally the friends of public and private faith and of public and personal liberty, that our governments are too unstable, that the public good is disregarded in the conflicts of rival parties, and that measures are too often decided, not according to the rules of justice and the rights of the minor party, but by the superior force of an interested and overbearing majority. However anxiously we may wish that these complaints had no foundation, the evidence of known facts will not permit us to deny that they are in some degree true. It will be found, indeed, on a candid review of our situation, that some of the distresses under which we labor have been erroneously charged on the operation of our governments; but it will be found, at the same time, that other causes will not alone account for many of our heaviest misfortunes; and, particularly, for that prevailing and increasing distrust of public engagements and alarm for private rights which are echoed from one end of the continent to the other. These must be chiefly, if not wholly, effects of the unsteadiness and injustice with which a factious spirit has tainted our public administration.

Faction Defined

By a faction I understand a number of citizens, whether amounting to a majority or minority of the whole, who are united and actuated by some common impulse of passion, or of interest, adverse to the rights of other citizens, or to the permanent and aggregate interests of the community.

There are two methods of curing the mischiefs of faction: the one, by removing its causes; the other, by controlling its effects.

There are again two methods of removing the causes of faction: the one, by destroying the liberty which is essential to its existence; the other, by giving to every citizen the same opinions, the same passions, and the same interests.

It could never be more truly said than of the first remedy that it was worse than the disease. Liberty is to faction what air is to fire, an aliment without which it instantly expires. But it could not be a less folly to abolish liberty, which is essential to political life, because it nourishes faction than it would be to wish the annihilation of air, which is essential to animal life, because it imparts to fire its destructive agency.

The second expedient is as impracticable as the first would be unwise. As long as the reason of man continues fallible, and he is at liberty to exercise it, different opinions will be formed. As long as the connection subsists between his reason and his self-love, his opinions and his passions will have a reciprocal influence on each other; and the former will be objects to which the latter will attach themselves. The diversity in the faculties of men, from which the rights of property originate, is not less an insuperable obstacle to a uniformity of interests. The protection of these faculties is the first object of government. From the protection of different and unequal faculties of acquiring property, the possession of different degrees and kinds of property immediately results; and from the influence of these on the sentiments and views of the respective proprietors ensues a division of the society into different interests and parties.

Faction's Origins in Human Nature

The latent causes of faction are thus sown in the nature of man; and we see them everywhere brought into different degrees of activity, according to the different circumstances of civil society. A zeal for different opinions concerning religion, concerning government, and many other points, as well of speculation as of practice; an attachment to different leaders ambitiously contending for pre-eminence and power; or to persons of other descriptions whose fortunes have been interesting to the human passions, have, in turn, divided mankind into parties, inflamed them with mutual animosity, and rendered them much more disposed to vex and oppress each other than to co-operate for their common good. So strong is this propensity of mankind to fall into mutual animosities that where no substantial occasion presents itself the most frivolous and fanciful distinctions have been sufficient to kindle their unfriendly passions and excite their most violent conflicts. But the most common and durable source of factions has been the various and unequal distribution of property. Those who hold and those who are without property have ever formed distinct interests in society. Those who are creditors, and those who are debtors, fall under a like discrimination. A landed interest, a manufacturing interest, a mercantile interest, a moneyed interest, with many lesser interests, grow up of necessity in civilized nations, and divide them into different classes, actuated by different sentiments and views. The regulation of these various and interfering interests forms the principal task of modern legislation and involves the spirit of party and faction in the necessary and ordinary operations of government.

No Person or Party Should Judge His Own Cause

No man is allowed to be a judge in his own cause, because his interest would certainly bias his judgment, and, not improbably, corrupt his integrity. With equal, nay with greater reason, a body of men are unfit to be both judges and parties at the same time; yet what are many of the most important acts of legislation but so many judicial determinations, not indeed concerning the rights of single persons, but concerning the rights of large bodies of citizens? And what are the different classes of legislators but advocates and parties to the causes which they determine? Is a law proposed concerning private debts? It is a question to which the creditors are parties on one side and the debtors on the other. Justice ought to hold the balance between them. Yet the parties are, and must be, themselves the judges; and the most numerous party, or in other words, the most powerful faction must be expected to prevail. Shall domestic manufacturers be encouraged, and in what degree, by restrictions on foreign manufacturers? are questions which would be differently decided by the landed and the manufacturing classes, and probably by neither with a sole regard to justice and the public good. The apportionment of taxes on the various descriptions of property is an act which seems to require the most exact impartiality; yet there is, perhaps, no legislative act in which greater opportunity and temptation are given to a predominant party to trample on the rules of justice. Every shilling with which they overburden the inferior number is a shilling saved to their own pockets.

It is in vain to say that enlightened statesmen will be able to adjust these clashing interests and render them all subservient to the public good. Enlightened statesmen will not always be at the helm. Nor, in many cases, can such an adjustment be made at all without taking into view indirect and remote considerations, which will rarely prevail over the immediate interest which one party may find in disregarding the rights of another or the good of the whole.

The Causes of Faction Cannot Be Contained, Only Its Effects

The inference to which we are brought is that the *causes* of faction cannot be removed and that relief is only to be sought in the means of controlling its *effects*.

If a faction consists of less than a majority, relief is supplied by the republican principle, which enables the majority to defeat its sinister views by regular vote. It may clog the administration, it may convulse the society; but it will be unable to execute and mask its violence under the forms of the Constitution. When a majority is included in a faction, the form of popular government, on the other hand, enables it to sacrifice to its ruling passion or interest both the public good and the rights of other citizens. To secure the public good and private rights against the danger of such a faction, and at the same time to preserve the spirit and the form of popular government, is then the great object to which our inquiries are directed. Let me add that it is the great desideratum by which alone this form of government can be rescued from the opprobrium under which it has so long labored and be recommended to the esteem and adoption of mankind.

By what means is this object attainable? Evidently by one of two only. Either the existence of the same passion or interest in a majority at the same time must be prevented, or the majority, having such coexistent passion or interest, must be rendered, by their number and local situation, unable to concert and carry into effect schemes of oppression. If the impulse and the opportunity be suffered to coincide, we well know that neither moral nor religious motives can be relied on as an adequate control. They are not found to be such on the injustice and violence of individuals, and lose their efficacy in proportion to the number combined together, that is, in proportion as their efficacy becomes needful.

A Pure Democracy Cannot Contain Faction

From this view of the subject it may be concluded that a pure democracy, by which I mean a society consisting of a small number of citizens, who assemble and administer the government in person, can admit of no cure for the mischiefs of faction. A common passion or interest will, in almost every case, be felt by a majority of the whole; a communication and concert results from the form of government itself; and there is nothing to check the inducements to sacrifice the weaker party or an obnoxious individual. Hence it is that such democracies have ever been spectacles of turbulence and contention; have ever been found incompatible with personal security or the rights of property; and have in general been as short in their lives as they have been violent in their deaths. Theoretic politicians, who have patronized this species of government, have erroneously supposed that by reducing mankind to a perfect equality in their political rights, they would at the same time be perfectly equalized and assimilated in their possessions, their opinions, and their passions.

The Difference Between a Democracy and a Republic

A republic, by which I mean a government in which the scheme of representation takes place, opens a different prospect and promises the cure for which we are seeking. Let us examine the points in which it varies from pure democracy, and we shall comprehend both the nature of the cure and the efficacy which it must derive from the Union.

The two great points of difference between a democracy and a republic are: first, the delegation of the government, in the latter, to a small number of citizens elected by the rest; secondly, the greater number of citizens and greater sphere of country over which the latter may be extended.

The Value of Distance from the Electorate

The effect of the first difference is, on the one hand, to refine and enlarge the public views by passing them through the medium of a chosen body of citizens, whose wisdom may best discern the true interest of their country and whose patriotism and love of justice will be least likely to sacrifice it to temporary or partial considerations. Under such a regulation it may well happen that the public voice, pronounced by the representatives of the people, will be more consonant to the public good than if pronounced by the people themselves, convened for the purpose. On the other hand, the effect may be inverted. Men of factious tempers, of local prejudices, or of sinister designs, may, by intrigue, by corruption, or by other means, first obtain the suffrages, and then betray the interests of the people. The question resulting is, whether small or extensive republics are most favorable to the election of proper guardians of the public weal; and it is clearly decided in favor of the latter by two obvious considerations.

In the first place it is to be remarked that however small the republic may be the representatives must be raised to a certain number in order to guard against the cabals of a few; and that however large it may be they must be limited to a certain number in order to guard against the confusion of a multitude. Hence, the number of representatives in the two cases not being in proportion to that of the constituents, and being proportionally greatest in the small republic, it follows that if the proportion of fit characters be not less in the large than in the small republic, the former will present a greater option, and consequently a greater probability of a fit choice.

In the next place, as each representative will be chosen by a greater number of citizens in the large than in the small republic, it will be more difficult for unworthy candidates to practice with success the vicious arts by which elections are too often carried; and the suffrages of the people being more free, will be more likely to center on men who possess the most attractive merit and the most diffusive and established characters.

The Problem of Too Few or Too Many Representatives

It must be confessed that in this, as in most other cases, there is a mean, on both sides of which inconveniences will be found to lie. By enlarging too much the number of electors, you render the representative too little acquainted with all their local circumstances and lesser interests; as by reducing it too much, you render him unduly attached to these, and too little fit to comprehend and pursue great and national objects. The federal Constitution forms a happy combination in this respect; the great and aggregate interests being referred to the national, the local and particular to the State legislatures.

Increasing a Republic's Size Reduces Prospects of Disruptive Faction

The other point of difference is the greater number of citizens and extent of territory which may be brought within the compass of republican than of democratic government; and it is this circumstance principally which renders factious combinations less to be dreaded in the former than in the latter. The smaller the society, the fewer probably will be the distinct parties and interests composing it; the fewer the distinct parties and interests, the more frequently will a majority be found of the same party; and the smaller the number of individuals composing a majority, and the smaller the compass within which they are placed, the more easily will they concert and execute their plans of oppression. Extend the sphere and you take in a greater variety of parties and interests; you make it less probable that a majority of the whole will have a common motive to invade the rights of other citizens; or if such a common motive exists, it will be more difficult for all who feel it to discover their own strength and to act in unison with each other. Besides other impediments, it may be remarked that where there is a consciousness of unjust or dishonorable purposes, communication is always checked by distrust in proportion to the number whose concurrence is necessary.

Hence, it clearly appears that the same advantage which a republic has over a democracy in controlling the effects of faction is enjoyed by a large over a small republic—is enjoyed by the Union over the States composing it. Does this advantage consist in the substitution of representatives whose enlightened views and virtuous sentiments render them superior to local prejudices and to schemes of injustice? It will not be denied that the representation of the Union will be most likely to possess these requisite endowments. Does it consist in the greater security afforded by a greater variety of parties, against the event of any one party being able to outnumber and oppress the rest? In an equal degree does the increased variety of parties comprised within the Union increase this security? Does it, in fine, consist in the greater obstacles opposed to the concert and accomplishment of the secret wishes of an unjust and interested majority? Here again the extent of the Union gives it the most palpable advantage.

The influence of factious leaders may kindle a flame within their particular States but will be unable to spread a general conflagration through the other States. A religious sect may degenerate into a political faction in a part of the Confederacy; but the variety of sects dispersed over the entire face of it must secure the national councils against any danger from that source. A rage for paper money, for an abolition of debts, for an equal division of property, or for any other improper or wicked project, will be less apt to pervade the whole body of the Union than a particular member of it, in the same proportion as such a malady is more likely to taint a particular county or district than an entire State.

In the extent and proper structure of the Union, therefore, we behold a republican remedy for the diseases most incident to republican government. And according to the degree of pleasure and pride we feel in being republicans ought to be our zeal in cherishing the spirit and supporting the character of federalists.

No. 15

Concerning the Defects of the Present Confederation in Relation to the Principle of Legislation for the States in Their Collective Capacities

Federalist No. 15 is a succinct enumeration of why the Articles of Confederation failed, the principal reason being the lack of a strong central governing body. The country is in debt, bills are not paid, the nation is powerless and lacks prestige. "We have neither troops, nor treasury, nor government," and "our ambassadors abroad are the mere pageants of mimic sovereignty." The legislature is that in name only, with no powers to enact and enforce legislation. Hamilton chronicles "the dark catalogue of our public misfortunes," asking "why has government been instituted at all? Because the passions of men will not conform to the dictates of reason and justice without constraint."

In the course of the preceding papers I have endeavored, my fellow-citizens, to place before you in a clear and convincing light the importance of Union to your political safety and happiness. I have unfolded to you a complication of dangers to which you would be exposed, should you permit that sacred knot which binds the people of America together to be severed or dissolved by ambition or by avarice, by jealousy or by misrepresentation. In the sequel of the inquiry through which I propose to accompany you, the truths intended to be inculcated will receive further confirmation from facts and arguments hitherto unnoticed. If the road over which you will still have to pass should in some places appear to you tedious or irksome, you will recollect that you are in quest of information on a subject the most momentous which can engage the attention of a free people, that the field through which you have to travel is in itself spacious, and that the difficulties of the journey have been unnecessarily increased by the mazes with which sophistry has beset the way. It will be my aim to remove the obstacles to your progress in as compendious a manner as it can be done, without sacrificing utility to dispatch.

In pursuance of the plan which I have laid down for the discussion of the subject, the point next in order to be examined is the "insufficiency of the present Confederation to the preservation of the Union." It may perhaps be asked what need there is of reasoning or proof to illustrate a position which is not either controverted or doubted, to which the understandings and feelings of all classes of men assent, and which in substance is admitted by the opponents as well as by the friends of the new Constitution. It must in truth be acknowledged that, however these may differ in other respects, they in general appear to harmonize in this sentiment at least: that there are material imperfections in our national system and that something is necessary to be done to rescue us from impending anarchy. The facts that support this opinion are no longer objects of speculation. They have forced themselves upon the sensibility of the people at large, and have at length extorted from those, whose mistaken policy has had the principal share in precipitating the extremity at which we are arrived, a reluctant confession of the reality of those defects in the scheme of our federal government which have been long pointed out and regretted by the intelligent friends of the Union.

"The Dark Catalogue of Our Public Misfortunes"

We may indeed with propriety be said to have reached almost the last stage of national humiliation. There is scarcely anything that can wound the pride or degrade the character of an independent nation which we do not experience. Are there engagements to the performance of which we are held by every tie respectable among men? These are the subjects of constant and unblushing violation. Do we owe debts to foreigners and to our own citizens contracted in a time of imminent peril for the preservation of our political existence? These remain without any proper or satisfactory provision for their discharge. Have we valuable territories and important posts in the possession of a foreign power which, by express stipulations, ought long since to have been surrendered? These are still retained to the prejudice of our interests, not less than of our rights. Are we in a condition to resent or to repel the aggression? We have neither troops, nor treasury, nor government.[1] Are we even in a condition to remonstrate with dignity? The just imputations on our own faith in respect to the same treaty ought first to be removed. Are we entitled by nature and compact to a free participation in the navigation of the Mississippi? Spain excludes us from it. Is public credit an indispensable resource in time of public danger? We seem to have abandoned its cause as desperate and irretrievable. Is commerce of importance to national wealth? Ours is at the lowest point of declension. Is respectability in the eyes of foreign powers a safeguard against foreign encroachments? The imbecility of our government even forbids them to treat with us. Our ambassadors abroad are the mere pageants of mimic sovereignty. Is a violent and unnatural decrease in the value of land a symptom of national distress? The price of improved land in most parts of the country is much lower than can be accounted for by the quantity of waste land at market, and can only be fully explained by that want of private and public confidence, which are so alarmingly prevalent among all ranks and which have a direct tendency to depreciate property of every kind. Is private credit the friend and patron of industry? That most useful kind which relates to borrowing and lending is reduced within the narrowest limits, and this still more from an opinion of insecurity than from a scarcity of money. To shorten an enumeration of particulars which can afford neither pleasure nor instruction, it may in general be demanded, what indication is there of national disorder, poverty, and insignificance that could befall a community so peculiarly blessed with natural advantages as we are, which does not form a part of the dark catalogue of our public misfortunes?

This is the melancholy situation to which we have been brought by those very maxims and counsels which would now deter us from adopting the proposed Constitution; and which, not content with having conducted us to the brink of a precipice, seem resolved to plunge us into the abyss that awaits us below. Here, my countrymen, impelled by every motive that ought to influence an enlightened people, let us make a firm stand for our safety, our tranquillity, our dignity, our reputation. Let us at last break the fatal charm which has too long seduced us from the paths of felicity and prosperity.

It is true, as has been before observed, that facts too stubborn to be resisted have produced a species of general assent to the abstract proposition that there exist material defects in our national system; but the usefulness of the concession on the part of the old adversaries of federal measures is destroyed by a strenuous opposition to a remedy upon the only principles that can give it a chance of success. While they admit that the government of the United States is destitute of energy, they contend against conferring upon it those powers which are requisite to supply that energy. They seem still to aim at things repugnant and irreconcilable; at an augmentation of federal authority without a diminution of State authority; at sovereignty in the Union and complete independence in the members. They still, in fine, seem to cherish with blind devotion the political monster of an *imperium in imperio.* This renders a full display of the principal defects of the Confederation necessary in order to show that the evils we experience do not proceed from minute or partial imperfections, but from fundamental errors in the structure of the building, which cannot be amended otherwise than by an alteration in the first principles and main pillars of the fabric.

A Legislature with No Power

The great and radical vice in the construction of the existing Confederation is in the principle of legislation for states or governments in their corporate or collective capacities and as contradistinguished from the individuals of whom they consist. Though this principle does not run through all the powers delegated to the Union, yet it pervades and governs those on which the efficacy of the rest depends. Except as to the rule of apportionment, the United States have an indefinite discretion to make requisitions for men and money; but they have no authority to raise either by regulations extending to the individual citizens of America. The consequence of this is that though in theory their resolutions concerning those objects are laws constitutionally binding on the members of the Union, yet in practice they are mere recommendations which the States observe or disregard at their option.

It is a singular instance of the capriciousness of the human mind that after all the admonitions we have had from experience on this head, there should still be found men who object to the new Constitution for deviating from a principle which has been found the bane of the old and which is in itself evidently incompatible with the idea of government; a principle, in short, which, if it is to be executed at all, must substitute the violent and sanguinary agency of the sword to the mild influence of the magistracy.

"Why Has Government Been Instituted at All?"

There is nothing absurd or impracticable in the idea of a league or alliance between independent nations for certain defined purposes precisely stated in a treaty regulating all the details of time, place, circumstance, and quantity, leaving nothing to future discretion, and depending for its execution on the good faith of the parties. Compacts of this kind exist among all civilized nations, subject to the usual vicissitudes of peace and war, of observance and nonobservance, as the interests or passions of the contracting powers dictate. In the early part of the present century there was an epidemical rage in Europe for this species of compacts, from which the politicians of the times fondly hoped for benefits which were never realized. With a view to establishing the equilibrium of power and the peace of that part of the world, all the resources of negotiations were exhausted, and triple and quadruple alliances were formed; but they were scarcely formed before they were broken, giving an instructive but afflicting lesson to mankind how little dependence is to be placed on treaties which have no other sanction than the obligations of good faith, and which oppose general considerations of peace and justice to the impulse of any immediate interest or passion.

If the particular States in this country are disposed to stand in a similar relation to each other, and to drop the project of a general discretionary superintendence, the scheme would indeed be pernicious and would entail upon us all the mischiefs which have been enumerated under the first head; but it would have the merit of being, at least, consistent and practicable. Abandoning all views towards a confederate government, this would bring us to a simple alliance offensive and defensive; and would place us in a situation to be alternate friends and enemies of each other, as our mutual jealousies and rivalships, nourished by the intrigues of foreign nations, should prescribe to us.

But if we are unwilling to be placed in this perilous situation; if we still will adhere to the design of a national government, or, which is the same thing, of a superintending power under the direction of a common council, we must resolve to incorporate into our plan those ingredients which may be considered as forming the characteristic difference between a league and a government; we must extend the authority of the Union to the persons of the citizens—the only proper objects of government.

Government implies the power of making laws. It is essential to the idea of a law that it be attended with a sanction; or, in other words, a penalty or punishment for disobedience. If there be no penalty annexed to disobedience, the resolutions or commands which pretend to be laws will, in fact, amount to nothing more than advice or recommendation. This penalty, whatever it may be, can only be inflicted in two ways: by the agency of the courts and ministers of justice, or by military force; by the coercion of the magistracy, or by the coercion of arms. The first kind can evidently apply only to men; the last kind must of necessity be employed against bodies politic, or communities, or States. It is evident that there is no process of a court by which the observance of the laws can in the last resort be enforced. Sentences may be denounced against them for violations of their duty; but these sentences can only be carried into execution by the sword. In an association where the general authority is confined to the collective bodies of the communities that compose it, every breach of the laws must involve a state of war; and military execution must become the only instrument of civil obedience. Such a state of things can certainly not deserve the name of government, nor would any prudent man choose to commit his happiness to it.

There was a time when we were told that breaches by the States of the regulations of the federal authority were not to be expected; that a sense of common interest would preside over the conduct of the respective members, and would beget a full compliance with all the constitutional requisitions of the Union. This language, at the present day, would appear as wild as a great part of what we now hear from the same quarter will be thought, when we shall have received further lessons from that best oracle of wisdom, experience. It at all times betrayed an ignorance of the true springs by which human conduct is actuated, and belied the original inducements to the establishment of civil power. Why has government been instituted at all? Because the passions of men will not conform to the dictates of reason and justice without constraint. Has it been found that bodies of men act with more rectitude or greater disinterestedness than individuals? The contrary of this has been inferred by all accurate observers of the conduct of mankind; and the inference is founded upon obvious reasons. Regard to reputation has a less active influence when the infamy of a bad action is to be divided among a number than when it is to fall singly upon one. A spirit of faction, which is apt to mingle its poison in the deliberations of all bodies of men, will often hurry the persons of whom they are composed into improprieties and excesses for which they would blush in a private capacity.

Power Checked by Public Scrutiny

In addition to all this, there is in the nature of sovereign power an impatience of control that disposes those who are invested with the exercise of it to look with an evil eye upon all external attempts to restrain or direct its operations. From this spirit it happens that in every political association which is formed upon the principle of uniting in a common interest a number of lesser sovereignties, there will be found a kind of eccentric tendency in the subordinate or inferior orbs by the operation of which there will be a perpetual effort in each to fly off from the common center. This tendency is not difficult to be accounted for. It has its origin in the love of power. Power controlled or abridged is almost always the rival and enemy of that power by which it is controlled or abridged. This simple proposition will teach us how little reason there is to expect that the persons intrusted with the administration of the affairs of the particular members of a confederacy will at all times be ready with perfect good humor and an unbiased regard to the public weal to execute the resolutions or decrees of the general authority. The reverse of this results from the constitution of man.

If, therefore, the measures of the Confederacy cannot be executed without the intervention of the particular administrations, there will be little prospect of their being executed at all. The rulers of the respective members, whether they have a constitutional right to do it or not, will undertake to judge of the propriety of the measures themselves. They will consider the conformity of the thing proposed or required to their immediate interests or aims; the momentary conveniences or inconveniences that would attend its adoption. All this will be done; and in a spirit of interested and suspicious scrutiny, without that knowledge of national circumstances and reasons of state, which is essential to a right judgment, and with that strong predilection in favor of local objects, which can hardly fail to mislead the decision. The same process must be repeated in every member of which the body is constituted; and the execution of the plans, framed by the councils of the whole, will always fluctuate on the discretion of the ill-informed and prejudiced opinion of every part. Those who have been conversant in the proceedings of popular assemblies; who have seen how difficult it often is, when there is no exterior pressure of circumstances, to bring them to harmonious resolutions on important points, will readily conceive how impossible it must be to induce a number of such assemblies, deliberating at a distance from each other, at different times and under different impressions, long to co-operate in the same views and pursuits.

In our case the concurrence of thirteen distinct sovereign wills is requisite under the Confederation to the complete execution of every important measure that proceeds from the Union. It has happened as was to have been foreseen. The measures of the Union have not been executed; and the delinquencies of the States have step by step matured themselves to an extreme, which has, at length, arrested all the wheels of the national government and brought them to an awful stand. Congress at this time scarcely possesses the means of keeping up the forms of administration, till the States can have time to agree upon a more substantial substitute for the present shadow of a federal government. Things did not come to this desperate extremity at once. The causes which have been specified produced at first only unequal and disproportionate degrees of compliance with the requisitions of the Union. The greater deficiencies of some States furnished the pretext of example and the temptation of interest to the complying, or to the least delinquent States. Why should we do more in proportion than those who are embarked with us in the same political voyage? Why should we consent to bear more than our proper share of the common burden? There were suggestions which human selfishness could not withstand, and which even speculative men, who looked forward to remote consequences, could not without hesitation combat. Each State yielding to the persuasive voice of immediate interest or convenience has successively withdrawn its support, till the frail and tottering edifice seems ready to fall upon our heads and to crush us beneath its ruins.

HAMILTON

No. 16

The Same Subject Continued in Relation to the Same Principle

The specter of anarchy, conflict, and despotism faces the young nation if it does not unite in the constitutional government being proposed. An independent judiciary and strong magistrates will help guard the nation "from the inroads of private licentiousness," Hamilton believes. The national government, to be effective, must have powers equal to the state governments, and "the majesty of the national authority must be manifested through the medium of the courts of justice."

The tendency of the principle of legislation for States, or communities, in their political capacities, as it has been exemplified by the experiment we have made of it, is equally attested by the events which have befallen all other governments of the confederate kind of which we have any account in exact proportion to its prevalence in those systems. The confirmations of this fact will be worthy of a distinct and particular examination. I shall content myself with barely observing here that of all the confederacies of antiquity which history has handed down to us, the Lycian and Achaean leagues, as far as there remain vestiges of them, appear to have been most free from the fetters of that mistaken principle, and were accordingly those which have best deserved and have most liberally received the applauding suffrages of political writers.

This exceptionable principle may as truly as emphatically be styled the parent of anarchy: It has been seen that delinquencies in the members of the

86

Union are its natural and necessary offspring; and that whenever they happen, the only constitutional remedy is force, and the immediate effect of the use of it, civil war.

Weak Government Encourages Violence

It remains to inquire how far so odious an engine of government in its application to us would even be capable of answering its end. If there should not be a large army constantly at the disposal of the national government it would either not be able to employ force at all, or, when this could be done, it would amount to a war between different parts of the Confederacy concerning the infractions of a league in which the strongest combination would be most likely to prevail, whether it consisted of those who supported or of those who resisted the general authority. It would rarely happen that the delinquency to be redressed would be confined to a single member, and if there were more than one who had neglected their duty, similarity of situation would induce them to unite for common defense. Independent of this motive of sympathy, if a large and influential State should happen to be the aggressing member, it would commonly have weight enough with its neighbors to win over some of them as associates to its cause. Specious arguments of danger to the general liberty could easily be contrived; plausible excuses for the deficiencies of the party could without difficulty be invented to alarm the apprehensions, inflame the passions, and conciliate the good will even of those States which were not chargeable with any violation or omission of duty. This would be the more likely to take place, as the delinquencies of the larger members might be expected sometimes to proceed from an ambitious premeditation in their rulers, with a view to getting rid of all external control upon their designs of personal aggrandizement; the better to effect which it is presumable they would tamper beforehand with leading individuals in the adjacent States. If associates could not be found at home, recourse would be had to the aid of foreign powers, who would seldom be disinclined to encouraging the dissensions of a Confederacy from the firm union of which they had so much to fear. When the sword is once drawn, the passions of men observe no bounds of moderation. The suggestions of wounded pride, the instigations of irritated resentment, would be apt to carry the States against which the arms of the Union were exerted to any extremes necessary to avenge the affront or to avoid the disgrace of submission. The first war of this kind would probably terminate in a dissolution of the Union.

A Dying Confederacy

This may be considered as the violent death of the Confederacy. Its more natural death is what we now seem to be on the point of experiencing, if the federal system be not speedily renovated in a more substantial form. It is not probable, considering the genius of this country, that the complying States would often be inclined to support the authority of the Union by engaging in a war against the noncomplying States. They would always be more ready to pursue the milder course of putting themselves upon an equal footing with the delinquent members by an imitation of their example. And the guilt of all would thus become the security of all. Our past experience has exhibited the operation of this spirit in its full light. There would, in fact, be an insuperable difficulty in ascertaining when force could with propriety be employed. In the article of pecuniary contribution, which would be the most usual source of delinquency, it would often be impossible to decide whether it had proceeded from disinclination or inability. The pretense of the latter would always be at hand. And the case must be very flagrant in which its fallacy could be detected with sufficient certainty to justify the harsh expedient of compulsion. It is easy to see that this problem alone, as often as it should occur, would open a wide field to the majority that happened to prevail in the national council for the exercise of factious views, of partiality, and of oppression.

The Specter of Despotism in the Absence of Union

It seems to require no pains to prove that the States ought not to prefer a national Constitution which could only be kept in motion by the instrumentality of a large army continually on foot to execute the ordinary requisitions or decrees of the government. And yet this is the plain alternative involved by those who wish to deny it the power of extending its operations to individuals. Such a scheme, if practicable at all, would instantly degenerate into a military despotism; but it will be found in every light impracticable. The resources of the Union would not be equal to the maintenance of an army considerable enough to confine the larger States within the limits of their duty; nor would the means ever be furnished of forming such an army in the first instance. Whoever considers the populousness and strength of several of these States singly at the present juncture, and looks forward to what they will become even at the distance of half a century, will at once dismiss as idle and visionary any scheme which aims at regulating their movements by laws to operate upon them in their collective capacities and to be executed by a coercion applicable to them in the same capacities. A project of this kind is little less romantic than the monster-taming spirit, attributed to the fabulous heroes and demigods of antiquity.

Even in those confederacies which have been composed of members smaller than many of our counties, the principle of legislation for sovereign States supported by military coercion has never been found effectual. It has rarely been attempted to be employed, but against the weaker members; and in most instances attempts to coerce the refractory and disobedient have been the signals of bloody wars, in which one half of the Confederacy has displayed its banners against the other half.

The National Government's Powers Must Equal State Governments' Powers

The result of these observations to an intelligent mind must be clearly this, that if it be possible at any rate to construct a federal government capable of regulating the common concerns and preserving the general tranquillity, it must be founded, as to the objects committed to its care, upon the reverse of the principle contended for by the opponents of the proposed Constitution. It must carry its agency to the persons of the citizens. It must stand in need of no intermediate legislations, but must itself be empowered to employ the arm of the ordinary magistrate to execute its own resolutions. The majesty of the national authority must be manifested through the medium of the courts of justice. The government of the Union, like that of each State, must be able to address itself immediately to the hopes and fears of individuals; and to attract to its support those passions which have the strongest influence upon the human heart. It must, in short, possess all the means, and have a right to resort to all the methods, of executing the powers with which it is intrusted, that are possessed and exercised by the governments of the particular States.

To this reasoning it may perhaps be objected that if any State should be disaffected to the authority of the Union it could at any time obstruct the execution of its laws, and bring the matter to the same issue of force, with the necessity of which the opposite scheme is reproached.

The plausibility of this objection will vanish the moment we advert to the essential difference between a mere noncompliance and a direct and active resistance. If the interposition of the State legislatures be necessary to give effect to a measure of the Union, they have only not to act, or to act evasively, and the measure is defeated. This neglect of duty may be disguised under affected but unsubstantial provisions so as not to appear, and of course not to excite any alarm in the people for the safety of the Constitution. The State leaders may even make a merit of their surreptitious invasions of it on the ground of some temporary convenience, exemption, or advantage.

The Need for Independent Judges

But if the execution of the laws of the national government should not require the intervention of the State legislatures, if they were to pass into immediate operation upon the citizens themselves, the particular governments could not interrupt their progress without an open and violent exertion of an unconstitutional power. No omissions nor evasions would answer the end. They would be obliged to act, and in such a manner as would leave no doubt that they had encroached on the national rights. An experiment of this nature would always be hazardous in the face of a constitution in any degree competent to its own defense, and of a people enlightened enough to distinguish between a legal exercise and an illegal usurpation of authority. The success of it would require not merely a factious majority in the legislature, but the concurrence of the courts of justice and of the body of the people. If the judges were not embarked in a conspiracy with the legislature, they would pronounce the resolutions of such a majority to be contrary to the supreme law of the land, unconstitutional, and void. If the people were not tainted with the spirit of their State representatives, they, as the natural guardians of the Constitution, would throw their weight into the national scale and give it a decided preponderancy in the contest. Attempts of this kind would not often be made with levity or rashness, because they could seldom be made without danger to the authors, unless in cases of a tyrannical exercise of the federal authority.

If opposition to the national government should arise from the disorderly conduct of refractory or seditious individuals, it could be overcome by the same means which are daily employed against the same evil under the State governments. The magistracy, being equally the ministers of the law of the land from whatever source it might emanate, would doubtless be as ready to guard the national as the local regulations from the inroads of private licentiousness. As to those partial commotions and insurrections which sometimes disquiet society from the intrigues of an inconsiderable faction, or from sudden or occasional ill humors that do not infect the great body of the community, the general government could command more extensive resources for the suppression of disturbances of that kind than would be in the power of any single member. And as to those mortal feuds which in certain conjunctures spread a conflagration through a whole nation, or through a very large proportion of it, proceeding either from weighty causes of discontent given by the government or from the contagion of some violent popular paroxysm, they do not fall within any ordinary rules of calculation. When they happen, they commonly amount to revolutions and dismemberments of empire. No form of government can always either avoid or control them. It is in vain to hope to guard against events too mighty for human foresight or precaution, and it would be idle to object to a government because it could not perform impossibilities.

HAMILTON

No. 23

The Necessity of a Government at Least Equally Energetic with the One Proposed

Hamilton argues an "energetic," by which he means powerful and effective, government is needed to give the new country security, regulate commerce, and balance state and federal interests. "Energetic" and "vigorous" are adjectives used often in The Federalist Papers *to describe the new Constitution. In employing them, the authors envision, not simply a theoretical construct, but a practical, working government, enjoying widespread popular participation and contributing to a stable, prosperous economy. Federalist No. 23 contains one of the papers' most detailed statements in support of national security, arguing that this function belongs with the national government, which should have the flexibility to respond to unforeseen "national exigencies" and should possess "the means which may be necessary to satisfy them."*

The necessity of a Constitution, at least equally energetic with the one proposed, to the preservation of the Union is the point at the examination of which we are now arrived.

This inquiry will naturally divide itself into three branches—the objects to be provided for by a federal government, the quantity of power necessary to the accomplishment of those objects, the persons upon whom that power ought to operate. Its distribution and organization will more properly claim our attention under the succeeding head.

National Security and the Regulation of Commerce

The principal purposes to be answered by union are these—the common defense of the members; the preservation of the public peace, as well against internal convulsions as external attacks; the regulation of commerce with other nations and between the States; the superintendence of our intercourse, political and commercial, with foreign countries.

The authorities essential to the common defense are these: to raise armies; to build and equip fleets; to prescribe rules for the government of both; to direct their operations; to provide for their support. These powers ought to exist without limitation, *because it is impossible to foresee or to define the extent and variety of national exigencies, and the correspondent extent and variety of the means which may be necessary to satisfy them.* The circumstances that endanger the safety of nations are infinite, and for this reason no constitutional shackles can wisely be imposed on the power to which the care of it is committed. This power ought to be coextensive with all the possible combinations of such circumstances; and ought to be under the direction of the same councils which are appointed to preside over the common defense.

This is one of those truths which to a correct and unprejudiced mind carries its own evidence along with it, and may be obscured, but cannot be made plainer by argument or reasoning. It rests upon axioms as simple as they are universal; the *means* ought to be proportioned to the *end;* the persons from whose agency the attainment of any *end* is expected ought to possess the *means* by which it is to be attained.

National Security Elaborated

Whether there ought to be a federal government intrusted with the care of the common defense is a question in the first instance open to discussion; but the moment it is decided in the affirmative, it will follow that that government ought to be clothed with all the powers requisite to complete execution of its trust. And unless it can be shown that the circumstances which may affect the public safety are reducible within certain determinate limits; unless the contrary of this position can be fairly and rationally disputed, it must be admitted as a necessary consequence that there can be no limitation of that authority which is to provide for the defense and protection of the community in any matter essential to its efficacy—that is, in any matter essential to the *formation, direction,* or *support* of the national forces.

Defective as the present Confederation has been proved to be, this principle appears to have been fully recognized by the framers of it; though they have not made proper or adequate provision for its exercise. Congress have an unlimited discretion to make requisitions of men and money; to govern the army and navy; to direct their operations. As their requisitions are made constitutionally binding upon the States, who are in fact under the most solemn obligations to furnish the supplies required of them, the intention evidently was that the United States should command whatever resources were by them judged requisite to the "common defense and general welfare." It was presumed that a sense of their true interests, and a regard to the dictates of good faith, would be found sufficient pledges for the punctual performance of the duty of the members to the federal head.

The experiment has, however, demonstrated that this expectation was ill-founded and illusory; and the observations made under the last head will, I imagine, have sufficed to convince the impartial and discerning that there is an absolute necessity for an entire change in the first principles of the system; that if we are in earnest about giving the Union energy and duration we must abandon the vain project of legislating upon the States in their collective capacities; we must extend the laws of the federal government to the individual citizens of America; we must discard the fallacious scheme of quotas and requisitions as equally impracticable and unjust. The result from all this is that the Union ought to be invested with full power to levy troops; to build and equip fleets; and to raise the revenues which will be required for the formation and support of an army and navy in the customary and ordinary modes practiced in other governments.

Balancing State and Federal Powers

If the circumstances of our country are such as to demand a compound instead of a simple, a confederate instead of a sole, government, the essential point which will remain to be adjusted will be to discriminate the objects, as far as it can be done, which shall appertain to the different provinces or departments of power; allowing to each the most ample authority for fulfilling the objects committed to its charge. Shall the Union be constituted the guardian of the common safety? Are fleets and armies and revenues necessary to this purpose? The government of the Union must be empowered to pass all laws, and to make all regulations which have relation to them. The same must be the case in respect to commerce, and to every other matter to which its jurisdiction is permitted to extend. Is the administration of justice between the citizens of the same State the proper department of the local governments? These must possess all the authorities which are connected with this object, and with every other that may be allotted to their particular cognizance and direction. Not to confer in each case a degree of power commensurate to the end would be to violate the most obvious rules of prudence and propriety, and improvidently to trust the great interests of the nation to hands which are disabled from managing them with vigor and success.

Who so likely to make suitable provisions for the public defense as that body to which the guardianship of the public safety is confided; which, as the center of information, will best understand the extent and urgency of the dangers that threaten; as the representative of the whole, will feel itself most deeply interested in the preservation of every part; which, from the responsibility implied in the duty assigned to it, will be most sensibly impressed with the necessity of proper exertions; and which, by the extension of its authority throughout the States, can alone establish uniformity and concert in the plans and measures by which the common safety is to be secured? Is there not a manifest inconsistency in devolving upon the federal government the care of the general defense and leaving in the State governments the *effective* powers by which it is to be provided for? Is not a want of co-operation the infallible consequence of such a system? And will not weakness, disorder, an undue distribution of the burdens and calamities of war, an unnecessary and intolerable increase of expense, be its natural and inevitable concomitants? Have we not had unequivocal experience of its effects in the course of the revolutions which we have just achieved?

Every view we may take of the subject, as candid inquirers after truth, will serve to convince us that it is both unwise and dangerous to deny the federal government an unconfined authority in respect to all those objects which are intrusted to its management. It will indeed deserve the most vigilant and careful attention of the people to see that it be modeled in such a manner as to admit of its being safely vested with the requisite powers. If any plan which has been, or may be, offered to our consideration should not, upon a dispassionate inspection, be found to answer this description, it ought to be rejected. A government, the constitution of which renders it unfit to be trusted with all the powers which a free people *ought to delegate* to *any government,* would be an unsafe and improper depository of the national interests. Wherever these can with propriety be confided, the coincident powers may safely accompany them. This is the true result of all just reasoning upon the subject. And the adversaries of the plan promulgated by the convention would have given a better impression of their candor if they had confined themselves to showing that the internal structure of the proposed government was such as to render it unworthy of the confidence of the people. They ought not to have wandered into inflammatory declamations and unmeaning cavils about the extent of the powers. The powers are not too extensive for the objects of federal administration, or, in other words, for the management of our national interests nor can any satisfactory argument be framed to show that they are chargeable with such an excess. If it be true, as has been insinuated by some of the writers on the other side, that the difficulty arises from the nature of the thing, and that the extent of the country will not permit us to form a government in which such ample powers can safely be reposed, it would prove that we ought to contract our views, and resort to the expedient of separate confederacies, which will move within more practicable spheres. For the absurdity must continually stare us in the face of confiding to a government the direction of the most essential national interests, without daring to trust to it the authorities which are indispensable to their proper and efficient management. Let us not attempt to reconcile contradictions, but firmly embrace a rational alternative.

I trust, however, that the impracticability of one general system cannot be shown. I am greatly mistaken if anything of weight has yet been advanced of this tendency; and I flatter myself that the observations which have been made in the course of these papers have served to place the reverse of that position in as clear a light as any matter still in the womb of time and experience is susceptible of. This, at all events, must be evident, that the very difficulty itself, drawn from the extent of the country, is the strongest argument in favor of an energetic government; for any other can certainly never preserve the Union of so large an empire. If we embrace the tenets of those who oppose the adoption of the proposed Constitution as the standard of our political creed we cannot fail to verify the gloomy doctrines which predict the impracticability of a national system pervading the entire limits of the present Confederacy.

No. 37

Concerning the Difficulties Which the Convention Must Have Experienced in the Formation of a Proper Plan

As in Federalists No. 10 and 51, Madison reflects on both the practical problems at hand and the general nature of government. His remarks are aimed at "those only who add to a sincere zeal for the happiness of their country, a temper favorable to a just estimate of the means of promoting it." Madison faces the problem of how to balance "energy" and "stability" in government with liberty and a republican structure. Madison applauds the convention for writing a Constitution free "from the pestilential influence of party animosities—the disease most incident to deliberative bodies." Madison again reflects on human nature in dark tones; the history of experiments in government represents "a history of factions, contentions, and disappointments, and may be classed among the most dark and degrading pictures which display the infirmities and depravities of the human character." He says the Constitution writers avoided such acrimony by both "a deep conviction of the necessity of sacrificing public opinions and partial interests to the public good, and by a despair of seeing this necessity diminished by delays or by new experiments."*

In reviewing the defects of the existing Confederation, and showing that they cannot be supplied by a government of less energy than that before the public, several of the most important principles of the latter fell of course under consideration. But as the ultimate object of these papers is to determine clearly and fully the merits of this Constitution, and the expediency of adopting it, our plan cannot be completed without taking a more critical and thorough survey of the work of the convention, without examining it on all sides, comparing it in all its parts, and calculating its probable effects. That this remaining task may be executed under impressions conducive to a just and fair result, some reflections must in this place be indulged, which candor previously suggests.

The Papers' Audience: Those with "a Sincere Zeal for the Happiness of Their Country"

It is a misfortune, inseparable from human affairs, that public measures are rarely investigated with that spirit of moderation which is essential to a just estimate of their real tendency to advance or obstruct the public good; and that this spirit is more apt to be diminished than promoted by those occasions which require an unusual exercise of it. To those who have been led by experience to attend to this consideration, it could not appear surprising that the act of the convention, which recommends so many important changes and innovations, which may be viewed in so many lights and relations, and which touches the springs of so many passions and interests, should find or excite dispositions unfriendly, both on one side and on the other, to a fair discussion and accurate judgment of its merits. In some, it has been too evident from their own publications that they have scanned the proposed Constitution, not only with a predisposition to censure, but with a predetermination to condemn; as the language held by others betrays an opposite predetermination or bias, which must render their opinion also of little moment in the question. In placing, however, these different characters on a level with respect to the weight of their opinions I wish not to insinuate that there may not be a material difference in the purity of their intentions. It is but just to remark in favor of the latter description that as our situation is universally admitted to be peculiarly critical, and to require indispensably that something should be done for our relief, the predetermined patron of what has been actually done may have taken his bias from the weight of these considerations, as well as from considerations of a sinister nature. The predetermined adversary, on the other hand, can have been governed by no venial motive whatever. The intentions of the first may be upright, as they may on the contrary be culpable. The views of the last cannot be upright, and must be culpable. But the truth is that these papers are not addressed to persons falling under either of these characters. They solicit the attention of those only who add to a sincere zeal for the happiness of their country, a temper favorable to a just estimate of the means of promoting it.

Persons of this character will proceed to an examination of the plan submitted by the convention, not only without a disposition to find or to magnify faults; but will see the propriety of reflecting that a faultless plan was not to be expected. Nor will they barely make allowances for the errors which may be chargeable on the fallibility to which the convention, as a body of men, were liable; but will keep in mind that they themselves also are but men and ought not to assume an infallibility in rejudging the fallible opinions of others.

With equal readiness will it be perceived that besides these inducements to candor, many allowances ought to be made for the difficulties inherent in the very nature of the undertaking referred to the convention.

The novelty of the undertaking immediately strikes us. It has been shown in the course of these papers that the existing Confederation is founded on principles which are fallacious; that we must consequently change this first foundation, and with it the superstructure resting upon it. It has been shown that the other confederacies which could be consulted as precedents have been vitiated by the same erroneous principles, and can therefore furnish no other light than that of beacons, which give warning of the course to be shunned, without pointing out that which ought to be pursued. The most that the convention could do in such a situation was to avoid the errors suggested by the past experience of other countries, as well as of our own; and to provide a convenient mode of rectifying their own errors, as future experience may unfold them.

Balancing Stability and Liberty

Among the difficulties encountered by the convention, a very important one must have lain in combining the requisite stability and energy in government with the inviolable attention due to liberty and to the republican form. Without substantially accomplishing this part of their undertaking, they would have very imperfectly fulfilled the object of their appointment, or the expectation of the public; yet that it could not be easily accomplished will be denied by no one who is unwilling to betray his ignorance of the subject. Energy in government is essential to that security against external and internal danger and to that prompt and salutary execution of the laws which enter into the very definition of good government. Stability in government is essential to national character and to the advantages annexed to it, as well as to that repose and confidence in the minds of the people, which are among the chief blessings of civil society. An irregular and mutable legislation is not more an evil in itself than it is odious to the people; and it may be pronounced with assurance that the people of this country, enlightened as they are with regard to the nature, and interested, as the great body of them are, in the effects of good government, will never be satisfied till some remedy be applied to the vicissitudes and uncertainties which characterize the State administrations. On comparing, however, these valuable ingredients with the vital principles of liberty, we must perceive at once the difficulty of mingling them together in their due proportions. The genius of republican liberty seems to demand on one side not only that all power should be derived from the people, but that those intrusted with it should be kept in dependence on the people by a short duration of their appointments; and that even during this short period the trust should be placed not in a few, but a number of hands. Stability, on the contrary, requires that the hands in which power is lodged should continue for a length of time the same. A frequent change of men will result from a frequent return of elections; and a frequent change of measures from a frequent change of men: whilst energy in government requires not only a certain duration of power, but the execution of it by a single hand.

How far the convention may have succeeded in this part of their work will better appear on a more accurate view of it. From the cursory view here taken, it must clearly appear to have been an arduous part.

"The Proper Line of Partition" Between the General and State Governments

Not less arduous must have been the task of marking the proper line of partition between the authority of the general and that of the State governments. Every man will be sensible of this difficulty in proportion as he has been accustomed to contemplate and discriminate objects extensive and complicated in their nature. The faculties of the mind itself have never yet been distinguished and defined with satisfactory precision by all the efforts of the most acute and metaphysical philosophers. Sense, perception, judgment, desire, volition, memory, imagination are found to be separated by such delicate shades and minute gradations that their boundaries have eluded the most subtle investigations, and remain a pregnant source of ingenious disquisition and controversy. The boundaries between the great kingdoms of nature, and, still more, between the various provinces and lesser portions into which they are subdivided, afford another illustration of the same important truth. The most sagacious and laborious naturalists have never yet succeeded in tracing with certainty the line which separates the district of vegetable life from the neighboring region of unorganized matter, or which marks the termination of the former and the commencement of the animal empire. A still greater obscurity lies in the distinctive characters by which the objects in each of these great departments of nature have been arranged and assorted.

When we pass from the works of nature, in which all the delineations are perfectly accurate and appear to be otherwise only from the imperfection of the eye which surveys them, to the institutions of man, in which the obscurity arises as well from the object itself as from the organ by which it is contemplated, we must perceive the necessity of moderating still further our expectations and hopes from the efforts of human sagacity. Experience has instructed us that no skill in the science of government has yet been able to discriminate and define, with sufficient certainty, its three great provinces—the legislative, executive, and judiciary; or even the privileges and powers of the different legislative branches. Questions daily occur in the course of practice which prove the obscurity which reigns in these subjects, and which puzzle the greatest adepts in political science.

The experience of ages, with the continued and combined labors of the most enlightened legislators and jurists, has been equally unsuccessful in delineating the several objects and limits of different codes of laws and different tribunals of justice. The precise extent of the common law, and the statute law, the maritime law, the ecclesiastical law, the law of corporations, and other local laws and customs, remains still to be clearly and finally established in Great Britain, where accuracy in such subjects has been more industriously pursued than in any other part of the world. The jurisdiction of her several courts, general and local, of law, of equity, of admiralty, etc., is not less a source of frequent and intricate discussions, sufficiently denoting the indeterminate limits by which they are respectively circumscribed. All new laws, though penned with the greatest technical skill and passed on the fullest and most mature deliberation, are considered as more or less obscure and equivocal, until their meaning be liquidated and ascertained by a series of particular discussions and adjudications. Besides the obscurity arising from the complexity of objects and the imperfection of the human faculties, the medium through which the

101

conceptions of men are conveyed to each other adds a fresh embarrassment. The use of words is to express ideas. Perspicuity, therefore, requires not only that the ideas should be distinctly formed, but that they should be expressed by words distinctly and exclusively appropriate to them. But no language is so copious as to supply words or phrases for every complex idea, or so correct as not to include many equivocally denoting different ideas. Hence it must happen that however accurately objects may be discriminated in themselves, and however accurately the discrimination may be considered, the definition of them may be rendered inaccurate by the inaccuracy of the terms in which it is delivered. And this unavoidable inaccuracy must be greater or less, according to the complexity and novelty of the objects defined. When the Almighty himself condescends to address mankind in their own language, his meaning, luminous as it must be, is rendered dim and doubtful by the cloudy medium through which it is communicated.

Here, then, are three sources of vague and incorrect definitions: indistinctness of the object, imperfection of the organ of conception, inadequateness of the vehicle of ideas. Any one of these must produce a certain degree of obscurity. The convention, in delineating the boundary between the federal and State jurisdictions, must have experienced the full effect of them all.

To the difficulties already mentioned may be added the interfering pretensions of the larger and smaller States. We cannot err in supposing that the former would contend for a participation in the government, fully proportioned to their superior wealth and importance; and that the latter would not be less tenacious of the equality at present enjoyed by them. We may well suppose that neither side would entirely yield to the other, and consequently that the struggle could be terminated only by compromise. It is extremely probable, also, that after the ratio of representation had been adjusted, this very compromise must have produced a fresh struggle between the same parties to give such a turn to the organization of the government and to the distribution of its powers as would increase the importance of the branches, in forming which they had respectively obtained the greatest share of influence. There are features in the Constitution which warrant each of these suppositions; and as far as either of them is well founded, it shows that the convention must have been compelled to sacrifice theoretical propriety to the force of extraneous considerations.

Nor could it have been the large and small States only which would marshal themselves in opposition to each other on various points. Other combinations, resulting from a difference of local position and policy, must have created additional difficulties. As every State may be divided into different districts, and its citizens into different classes, which give birth to contending interests and local jealousies, so the different parts of the United States are distinguished from each other by a variety of circumstances, which produce a like effect on a larger scale. And although this variety of interests, for reasons sufficiently explained in a former paper, may have a salutary influence on the administration of the government when formed, yet every one must be sensible of the contrary influence which must have been experienced in the task of forming it.

The Convention's Achievement

Would it be wonderful if, under the pressure of all these difficulties, the convention should have been forced into some deviations from that artificial structure and regular symmetry which an abstract view of the subject might lead an ingenious theorist to bestow on a Constitution planned in his closet or in his imagination? The real wonder is that so many difficulties should have been surmounted, and surmounted with a unanimity almost as unprecedented as it must have been unexpected. It is impossible for any man of candor to reflect on this circumstance without partaking of the astonishment. It is impossible for the man of pious reflection not to perceive in it a finger of that Almighty hand which has been so frequently and signally extended to our relief in the critical stages of the revolution.

The Need for Action

We had occasion in a former paper to take notice of the repeated trials which have been unsuccessfully made in the United Netherlands for reforming the baneful and notorious vices of their constitution. The history of almost all the great councils and consultations held among mankind for reconciling their discordant opinions, assuaging their mutual jealousies and adjusting their respective interests, is a history of factions, contentions, and disappointments, and may be classed among the most dark and degrading pictures which display the infirmities and depravities of the human character. If in a few scattered instances a brighter aspect is presented, they serve only as exceptions to admonish us of the general truth; and by their luster to darken the gloom of the adverse prospect to which they are contrasted. In resolving the causes from which these exceptions result, and applying them to the particular instances before us, we are necessarily led to two important conclusions. The first is that the convention must have enjoyed, in a very singular degree, an exemption from the pestilential influence of party animosities—the disease most incident to deliberative bodies and most apt to contaminate their proceedings. The second conclusion is that all the deputations composing the convention were either satisfactorily accommodated by the final act, or were induced to accede to it by a deep conviction of the necessity of sacrificing private opinions and partial interests to the public good, and by a despair of seeing this necessity diminished by delays or by new experiments.

No. 39

The Conformity of the Plan to Republican Principles: An Objection in Respect to the Powers of the Convention Examined

Republican government is limited government, deriving its powers from the people, administered by people holding office for limited terms or during good behavior, meaning during a time when they execute their office responsibly and without corruption. Madison believes government's powers are "founded on the assent and ratification of the people ... given by deputies elected for the special purpose." The states retain their distinct powers and the Constitution is "neither a national nor a federal constitution, but a composition of both." He adds, "In its foundation it is federal, not national; in the source from which the ordinary powers of the government are drawn, it is partly federal and partly national; in the operation of these powers, it is national, not federal; in the extent of them, again, it is federal, not national; and, finally, in the authoritative mode of introducing amendments, it is neither wholly federal nor wholly national."

The last paper having concluded the observations which were meant to introduce a candid survey of the plan of government reported by the convention, we now proceed to the execution of that part of our undertaking.

The first question that offers itself is whether the general form and aspect of the government be strictly republican. It is evident that no other form would be reconcilable with the genius of the people of America; with the fundamental principles of the Revolution; or with that honorable determination which animates every votary of freedom to rest all our political experiments on the capacity of mankind for self-government. If the plan of the convention, therefore, be found to depart from the republican character, its advocates must abandon it as no longer defensible.

Republican (Limited) Government Defined

What, then, are the distinctive characters of the republican form? Were an answer to this question to be sought, not by recurring to principles but in the application of the term by political writers to the constitutions of different States, no satisfactory one would ever be found. Holland, in which no particle of the supreme authority is derived from the people, has passed almost universally under the denomination of a republic. The same title has been bestowed on Venice, where absolute power over the great body of the people is exercised in the most absolute manner by a small body of hereditary nobles. Poland, which is a mixture of aristocracy and of monarchy in their worst forms, has been dignified with the same appellation. The government of England, which has one republican branch only, combined with an hereditary aristocracy and monarchy, has with equal impropriety been frequently placed on the list of republics. These examples, which are nearly as dissimilar to each other as to a genuine republic, show the extreme inaccuracy with which the term has been used in political disquisitions.

If we resort for a criterion to the different principles on which different forms of government are established, we may define a republic to be, or at least may bestow that name on, a government which derives all its powers directly or indirectly from the great body of the people, and is administered by persons holding their offices during pleasure for a limited period, or during good behavior. It is *essential* to such a government that it be derived from the great body of the society, not from an inconsiderable proportion or a favored class of it; otherwise a handful of tyrannical nobles, exercising their oppressions by a delegation of their powers, might aspire to the rank of republicans and claim for their government the honorable title of republic. It is *sufficient* for such a government that the persons administering it be appointed, either directly or indirectly, by the people; and that they hold their appointments by either of the tenures just specified; otherwise every government in the United States, as well as every other popular government that has been or can be well organized or well executed, would be degraded from the republican character. According to the constitution of every State in the Union, some or other of the officers of government are appointed indirectly only by the people. According to most of them, the chief magistrate himself is so appointed. And according to one, this mode of appointment is extended to one of the co-ordinate branches of the legislature. According to all the constitutions, also, the tenure of the highest offices is extended to a definite period, and in many instances, both within the legislative and executive departments, to a period of years. According to the provisions of most of the constitutions, again, as well as according to the most respectable and received opinions on the subject, the members of the judiciary department are to retain their offices by the firm tenure of good behavior.

On comparing the Constitution planned by the convention with the standard here fixed, we perceived at once that it is, in the most rigid sense, conformable to it. The House of Representatives, like that of one branch at least of all the State legislatures, is elected immediately by the great body of the people. The Senate, like the present Congress and the Senate of Maryland, derives its appointment indirectly from the people. The President is indirectly derived from the choice of the people, according to the example in most of the States. Even the judges, with all other officers of the Union, will, as in the several States, be the choice, though a remote choice, of the people themselves. The duration of the appointments is equally conformable to the republican standard and to the model of State constitutions. The House of Representatives is periodically elective, as in all the States; and for the period of two years, as in the State of South Carolina. The Senate is elective for the period of six years, which is but one year more than the period of the Senate of Maryland, and but two more than that of the Senates of New York and Virginia. The President is to continue in office for the period of four years; as in New York and Delaware the chief magistrate is elected for three years, and in South Carolina for two years. In the other States the election is annual. In several of the States, however, no explicit provision is made for the impeachment of the chief magistrate. And in Delaware and Virginia he is not impeachable till out of office. The President of the United States is impeachable at any time during his continuance in office. The tenure by which the judges are to hold their places is, as it unquestionably ought to be, that of good behavior. The tenure of the ministerial offices generally will be a subject of legal regulation, conformably to the reason of the case and the example of the State constitutions.

Could any further proof be required of the republican complexion of this system, the most decisive one might be found in its absolute prohibition of titles of nobility, both under the federal and the State governments; and in its express guaranty of the republican form to each of the latter.

The States' Role in Republican Government

"But it was not sufficient," say the adversaries of the proposed Constitution, "for the convention to adhere to the republican form. They ought with equal care to have preserved the *federal* form, which regards the Union as a *Confederacy* of sovereign states; instead of which they have framed a *national* government, which regards the Union as a *consolidation* of the States." And it is asked by what authority this bold and radical innovation was undertaken? The handle which has been made of this objection requires that it should be examined with some precision.

Without inquiring into the accuracy of the distinction on which the objection is founded, it will be necessary to a just estimate of its force, first, to ascertain the real character of the government in question; secondly, to inquire how far the convention were authorized to propose such a government; and thirdly, how far the duty they owed to their country could supply any defect of regular authority.

First.—In order to ascertain the real character of the government, it may be considered in relation to the foundation on which it is to be established; to the sources from which its ordinary powers are to be drawn; to the operation of those powers; to the extent of them; and to the authority by which future changes in the government are to be introduced.

On examining the first relation, it appears, on one hand, that the Constitution is to be founded on the assent and ratification of the people of America, given by deputies elected for the special purpose; but, on the other, that this assent and ratification is to be given by the people, not as individuals composing one entire nation, but as composing the distinct and independent States to which they respectively belong. It is to be the assent and ratification of the several States, derived from the supreme authority in each State—the authority of the people themselves. The act, therefore, establishing the Constitution will not be a *national* but a *federal* act.

That it will be a federal and not a national act, as these terms are understood by the objectors—the act of the people, as forming so many independent States, not as forming one aggregate nation—is obvious from this single consideration: that it is to result neither from the decision of a *majority* of the people of the Union, nor from that of a *majority* of the States. It must result from the *unanimous* assent of the several States that are parties to it, differing no otherwise from their ordinary assent than in its being expressed, not by the legislative authority, but by that of the people themselves. Were the people regarded in this transaction as forming one nation, the will of the majority of the whole people of the United States would bind the minority, in the same manner as the majority in each State must bind the minority; and the will of the majority must be determined either by a comparison of the individual votes, or by considering the will of the majority of the States as evidence of the will of a majority of the people of the United States. Neither of these rules has been adopted. Each State, in ratifying the Constitution, is considered as a sovereign body independent of all others, and only to be bound by its own voluntary act. In this relation, then, the new Constitution will, if established, be a *federal* and not a *national* constitution.

Balancing Federal and National Powers

The next relation is to the sources from which the ordinary powers of government are to be derived. The House of Representatives will derive its powers from the people of America; and the people will be represented in the same proportion and on the same principle as they are in the legislature of a particular State. So far the government is *national,* not *federal.* The Senate, on the other hand, will derive its powers from the States as political and coequal societies; and these will be represented on the principle of equality in the Senate, as they now are in the existing Congress. So far the government is *federal,* not *national.* The executive power will be derived from a very compound source. The immediate election of the President is to be made by the States in their political characters. The votes allotted to them are in a compound ratio, which considers them partly as distinct and coequal societies, partly as unequal members of the same society. The eventual election, again, is to be made by that branch of the legislature which consists of the national representatives; but in this particular act they are to be thrown into the form of individual delegations from so many distinct and coequal bodies politic. From this aspect of the government it appears to be of a mixed character, presenting at least as many *federal* as *national* features.

The difference between a federal and national government, as it relates to the *operation of the government*, is by the adversaries of the plan of the convention supposed to consist in this, that in the former the powers operate on the political bodies composing the Confederacy in their political capacities; in the latter, on the individual citizens composing the nation in their individual capacities. On trying the Constitution by this criterion, it falls under the *national* not the *federal* character; though perhaps not so completely as has been understood. In several cases, and particularly in the trial of controversies to which States may be parties, they must be viewed and proceeded against in their collective and political capacities only. But the operation of the government on the people in their individual capacities, in its ordinary and most essential proceedings, will, in the sense of its opponents, on the whole, designate it, in this relation, a *national* government.

But if the government be national with regard to the *operation* of its powers, it changes its aspect again when we contemplate it in relation to the extent of its powers. The idea of a national government involves in it not only an authority over the individual citizens, but an indefinite supremacy over all persons and things, so far as they are objects of lawful government. Among a people consolidated into one nation, this supremacy is completely vested in the national legislature. Among communities united for particular purposes, it is vested partly in the general and partly in the municipal legislatures. In the former case, all local authorities are subordinate to the supreme; and may be controlled, directed, or abolished by it at pleasure. In the latter, the local or municipal authorities form distinct and independent portions of the supremacy, no more subject, within their respective spheres, to the general authority than the general authority is subject to them, within its own sphere. In this relation, then, the proposed government cannot be deemed a *national* one; since its jurisdiction extends to certain enumerated objects only, and leaves to the several States a residuary and inviolable sovereignty over all other objects. It is true that in controversies relating to the boundary between the two jurisdictions, the tribunal which is ultimately to decide is to be established under the general government. But this does not change the principle of the case. The decision is to be impartially made, according to the rules of the Constitution; and all the usual and most effectual precautions are taken to secure this impartiality. Some such tribunal is clearly essential to prevent an appeal to the sword and a dissolution of the compact; and that it ought to be established under the general rather than under the local governments, or, to speak more properly, that it could be safely established under the first alone, is a position not likely to be combated.

Neither Wholly National nor Wholly Federal

If we try the Constitution by its last relation to the authority by which amendments are to be made, we find it neither wholly *national* nor wholly *federal*. Were it wholly national, the supreme and ultimate authority would reside in the *majority* of the people of the Union; and this authority would be competent at all times, like that of a majority of every national society to alter or abolish its established government. Were it wholly federal, on the other hand, the concurrence of each State in the Union would be essential to every alteration that would be binding on all. The mode provided by the plan of the convention is not founded on either of these principles. In requiring more than a majority, and particularly in computing the proportion by *States*, not by *citizens*, it departs from the national and advances towards the *federal* character; in rendering the concurrence of less than the whole number of States sufficient, it loses again *federal* and partakes of the *national* character.

The proposed Constitution, therefore, even when tested by the rules laid down by its antagonists, is, in strictness, neither a national nor a federal Constitution, but a composition of both. In its foundation it is federal, not national; in the sources from which the ordinary powers of the government are drawn, it is partly federal and partly national; in the operation of these powers, it is national, not federal; in the extent of them, again, it is federal, not national; and, finally in the authoritative mode of introducing amendments, it is neither wholly federal nor wholly national.

No. 47

The Meaning of the Maxim, Which Requires a Separation of the Departments of Power, Examined and Ascertained

Central to the Federalist *argument is the fact that in a republic, powers are separated clearly between the executive, legislative, and judicial branches of government and between the national and state governments. In this paper, Madison draws on Montesquieu and cites the Massachusetts state constitution as an example of powers clearly separated among the three parts of government. He also reviews several other state constitutions with regard to how powers are divided and notes, "The accumulation of all powers, legislative, executive, and judiciary, in the same hands, whether of one, a few, or many, and whether hereditary, self-appointed, or elective, may justly be pronounced the very definition of tyranny."*

Having reviewed the general form of the proposed government and the general mass of power allotted to it, I proceed to examine the particular structure of this government, and the distribution of this mass of power among its constituent parts.

Separation of Powers

One of the principal objections inculcated by the more respectable adversaries to the Constitution is its supposed violation of the political maxim that the legislative, executive, and judiciary departments ought to be separate and distinct. In the structure of the federal government no regard, it is said, seems to have been paid to this essential precaution in favor of liberty. The several departments of power are distributed and blended in such a manner as at once to destroy all symmetry and beauty of form, and to expose some of the essential parts of the edifice to the danger of being crushed by the disproportionate weight of other parts. No political truth is certainly of greater intrinsic value, or is stamped with the authority of more enlightened patrons of liberty than that on which the objection is founded. The accumulation of all powers, legislative, executive, and judiciary, in the same hands, whether of one, a few, or many, and whether hereditary, self-appointed, or elective, may justly be pronounced the very definition of tyranny. Were the federal Constitution, therefore, really chargeable with this accumulation of power, or with a mixture of powers, having a dangerous tendency to such an accumulation, no further arguments would be necessary to inspire a universal reprobation of the system. I persuade myself, however, that it will be made apparent to everyone that the charge cannot be supported, and that the maxim on which it relies has been totally misconceived and misapplied. In order to form correct ideas on this important subject it will be proper to investigate the sense in which the preservation of liberty requires that the three great departments of power should be separate and distinct.

The oracle who is always consulted and cited on this subject is the celebrated Montesquieu. If he be not the author of this invaluable precept in the science of politics, he has the merit at least of displaying and recommending it most effectually to the attention of mankind. Let us endeavor, in the first place, to ascertain his meaning on this point.

The British Constitution was to Montesquieu what Homer has been to the didactic writers on epic poetry. As the latter have considered the work of the immortal bard as the perfect model from which the principles and rules of the epic art were to be drawn, and by which all similar works were to be judged, so this great political critic appears to have viewed the Constitution of England as the standard, or to use his own expression, as the mirror of political liberty; and to have delivered, in the form of elementary truths, the several characteristic principles of that particular system. That we may be sure, then, not to mistake his meaning in this case, let us recur to the source from which the maxim was drawn.

On the slightest view of the British Constitution, we must perceive that the legislative, executive, and judiciary departments are by no means totally separate and distinct from each other. The executive magistrate forms an integral part of the legislative authority. He alone has the prerogative of making treaties with foreign sovereigns which, when made, have, under certain limitations, the force of legislative acts. All the members of the judiciary department are appointed by him, can be removed by him on the address of the two Houses of Parliament, and form, when he pleases to consult them, one of his constitutional councils. One branch of the legislative department forms also a great constitutional council to the executive chief, as, on another hand, it is the sole depositary of judicial power in cases of impeachment, and is invested with the supreme appellate jurisdiction in all other cases. The judges, again, are so far connected with the legislative department as often to attend and participate in its deliberations, though not admitted to a legislative vote.

Montesquieu on Separation of Powers

From these facts, by which Montesquieu was guided, it may clearly be inferred that in saying "There can be no liberty where the legislative and executive powers are united in the same person, or body of magistrates," or, "if the power of judging be not separated from the legislative and executive powers," he did not mean that these departments ought to have no *partial agency* in, or no *control* over, the acts of each other. His meaning, as his own words import, and still more conclusively as illustrated by the example in his eye, can amount to no more than this, that where the *whole* power of one department is exercised by the same hands which possess the *whole* power of another department, the fundamental principles of a free constitution are subverted. This would have been the case in the constitution examined by him, if the king, who is the sole executive magistrate, had possessed also the complete legislative power, or the supreme administration of justice; or if the entire legislative body had possessed the supreme judiciary, or the supreme executive authority. This, however, is not among the vices of that constitution. The magistrate in whom the whole executive power resides cannot of himself make a law, though he can put a negative on every law; nor administer justice in person, though he has the appointment of those who do administer it. The judges can exercise no executive prerogative, though they are shoots from the executive stock; nor any legislative function, though they may be advised by the legislative councils. The entire legislature can perform no judiciary act, though by the joint act of two of its branches the judges may be removed from their offices, and though one of its branches is possessed of the judicial power in the last resort. The entire legislature, again, can exercise no executive prerogative, though one of its branches constitutes the supreme executive magistracy, and another, on the impeachment of a third, can try and condemn all the subordinate officers in the executive department.

Need for an Independent Judiciary

The reasons on which Montesquieu grounds his maxim are a further demonstration of his meaning. "When the legislative and executive powers are united in the same person or body," says he, "there can be no liberty, because apprehensions may arise lest *the same* monarch or senate should *enact* tyrannical laws to *execute* them in a tyrannical manner." Again: "Were the power of judging joined with the legislative, the life and liberty of the subject would be exposed to arbitrary control, for *the judge* would then be *the legislator.* Were it joined to the executive power, *the judge* might behave with all the violence of *an oppressor.*" Some of these reasons are more fully explained in other passages; but briefly stated as they are here they sufficiently establish the meaning which we have put on this celebrated maxim of this celebrated author.

State Constitutions as Examples

If we look into the constitutions of the several States we find that, notwithstanding the emphatical and, in some instances, the unqualified terms in which this axiom has been laid down, there is not a single instance in which the several departments of power have been kept absolutely separate and distinct. New Hampshire, whose constitution was the last formed, seems to have been fully aware of the impossibility and inexpediency of avoiding any mixture whatever of these departments, and has qualified the doctrine by declaring "that the legislative, executive, and judiciary powers ought to be kept as separate from, and independent of, each other *as the nature of a free government will admit; or as is consistent with that chain of connection that binds the whole fabric of the constitution in one indissoluble bond of unity and amity.*" Her constitution accordingly mixes these departments in several respects. The Senate, which is a branch of the legislative department, is also a judicial tribunal for the trial of impeachments. The President, who is the head of the executive department, is the presiding member also of the Senate; and, besides an equal vote in all cases, has a casting vote in case of a tie. The executive head is himself eventually elective every year by the legislative department, and his council is every year chosen by and from the members of the same department. Several of the officers of state are also appointed by the legislature. And the members of the judiciary department are appointed by the executive department.

The constitution of Massachusetts has observed a sufficient though less pointed caution in expressing this fundamental article of liberty. It declares "that the legislative department shall never exercise the executive and judicial powers, or either of them; the executive shall never exercise the legislative and judicial powers, or either of them; the judicial shall never exercise the legislative and executive powers, or either of them." This declaration corresponds precisely with the doctrine of Montesquieu, as it has been explained, and is not in a single point violated by the plan of the convention. It goes no farther than to prohibit any one of the entire departments from exercising the powers of another department. In the very Constitution to which it is prefixed, a partial mixture of powers has been admitted. The executive magistrate has a qualified negative on the legislative body, and the Senate, which is a part of the legislature, is a court of impeachment for members both of the executive and judiciary departments. The members of the judiciary department, again, are appointed by the executive department, and removable by the same authority on the address of the two legislative branches. Lastly, a number of the officers of government are annually appointed by the legislative department. As the appointment to offices, particularly executive offices, is in its nature an executive function, the compilers of the Constitution have, in this last point at least, violated the rule established by themselves.

I pass over the constitutions of Rhode Island and Connecticut, because they were formed prior to the Revolution and even before the principle under examination had become an object of political attention.

The constitution of New York contains no declaration on this subject, but appears very clearly to have been framed with an eye to the danger of improperly blending the different departments. It gives, nevertheless, to the executive magistrate, a partial control over the legislative department; and, what is more, gives a like control to the judiciary department; and even blends the executive and judiciary departments in the exercise of this control. In its council of appointment members of the legislative are associated with the executive authority, in the appointment of officers, both executive and judiciary. And its court for the trial of impeachments and correction of errors is to consist of one branch of the legislature and the principal members of the judiciary department.

The constitution of New Jersey has blended the different powers of government more than any of the preceding. The governor, who is the executive magistrate, is appointed by the legislature; is chancellor and ordinary, or surrogate of the State; is a member of the Supreme Court of Appeals, and president, with a casting vote, of one of the legislative branches. The same legislative branch acts again as executive council to the governor, and with him constitutes the Court of Appeals. The members of the judiciary department are appointed by the legislative department, and removable by one branch of it, on the impeachment of the other.

According to the constitution of Pennsylvania, the president, who is the head of the executive department, is annually elected by a vote in which the legislative department predominates. In conjunction with an executive council, he appoints the members of the judiciary department and forms a court of impeachment for trial of all officers, judiciary as well as executive. The judges of the Supreme Court and justices of the peace seem also to be removable by the legislature; and the executive power of pardoning, in certain cases, to be referred to the same department. The members of the executive council are made ex officio justices of peace throughout the State.

In Delaware the chief executive magistrate is annually elected by the legislative department. The speakers of the two legislative branches are vice-presidents in the executive department. The executive chief, with six others appointed, three by each of the legislative branches, constitutes the Supreme Court of Appeals; he is joined with the legislative department in the appointment of the other judges. Throughout the States it appears that the members of the legislature may at the same time be justices of the peace; in this State, the members of one branch of it are ex officio justices of the peace; as are also the members of the executive council. The principal officers of the executive department are appointed by the legislative; and one branch of the latter forms a court of impeachments. All officers may be removed on address of the legislature.

Maryland has adopted the maxim in the most unqualified terms; declaring that the legislative, executive, and judicial powers of government ought to be forever separate and distinct from each other. Her constitution, notwithstanding, makes the executive magistrate appointable by the legislative department; and the members of the judiciary by the executive department.

The language of Virginia is still more pointed on this subject. Her constitution declares "that the legislative, executive, and judiciary departments shall be separate and distinct; so that neither exercises the powers properly belonging to the other; nor shall any person exercise the powers of more than one of them at the same time, except that the justices of county courts shall be eligible to either House of Assembly." Yet we find not only this express exception with respect to the members of the inferior courts, but that the chief magistrate, with his executive council, are appointable by the legislature; that two members of the latter are triennially displaced at the pleasure of the legislature; and that all the principal offices, both executive and judiciary, are filled by the same department. The executive prerogative of pardon, also, is in one case vested in the legislative department.

The constitution of North Carolina, which declares "that the legislative, executive, and supreme judicial powers of government ought to be forever separate and distinct from each other," refers, at the same time, to the legislative department, the appointment not only of the executive chief, but all the principal officers within both that and the judiciary department. In South Carolina, the constitution makes the executive magistracy eligible by the legislative department. It gives to the latter, also, the appointment of the members of the judiciary department, including even justices of the peace and sheriffs; and the appointment of officers in the executive department, down to captains in the army and navy of the State.

In the constitution of Georgia where it is declared "that the legislative, executive, and judiciary departments shall be separate and distinct, so that neither exercise the powers properly belonging to the other," we find that the executive department is to be filled by appointments of the legislature; and the executive prerogative of pardon to be finally exercised by the same authority. Even justices of the peace are to be appointed by the legislature.

In citing these cases, in which the legislative, executive, and judiciary departments have not been kept totally separate and distinct, I wish not to be regarded as an advocate for the particular organizations of the several State governments. I am fully aware that among the many excellent principles which they exemplify they carry strong marks of the haste, and still stronger of the inexperience, under which they were framed. It is but too obvious that in some instances the fundamental principle under consideration has been violated by too great a mixture, and even an actual consolidation of the different powers; and that in no instance has a competent provision been made for maintaining in practice the separation delineated on paper. What I have wished to evince is that the charge brought against the proposed Constitution of violating the sacred maxim of free government is warranted neither by the real meaning annexed to that maxim by its author, nor by the sense in which it has hitherto been understood in America. This interesting subject will be resumed in the ensuing paper.

No. 48

The Same Subject Continued with a View to the Means of Giving Efficacy in Practice to That Maxim

Here Madison deals with the legislative branch's proclivity to absorb and consolidate power belonging to other branches. This can result in a "tyrannical concentration of all the powers of government in the same hands." Madison writes, ". . . power is of an encroaching nature and . . . ought to be effectually restrained from passing the limits assigned to it." Once again, Madison states his fear of inadequate "parchment barriers" between divisions of government and uncontrolled power loose in the body politic, and once again he proposes means to contain it through checks and balances and the separation of powers. The Virginia constitution is cited. Its flaw is that there is no clearly stated barrier between the powers of the three branches of government, with the legislature in control of the public purse, including expenditures of the executive and the judiciary, causing those branches to be subservient to the legislature. Madison uses a quote from his friend Thomas Jefferson, in the latter's Notes on the State of Virginia: *"One hundred and seventy-three despots would surely be as oppressive as one." As for the constitution of another important state, Pennsylvania, a commission of inquiry found "that the Constitution had been flagrantly violated by the legislature in a variety of important instances."*

> *The conclusion drawn from the study of the two state constitutions is that "a mere demarcation on parchment of the constitutional limits of the several departments is not a sufficient guard against those encroachments which lead to a tyrannical concentration of all the powers of government in the same hands."*

It was shown in the last paper that the political apothegm there examined does not require that the legislative, executive, and judiciary departments should be wholly unconnected with each other. I shall undertake, in the next place, to show that unless these departments be so far connected and blended as to give to each a constitutional control over the others, the degree of separation which the maxim requires, as essential to a free government, can never in practice be duly maintained.

It is agreed on all sides that the powers properly belonging to one of the departments ought not to be directly and completely administered by either of the other departments. It is equally evident that none of them ought to possess, directly or indirectly, an overruling influence over the others in the administration of their respective powers. It will not be denied that power is of an encroaching nature and that it ought to be effectually restrained from passing the limits assigned to it. After discriminating, therefore, in theory, the several classes of power, as they may in their nature be legislative, executive, or judiciary, the next and most difficult task is to provide some practical security for each, against the invasion of the others. What this security ought to be is the great problem to be solved.

The Failure of "Parchment Barriers"

Will it be sufficient to mark, with precision, the boundaries of these departments in the constitution of the government, and to trust to these parchment barriers against the encroaching spirit of power? This is the security which appears to have been principally relied on by the compilers of most of the American constitutions. But experience assures us that the efficacy of the provision has been greatly overrated; and that some more adequate defense is indispensably necessary for the more feeble against the more powerful members of the government. The legislative department is everywhere extending the sphere of its activity and drawing all power into its impetuous vortex.

The founders of our republics have so much merit for the wisdom which they have displayed that no task can be less pleasing than that of pointing out the errors into which they have fallen. A respect for truth, however, obliges us to remark that they seem never for a moment to have turned their eyes from the danger, to liberty, from the overgrown and all-grasping prerogative of an hereditary magistrate, supported and fortified by an hereditary branch of the legislative authority. They seem never to have recollected the danger from legislative usurpations, which, by assembling all power in the same hands, must lead to the same tyranny as is threatened by executive usurpations.

Dangers of a "Too-Strong" Legislature

In a government where numerous and extensive prerogatives are placed in the hands of an hereditary monarch, the executive department is very justly regarded as the source of danger, and watched with all the jealousy which a zeal for liberty ought to inspire. In a democracy, where a multitude of people exercise in person the legislative functions and are continually exposed, by their incapacity for regular deliberation and concerted measures, to the ambitious intrigues of their executive magistrates, tyranny may well be apprehended, on some favorable emergency, to start up in the same quarter. But in a representative republic where the executive magistracy is carefully limited, both in the extent and the duration of its power; and where the legislative power is exercised by an assembly, which is inspired by a supposed influence over the people with an intrepid confidence in its own strength; which is sufficiently numerous to feel all the passions which actuate a multitude, yet not so numerous as to be incapable of pursuing the objects of its passions by means which reason prescribes; it is against the enterprising ambition of this department that the people ought to indulge all their jealousy and exhaust all their precautions.

The legislative department derives a superiority in our governments from other circumstances. Its constitutional powers being at once more extensive, and less susceptible of precise limits, it can, with the greater facility, mask, under complicated and indirect measures, the encroachments which it makes on the co-ordinate departments. It is not unfrequently a question of real nicety in legislative bodies whether the operation of a particular measure will, or will not, extend beyond the legislative sphere. On the other side, the executive power being restrained within a narrower compass and being more simple in its nature, and the judiciary being described by landmarks still less uncertain, projects of usurpation by either of these departments would immediately betray and defeat themselves.

Nor is this all: as the legislative department alone has access to the pockets of the people, and has in some constitutions full discretion, and in all a prevailing influence, over the pecuniary rewards of those who fill the other departments, a dependence is thus created in the latter, which gives still greater facility to encroachments of the former.

I have appealed to our own experience for the truth of what I advance on this subject. Were it necessary to verify this experience by particular proofs, they might be multiplied without end. I might collect vouchers in abundance from the records and archives of every State in the Union. But as a more concise and at the same time equally satisfactory evidence, I will refer to the example of two States, attested by two unexceptionable authorities.

Thomas Jefferson on Separating Powers to Avoid Despotism

The first example is that of Virginia, a State which, as we have seen, has expressly declared in its constitution that the three great departments ought not to be intermixed. The authority in support of it is Mr. Jefferson, who, besides his other advantages for remarking the operation of the government, was himself the chief magistrate of it. In order to convey fully the ideas with which his experience had impressed him on this subject, it will be necessary to quote a passage of some length from his very interesting *Notes on the State of Virginia*, p. 195. "All the powers of government, legislative, executive, and judiciary, result to the legislative body. The concentrating these in the same hands is precisely the definition of despotic government. It will be no alleviation that these powers will be exercised by a plurality of hands, and not by a single one. One hundred and seventy-three despots would surely be as oppressive as one. Let those who doubt it turn their eyes on the republic of Venice. As little will it avail us that they are chosen by ourselves. An *elective despotism* was not the government we fought for; but one which should not only be founded on free principles, but in which the powers of government should be so divided and balanced among several bodies of magistracy as that no one could transcend their legal limits without being effectually checked and restrained by the others. For this reason that convention which passed the ordinance of government laid its foundation on this basis, that the legislative, executive, and judiciary departments should be separate and distinct, so that no person should exercise the powers of more than one of them at the same time. *But no*

123

barrier was provided between these several powers. The judiciary and the executive members were left dependent on the legislative for their subsistence in office, and some of them for their continuance in it. If, therefore, the legislature assumes executive and judiciary powers, no opposition is likely to be made; nor, if made, can be effectual; because in that case they may put their proceedings into the form of acts of Assembly, which will render them obligatory on the other branches. They have accordingly, *in many* instances, *decided rights* which should have been left to *judiciary controversy,* and *the direction of the executive, during the whole time of their session, is becoming habitual and familiar."*

Pennsylvania's Legislature "Flagrantly Violates" the Constitution

The other State which I shall have for an example is Pennsylvania; and the other authority, the Council of Censors, which assembled in the years 1783 and 1784. A part of the duty of this body, as marked out by the Constitution, was to "inquire whether the Constitution had been preserved inviolate in every part; and whether the legislative and executive branches of government had performed their duty as guardians of the people, or assumed to themselves, or exercised, other or greater powers than they are entitled to by the Constitution." In the execution of this trust, the council were necessarily led to a comparison of both the legislative and executive proceedings with the constitutional powers of these departments; and from the facts enumerated, and to the truth of most of which both sides in the council subscribed, it appears that the Constitution had been flagrantly violated by the legislature in a variety of important instances.

A great number of laws had been passed violating, without any apparent necessity, the rule requiring that all bills of a public nature shall be previously printed for the consideration of the people; although this is one of the precautions chiefly relied on by the Constitution against improper acts of the legislature.

The constitutional trial by jury had been violated and powers assumed which had not been delegated by the Constitution.

Executive powers had been usurped.

The salaries of the judges, which the Constitution expressly requires to be fixed, had been occasionally varied; and cases belonging to the judiciary department frequently drawn within legislative cognizance and determination.

Those who wish to see the several particulars falling under each of these heads may consult the journals of the council which are in print. Some of them, it will be found, may be imputable to peculiar circumstances connected with the war; but the greater part of them may be considered as the spontaneous shoots of an ill-constituted government.

It appears, also, that the executive department had not been innocent of frequent breaches of the Constitution. There are three observations, however, which ought to be made on this head: *first,* a great proportion of the instances were either immediately produced by the necessities of the war, or recommended by Congress or the commander-in-chief; *second,* in most of the other instances they conformed either to the declared or the known sentiments of the legislative department; *third,* the executive department of Pennsylvania is distinguished from that of the other States by the number of members composing it. In this respect, it has as much affinity to a legislative assembly as to an executive council. And being at once exempt from the restraint of an individual responsibility for the acts of the body, and deriving confidence from mutual example and joint influence, unauthorized measures would, of course, be more freely hazarded, than where the executive department is administered by a single hand, or by a few hands.

The conclusion which I am warranted in drawing from these observations is that a mere demarcation on parchment of the constitutional limits of the several departments is not a sufficient guard against those encroachments which lead to a tyrannical concentration of all the powers of government in the same hands.

No. 49

The Same Subject Continued with the Same View

The papers continue their strong case for a republican government but seek clear restraints on governmental power. This is considerably different from a pure democracy, where popular will and impulse rule. Madison's opposition to "direct democracy" is restated here. Madison believes there should be provisions to amend the Constitution, but such changes should be infrequent and difficult to enact to avoid turning momentary political passions into immutable law.

The author of the *Notes on the State of Virginia,* quoted in the last paper, has subjoined to that valuable work the draught of a constitution, which had been prepared in order to be laid before a convention expected to be called in 1783, by the legislature, for the establishment of a constitution for that commonwealth. The plan, like everything from the same pen, marks a turn of thinking, original, comprehensive, and accurate; and is the more worthy of attention as it equally displays a fervent attachment to republican government and an enlightened view of the dangerous propensities against which it ought to be guarded. One of the precautions which he proposes, and on which he appears ultimately to rely as a palladium to the weaker departments of power against the invasions of the stronger, is perhaps altogether his own, and as it immediately relates to the subject of our present inquiry, ought not to be overlooked.

His proposition is "that whenever any two of the three branches of government shall concur in opinion, each by the voices of two thirds of their whole number, that a convention is necessary for altering the Constitution, or *correcting breaches of it,* a convention shall be called for the purpose."

As the people are the only legitimate fountain of power, and it is from them that the constitutional charter, under which the several branches of government hold their power, is derived, it seems strictly consonant to the republican theory to recur to the same original authority, not only whenever it may be necessary to enlarge, diminish, or new-model the powers of government, but also whenever any one of the departments may commit encroachments on the chartered authorities of the others. The several departments being perfectly co-ordinate by the terms of their common commission, neither of them, it is evident, can pretend to an exclusive or superior right of settling the boundaries between their respective powers; and how are the encroachments of the stronger to be prevented, or the wrongs of the weaker to be redressed, without an appeal to the people themselves, who, as the grantors of the commission, can alone declare its true meaning, and enforce its observance?

How Can the Constitution Be Changed?

There is certainly great force in this reasoning, and it must be allowed to prove that a constitutional road to the decision of the people ought to be marked out and kept open, for certain great and extraordinary occasions. But there appear to be insuperable objections against the proposed recurrence to the people, as a provision in all cases for keeping the several departments of power within their constitutional limits.

In the first place, the provision does not reach the case of a combination of two of the departments against the third. If the legislative authority, which possesses so many means of operating on the motives of the other departments, should be able to gain to its interest either of the others, or even one third of its members, the remaining department could derive no advantage from this remedial provision. I do not dwell, however, on this objection, because it may be thought to lie rather against the modifications of the principle, than against the principle itself.

In the next place, it may be considered as an objection inherent in the principle that as every appeal to the people would carry an implication of some defect in the government, frequent appeals would, in great measure, deprive the government of that veneration which time bestows on everything, and without which perhaps the wisest and freest governments would not possess the requisite stability. If it be true that all governments rest on opinion, it is no less true that the strength of opinion in each individual, and its practical influence on his conduct, depend much on the number which he supposes to have entertained the same opinion. The reason of man, like man himself, is timid and cautious when left alone, and acquires firmness and confidence in proportion to the number with which it is associated. When the examples which fortify opinion are *ancient* as well as *numerous,* they are known to have a double effect. In a nation of philosophers, this consideration ought to be disregarded. A reverence for the laws would be sufficiently inculcated by the voice of an enlightened reason. But a nation of philosophers is as little to be expected as the philosophical race of kings wished for by Plato. And in every other nation, the most rational government will not find it a superfluous advantage to have the prejudices of the community on its side.

"The Danger of Disturbing the Public Tranquillity"

The danger of disturbing the public tranquillity by interesting too strongly the public passions is a still more serious objection against a frequent reference of constitutional questions to the decision of the whole society. Notwithstanding the success which has attended the revisions of our established forms of government and which does so much honor to the virtue and intelligence of the people of America, it must be confessed that the experiments are of too ticklish a nature to be unnecessarily multiplied. We are to recollect that all the existing constitutions were formed in the midst of a danger which repressed the passions most unfriendly to order and concord; of an enthusiastic confidence of the people in their patriotic leaders, which stifled the ordinary diversity of opinions on great national questions; of a universal ardor for new and opposite forms, produced by a universal resentment and indignation against the ancient government; and whilst no spirit of party connected with the changes to be made, or the abuses to be reformed, could mingle its leaven in the operation. The future situations in which we must expect to be usually placed do not present any equivalent security against the danger which is apprehended.

But the greatest objection of all is that the decisions which would probably result from such appeals would not answer the purpose of maintaining the constitutional equilibrium of the government. We have seen that the tendency of republican governments is to an aggrandizement of the legislative at the expense of the other departments. The appeals to the people, therefore, would usually be made by the executive and judiciary departments. But whether made by one side or the other, would each side enjoy equal advantages on the trial? Let us view their different situations. The members of the executive and judiciary departments are few in number, and can be personally known to a small part only of the people. The latter, by the mode of their appointment, as well as by the nature and permanency of it, are too far removed from the people to share much in their prepossessions. The former are generally the objects of jealousy and their administration is always liable to be discolored and rendered unpopular. The members of the legislative department, on the other hand, are numerous. They are distributed and dwell among the people at large. Their connections of blood, of friendship, and of acquaintance embrace a great proportion of the most influential part of the society. The nature of their public trust implies a personal influence among the people, and that they are more immediately the confidential guardians of the rights and liberties of the people. With these advantages it can hardly be supposed that the adverse party would have an equal chance for a favorable issue.

But the legislative party would not only be able to plead their cause most successfully with the people. They would probably be constituted themselves the judges. The same influence which had gained them an election into the legislature would gain them a seat in the convention. If this should not be the case with all, it would probably be the case with many, and pretty certainly with those leading characters, on whom everything depends in such bodies. The convention, in short, would be composed chiefly of men who had been, who actually were, or who expected to be, members of the department whose conduct was arraigned. They would consequently be parties to the very question to be decided by them.

It might, however, sometimes happen, that appeals would be made under circumstances less adverse to the executive and judiciary departments. The usurpations of the legislature might be so flagrant and so sudden, as to admit of no specious coloring. A strong party among themselves might take side with the other branches. The executive power might be in the hands of a peculiar favorite of the people. In such a posture of things, the public decision might be less swayed by prepossessions in favor of the legislative party. But still it could never be expected to turn on the true merits of the question. It would inevitably be connected with the spirit of pre-existing parties, or of parties springing out of the question itself. It would be connected with persons of distinguished character and extensive influence in the community. It would be pronounced by the very men who had been agents in, or opponents of, the measures to which the decision would relate. The *passions,* therefore, not the *reason,* of the public would sit in judgment. But it is the reason, alone, of the public, that ought to control and regulate the government. The passions ought to be controlled and regulated by the government.

We found in the last paper that mere declarations in the written Constitution are not sufficient to restrain the several departments within their legal rights. It appears in this that occasional appeals to the people would be neither a proper nor an effectual provision for that purpose. How far the provisions of a different nature contained in the plan above quoted might be adequate I do not examine. Some of them are unquestionably founded on sound political principles, and all of them are framed with singular ingenuity and precision.

No. 51

The Same Subject Continued with the Same View and Concluded

Like Federalist No. 10, Federalist No. 51 *contains some of Madison's most carefully wrought observations about human society and its governance. For Madison, the key to securing stable government and protecting civic rights comes in balancing "the multiplicity of interests" contained in a diverse society.*

The concentration of power in any single place can be avoided through the Constitution, and "ambition must be made to counteract ambition. The interest of the man must be connected with the constitutional rights of the place. It may be a reflection on human nature that such devices should be necessary to control the abuses of government." He then writes, "But what is government itself but the greatest of all reflections on human nature? If men were angels, no government would be necessary." He continues, "You must first enable the government to control the governed; and in the next place oblige it to control itself." That is the problem of democratic governance stated in its most reduced form.

Madison calls the American experiment a "compound republic," in which the people surrender power to two distinct governments, after which power is further "subdivided among distinct and separate departments. Hence a double security arises to the rights of the people. The different governments will control each other, at the same time that each will be controlled by itself." Not only must the society be protected against the oppression of its rulers, but one part of the society must be safeguarded "against the injustice of the other part." He states, "Justice is the end of government. It is the end of civil society. It ever has been and ever will be pursued until it is obtained, or until liberty be lost in the pursuit."

Once more Madison draws on the "enlarged spheres" argument; the more the society is broken into parts reflecting interests and classes, the more rights will be protected, just as the more numerous religious denominations become, the better are prospects for religious liberty flourishing. "The larger the society, provided it lie within a practicable sphere, the more duly capable it will be of self-government."

To what expedient, then, shall we finally resort, for maintaining in practice the necessary partition of power among the several departments as laid down in the Constitution? The only answer that can be given is that as all these exterior provisions are found to be inadequate the defect must be supplied, by so contriving the interior structure of the government as that its several constituent parts may, by their mutual relations, be the means of keeping each other in their proper places. Without presuming to undertake a full development of this important idea I will hazard a few general observations which may perhaps place it in a clearer light, and enable us to form a more correct judgment of the principles and structure of the government planned by the convention.

In order to lay a due foundation for that separate and distinct exercise of the different powers of government, which to a certain extent is admitted on all hands to be essential to the preservation of liberty, it is evident that each department should have a will of its own; and consequently should be so constituted that the members of each should have as little agency as possible in the appointment of the members of the others. Were this principle rigorously adhered to, it would require that all the appointments for the supreme executive, legislative, and judiciary magistracies should be drawn from the same fountain of authority, the people, through channels having no communication whatever with one another. Perhaps such a plan of constructing the several departments would be less difficult in practice than it may in contemplation appear. Some difficulties, however, and some additional expense would attend the execution of it. Some deviations, therefore, from the principle must be admitted. In the constitution of the judiciary department in particular, it might be inexpedient to insist rigorously on the principle: first, because peculiar qualifications being essential in the members, the primary consideration ought to be to select that mode of choice which best secures these qualifications; second, because the permanent tenure by which the appointments are held in that department must soon destroy all sense of dependence on the authority conferring them.

"If Men Were Angels, No Government Would Be Necessary"

It is equally evident that the members of each department should be as little dependent as possible on those of the others for the emoluments annexed to their offices. Were the executive magistrate, or the judges, not independent of the legislature in this particular, their independence in every other would be merely nominal.

But the great security against a gradual concentration of the several powers in the same department consists in giving to those who administer each department the necessary constitutional means and personal motives to resist encroachments of the others. The provision for defense must in this, as in all other cases, be made commensurate to the danger of attack. Ambition must be made to counteract ambition. The interest of the man must be connected with the constitutional rights of the place. It may be a reflection on human nature that such devices should be necessary to control the abuses of government. But what is government itself but the greatest of all reflections on human nature? If men were angels, no government would be necessary. If angels were to govern men, neither external nor internal controls on government would be necessary. In framing a government which is to be administered by men over men, the great difficulty lies in this: you must first enable the government to control the governed; and in the next place oblige it to control itself. A dependence on the people is, no doubt, the primary control on the government; but experience has taught mankind the necessity of auxiliary precautions.

This policy of supplying, by opposite and rival interests, the defect of better motives, might be traced through the whole system of human affairs, private as well as public. We see it particularly displayed in all the subordinate distributions of power, where the constant aim is to divide and arrange the several offices in such a manner as that each may be a check on the other—that the private interest of every individual may be a sentinel over the public rights. These inventions of prudence cannot be less requisite in the distribution of the supreme powers of the State.

But it is not possible to give to each department an equal power of self-defense. In republican government, the legislative authority necessarily predominates. The remedy for this inconveniency is to divide the legislature into different branches; and to render them, by different modes of election and different principles of action, as little connected with each other as the nature of their common functions and their common dependence on the society will admit. It may even be necessary to guard against dangerous encroachments by still further precautions. As the weight of the legislative authority requires that it should be thus divided, the weakness of the executive may require, on the other hand, that it should be fortified. An absolute negative on the legislature appears, at first view, to be the natural defense with which the executive magistrate should be armed. But perhaps it would be neither altogether safe nor alone sufficient. On ordinary occasions it might not be exerted with the requisite firmness, and on extraordinary occasions it might be perfidiously abused. May not this defect of an absolute negative be supplied by some qualified connection between this weaker department and the weaker branch of the stronger department, by which the latter may be led to support the constitutional rights of the former, without being too much detached from the rights of its own department?

If the principles on which these observations are founded be just, as I persuade myself they are, and they be applied as a criterion to the several State constitutions, and to the federal Constitution, it will be found that if the latter does not perfectly correspond with them, the former are infinitely less able to bear such a test.

There are, moreover, two considerations particularly applicable to the federal system of America, which place that system in a very interesting point of view.

The Compound Republic

First. In a single republic, all the power surrendered by the people is submitted to the administration of a single government; and the usurpations are guarded against by a division of the government into distinct and separate departments. In the compound republic of America, the power surrendered by the people is first divided between two distinct governments, and then the portion allotted to each subdivided among distinct and separate departments. Hence a double security arises to the rights of the people. The different governments will control each other, at the same time that each will be controlled by itself.

"To Guard One Part of the Society Against the Injustice of the Other Part"

Second. It is of great importance in a republic not only to guard the society against the oppression of its rulers, but to guard one part of the society against the injustice of the other part. Different interests necessarily exist in different classes of citizens. If a majority be united by a common interest, the rights of the minority will be insecure. There are but two methods of providing against this evil: the one by creating a will in the community independent of the majority—that is, of the society itself; the other, by comprehending in the society so many separate descriptions of citizens as will render an unjust combination of a majority of the whole very improbable, if not impracticable. The first method prevails in all governments possessing an hereditary or self-appointed authority. This, at best, is but a precarious security; because a power independent of the society may as well espouse the unjust views of the major as the rightful interests of the minor party, and may possibly be turned against both parties. The second method will be exemplified in the federal republic of the United States. Whilst all authority in it will be derived from and dependent on the society, the society itself will be broken into so many parts, interests and classes of citizens, that the rights of individuals, or of the minority, will be in little danger from interested combinations of the majority. In a free government the security for civil rights must be the same as that for religious rights. It consists in the one case in the multiplicity of interests, and in the other in the multiplicity of sects. The degree of security in both cases will depend on the number of interests and sects; and this may be presumed to depend on the extent of country and number of people comprehended under the same government. This view of the subject must particularly recommend a proper federal system to all the sincere and considerate friends of republican government, since it shows that in exact proportion as the territory of the Union may be formed into more circumscribed Confederacies, or States, oppressive combinations of a majority will be facilitated; the best security, under the republican forms, for the rights of every class of citizen, will be diminished; and consequently the stability and independence of some member of the government, the only other security, must be proportionally increased. Justice is the end of government. It is the end of civil society. It ever has been and ever will be pursued until it be obtained, or until liberty be lost in the pursuit. In a society under the forms of which the stronger faction can readily unite and oppress the weaker, anarchy may as truly be said to reign as in a state of nature, where the weaker individual is not secured against the violence of the stronger; and as, in the latter state, even the stronger individuals are prompted, by the uncertainty of their condition, to submit to a government which may protect the weak as well as themselves; so, in the former state, will the more powerful factions or parties be gradually induced, by a like motive, to wish for a government which will protect all parties, the weaker as well as the more powerful. It can be little doubted that if the State of Rhode Island was separated from the Confederacy and left to itself, the insecurity of rights under the popular form of government within such narrow limits would be displayed by such reiterated oppressions of factious majorities that some power altogether independent of the people would soon be called for by the voice of the very factions whose misrule had proved the necessity of it. In the extended republic of the United States, and among the great variety of interests, parties, and sects which it embraces, a coalition of a majority of the whole society could seldom take place on any other principles than those of justice and the general good; whilst there being thus less danger to a minor from the will of a major party, there must be less pretext, also, to provide for the security of the former, by introducing into the government a will not dependent on the latter, or, in other words, a will independent of the society itself. It is no less certain than it is important, notwithstanding the contrary opinions which have been entertained, that the larger the society, provided it lie within a practicable sphere, the more duly capable it will be of self-government. And happily for the *republican cause,* the practicable sphere may be carried to a very great extent by a judicious modification and mixture of the *federal principle.*

No. 62

Concerning the Constitution of the Senate with Regard to the Qualifications of the Members, the Manner of Appointing Them, the Equality of Representation, the Number of the Senators and the Duration of Their Appointments

Seven previous Federalist Papers *discuss election to the House of Representatives. In them Madison argues for a two-year term and notes in No. 55, "No political problem is less susceptible of a precise solution than that which relates to the number most convenient for a representative legislature." In No. 62, probably written by Madison, the republican nature of the Senate's structure is affirmed and its powers carefully delineated. "Liberty may be endangered by the abuses of liberty as well as by the abuses of power," he observes.*

Madison cautions against too rapid a turnover in the Senate, which risks creating a mutable or unstable government where special interest groups, knowledgeable in the ways of Congress, could feed from the public trough. Madison says, "Another effect of public instability is the unreasonable advantage it gives to the sagacious, the enterprising, and the moneyed few over the industrious and uninformed mass of the public. Every new regulation concerning commerce or revenue, or in any manner affecting the value of the different species of property, presents a new harvest to those who watch the change, and can trace its consequences; a harvest, reared not by themselves, but by the toils and cares of the great body of their fellow-citizens. This is the state of things in which it may be said with some truth that laws are made for the few, not for the many."

Having examined the constitution of the House of Representatives, and answered such of the objections against it as seemed to merit notice, I enter next on the examination of the Senate. The heads into which this member of the government may be considered are: I. The qualifications of senators; II. The appointment of them by the State legislatures; III. The equality of representation in the Senate; IV. The number of senators, and the term for which they are to be elected; V. The powers vested in the Senate.

Qualifications

I. The qualifications proposed for senators, as distinguished from those of representatives, consist in a more advanced age and a longer period of citizenship. A senator must be thirty years of age at least; as a representative must be twenty-five. And the former must have been a citizen nine years; as seven years are required for the latter. The propriety of these distinctions is explained by the nature of the senatorial trust, which, requiring greater extent of information and stability of character, requires at the same time that the senator should have reached a period of life most likely to supply these advantages; and which, participating immediately in transactions with foreign nations, ought to be exercised by none who are not thoroughly weaned from the prepossessions and habits incident to foreign birth and education. The term of nine years appears to be a prudent mediocrity between a total exclusion of adopted citizens, whose merits and talents may claim a share in the public confidence, and an indiscriminate and hasty admission of them, which might create a channel for foreign influence on the national councils.

II. It is equally unnecessary to dilate on the appointment of senators by the State legislatures. Among the various modes which might have been devised for constituting this branch of the government, that which has been proposed by the convention is probably the most congenial with the public opinion. It is recommended by the double advantage of favoring a select appointment, and of giving to the State governments such an agency in the formation of the federal government as must secure the authority of the former, and may form a convenient link between the two systems.

III. The equality of representation in the Senate is another point which, being evidently the result of compromise between the opposite pretensions of the large and the small States, does not call for much discussion. If indeed it be right that among a people thoroughly incorporated into one nation every district ought to have a *proportional* share in the government and that among independent and sovereign States, bound together by a simple league, the parties, however unequal in size, ought to have an *equal* share in the common councils, it does not appear to be without some reason that in a compound republic, partaking both of the national and federal character, the government ought to be founded on a mixture of the principles of proportional and equal representation. But it is superfluous to try, by the standard of theory, a part of the Constitution which is allowed on all hands to be the result, not of theory, but "of a spirit of amity, and that mutual deference and concession which the peculiarity of our political situation rendered indispensable." A common government, with powers equal to its objects, is called for by the voice, and still more loudly by the political situation, of America. A government founded on principles more consonant to the wishes of the larger States is not likely to be obtained from the smaller States. The only option, then, for the former lies between the proposed government and a government still more objectionable. Under this alternative, the advice of prudence must be to embrace the lesser evil; and instead of indulging a fruitless anticipation of the possible mischiefs which may ensue, to contemplate rather the advantageous consequences which may qualify the sacrifice.

In this spirit it may be remarked that the equal vote allowed to each State is at once a constitutional recognition of the portion of sovereignty remaining in the individual States and an instrument for preserving that residuary sovereignty. So far the equality ought to be no less acceptable to the large than to the small States; since they are not less solicitous to guard, by every possible expedient, against an improper consolidation of the States into one simple republic.

Another advantage accruing from this ingredient in the constitution of the Senate is the additional impediment it must prove against improper acts of legislation. No law or resolution can now be passed without the concurrence, first, of a majority of the people, and then of a majority of the States. It must be acknowledged that this complicated check on legislation may in some instances be injurious as well as beneficial; and that the peculiar defense which it involves in favor of the smaller States would be more rational if any interests common to them and distinct from those of the other States would otherwise be exposed to peculiar danger. But as the larger States will always be able, by their power over the supplies, to defeat unreasonable exertions of this prerogative of the lesser States, and as the facility and excess of lawmaking seem to be the diseases to which our governments are most liable, it is not impossible that this part of the Constitution may be more convenient in practice than it appears to many in contemplation.

Number of Senators, Duration of Appointment

IV. The number of senators and the duration of their appointment come next to be considered. In order to form an accurate judgment on both these points it will be proper to inquire into the purposes which are to be answered by a senate; and in order to ascertain these it will be necessary to review the inconveniences which a republic must suffer from the want of such an institution.

First. It is a misfortune incident to republican government, though in a less degree than to other governments, that those who administer it may forget their obligations to their constituents and prove unfaithful to their important trust. In this point of view a senate, as a second branch of the legislative assembly distinct from and dividing the power with a first, must be in all cases a salutary check on the government. It doubles the security to the people by requiring the concurrence of two distinct bodies in schemes of usurpation or perfidy, where the ambition or corruption of one would otherwise be sufficient. This is a precaution founded on such clear principles, and now so well understood in the United States, that it would be more than superfluous to enlarge on it. I will barely remark that as the improbability of sinister combinations will be in proportion to the dissimilarity in the genius of the two bodies, it must be politic to distinguish them from each other by every circumstance which will consist with a due harmony in all proper measures, and with the genuine principles of republican government.

Second. The necessity of a senate is not less indicated by the propensity of all single and numerous assemblies to yield to the impulse of sudden and violent passions, and to be seduced by factious leaders into intemperate and pernicious resolutions. Examples on this subject might be cited without number; and from proceedings within the United States, as well as from the history of other nations. But a position that will not be contradicted need not be proved. All that need be remarked is that a body which is to correct this infirmity ought itself to be free from it, and consequently ought to be less numerous. It ought, moreover, to possess great firmness, and consequently ought to hold its authority by a tenure of considerable duration.

Third. Another defect to be supplied by a senate lies in a want of due acquaintance with the objects and principles of legislation. It is not possible that an assembly of men called for the most part from pursuits of a private nature, continued in appointment for a short time and led by no permanent motive to devote the intervals of public occupation to a study of the laws, the affairs, and the comprehensive interests of their country, should, if left wholly to themselves, escape a variety of important errors in the exercise of their legislative trust. It may be affirmed, on the best grounds, that no small share of the present embarrassments of America is to be charged on the blunders of our governments; and that these have proceeded from the heads rather than the hearts of most of the authors of them. What indeed are all the repealing, explaining, and amending laws, which fill and disgrace our voluminous codes, but so many monuments of deficient wisdom; so many impeachments exhibited by each succeeding against each preceding session; so many admonitions to the people of the value of those aids which may be expected from a well-constituted senate?

A good government implies two things: first, fidelity to the object of government, which is the happiness of the people; secondly, a knowledge of the means by which that object can be best attained. Some governments are deficient in both these qualities; most governments are deficient in the first. I scruple not to assert that in American governments too little attention has been paid to the last. The federal Constitution avoids this error; and what merits particular notice, it provides for the last in a mode which increases the security for the first.

Fourth. The mutability in the public councils arising from a rapid succession of new members, however qualified they may be, points out, in the strongest manner, the necessity of some stable institution in the government. Every new election in the States is found to change one half of the representatives. From this change of men must proceed a change of opinions; and from a change of opinions, a change of measures. But a continual change even of good measures is inconsistent with every rule of prudence and every prospect of success. The remark is verified in private life, and becomes more just, as well as more important, in national transactions.

To trace the mischievous effects of a mutable government would fill a volume. I will hint a few only, each of which will be perceived to be a source of innumerable others.

In the first place, it forfeits the respect and confidence of other nations, and all the advantages connected with national character. An individual who is observed to be inconstant to his plans, or perhaps to carry on his affairs without any plan at all, is marked at once by all prudent people as a speedy victim to his own unsteadiness and folly. His more friendly neighbors may pity him, but all will decline to connect their fortunes with his; and not a few will seize the opportunity of making their fortunes out of his. One nation is to another what one individual is to another; with this melancholy distinction, perhaps, that the former, with fewer of the benevolent emotions than the latter, are under fewer restraints also from taking undue advantage of the indiscretions of each other. Every nation, consequently, whose affairs betray a want of wisdom and stability, may calculate on every loss which can be sustained from the more systematic policy of its wiser neighbors. But the best instruction on this subject is unhappily conveyed to America by the example of her own situation. She finds that she is held in no respect by her friends; that she is the derision of her enemies; and that she is a prey to every nation which has an interest in speculating on her fluctuating councils and embarrassed affairs.

The internal effects of a mutable policy are still more calamitous. It poisons the blessings of liberty itself. It will be of little avail to the people that the laws are made by men of their own choice if the laws be so voluminous that they cannot be read, or so incoherent that they cannot be understood; if they be repealed or revised before they are promulgated, or undergo such incessant changes that no man, who knows what the law is today, can guess what it will be tomorrow. Law is defined to be a rule of action; but how can that be a rule, which is little known, and less fixed?

Another effect of public instability is the unreasonable advantage it gives to the sagacious, the enterprising, and the moneyed few over the industrious and uninformed mass of the people. Every new regulation concerning commerce or revenue, or in any manner affecting the value of the different species of property, presents a new harvest to those who watch the change, and can trace its consequences; a harvest, reared not by themselves, but by the toils and cares of the great body of their fellow-citizens. This is a state of things in which it may be said with some truth that laws are made for the *few*, not for the *many*.

In another point of view, great injury results from an unstable government. The want of confidence in the public councils damps every useful undertaking, the success and profit of which may depend on a continuance of existing arrangements. What prudent merchant will hazard his fortunes in any branch of commerce when he knows not but that his plans may be rendered unlawful before they can be executed? What farmer or manufacturer will lay himself out for the encouragement given to any particular cultivation or establishment, when he can have no assurance that his preparatory labors and advances will not render him a victim to an inconstant government? In a word, no great improvement or laudable enterprise can go forward which requires the auspices of a steady system of national policy.

But the most deplorable effect of all is that diminution of attachment and reverence which steals into the hearts of the people towards a political system which betrays so many marks of infirmity, and disappoints so many of their flattering hopes. No government, any more than an individual, will long be respected without being truly respectable; nor be truly respectable without possessing a certain portion of order and stability.

MADISON

No. 63

A Further View of the Constitution of the Senate in Regard to the Duration of Appointment of Its Members

In the second of five papers on the Senate, the author says "some temperate and respectable body of citizens" is needed "to check the misguided career and to suspend the blow meditated by the people against themselves, until reason, justice, and truth can regain their authority over the public mind." Such senators would be called on to act in "those particular moments in public affairs when the people, stimulated by some irregular passion, or some illicit advantage, or misled by the artful misrepresentations of interested men, may call for measures which they themselves will afterwards be the most ready to lament and condemn."

A *fifth* desideratum, illustrating the utility of a senate, is the want of a due sense of national character. Without a select and stable member of the government, the esteem of foreign powers will not only be forfeited by an unenlightened and variable policy, proceeding from the causes already mentioned, but the national councils will not possess that sensibility to the opinion of the world which is perhaps not less necessary in order to merit than it is to obtain its respect and confidence.

An attention to the judgment of other nations is important to every government for two reasons; the one is that independently of the merits of any particular plan or measure, it is desirable, on various accounts, that it should appear to other nations as the offspring of a wise and honorable policy; the second is that in doubtful cases, particularly where the national councils may be warped by some strong passion or momentary interest, the presumed or known opinion of the impartial world may be the best guide that can be followed. What has not America lost by her want of character with foreign nations; and how many errors and follies would she not have avoided, if the justice and propriety of her measures had, in every instance, been previously tried by the light in which they would probably appear to the unbiased part of mankind?

Yet however requisite a sense of national character may be, it is evident that it can never be sufficiently possessed by a numerous and changeable body. It can only be found in a number so small that a sensible degree of the praise and blame of public measures may be the portion of each individual; or in an assembly so durably invested with public trust that the pride and consequence of its members may be sensibly incorporated with the reputation and prosperity of the community. The half-yearly representatives of Rhode Island would probably have been little affected in their deliberations on the iniquitous measures of that State by arguments drawn from the light in which such measures would be viewed by foreign nations, or even by the sister States; whilst it can scarcely be doubted that if the concurrence of a select and stable body had been necessary, a regard to national character alone would have prevented the calamities under which that misguided people is now laboring.

I add, as a *sixth* defect, the want, in some important cases, of a due responsibility in the government to the people, arising from that frequency of elections which in other cases produces this responsibility. This remark will, perhaps, appear not only new, but paradoxical. It must nevertheless be acknowledged, when explained, to be as undeniable as it is important.

Responsibility, in order to be reasonable, must be limited to objects within the power of the responsible party, and in order to be effectual, must relate to operations of that power, of which a ready and proper judgment can be formed by the constituents. The objects of government may be divided into two general classes: the one depending on measures which have singly an immediate and sensible operation; the other depending on a succession of well-chosen and well-connected measures, which have a gradual and perhaps unobserved operation. The importance of the latter description to the collective and permanent welfare of every country needs no explanation. And yet it is evident that an assembly elected for so short a term as to be unable to provide more than one or two links in a chain of measures, on which the general welfare may essentially depend, ought not to be answerable for the final result any more than a steward or tenant, engaged for one year, could be justly made to answer for places or improvements which could not be accomplished in less than half a dozen years. Nor is it possible for the people to estimate the *share* of influence which their annual assemblies may respectively have on events resulting from the mixed transactions of several years. It is sufficiently difficult, at any rate, to preserve a personal responsibility in the members of a *numerous* body, for such acts of the body as have an immediate, detached, and palpable operation on its constituents.

The proper remedy for this defect must be an additional body in the legislative department, which, having sufficient permanency to provide for such objects as require a continued attention, and a train of measures, may be justly and effectually answerable for the attainment of those objects.

A "Temperate and Respectable Body of Citizens"

Thus far I have considered the circumstances which point out the necessity of a well-constructed Senate only as they relate to the representatives of the people. To a people as little blinded by prejudice or corrupted by flattery as those whom I address, I shall not scruple to add that such an institution may be sometimes necessary as a defense to the people against their own temporary errors and delusions. As the cool and deliberate sense of the community ought, in all governments, and actually will, in all free governments, ultimately prevail over the views of its rulers; so there are particular moments in public affairs when the people, stimulated by some irregular passion, or some illicit advantage, or misled by the artful misrepresentations of interested men, may call for measures which they themselves will afterwards be the most ready to lament and condemn. In these critical moments, how salutary will be the interference of some temperate and respectable body of citizens, in order to check the misguided career and to suspend the blow meditated by the people against themselves, until reason, justice, and truth can regain their authority over the public mind? What bitter anguish would not the people of Athens have often escaped if their government had contained so provident a safeguard against the tyranny of their own passions? Popular liberty might then have escaped the indelible reproach of decreeing to the same citizens the hemlock on one day and statues on the next.

It may be suggested that a people spread over an extensive region cannot, like the crowded inhabitants of a small district, be subject to the infection of violent passions or to the danger of combining in pursuit of unjust measures. I am far from denying that this is a distinction of peculiar importance. I have, on the contrary, endeavored in a former paper to show that it is one of the principal recommendations of a confederated republic. At the same time, this advantage ought not to be considered as superseding the use of auxiliary precautions. It may even be remarked that the same extended situation which will exempt the people of America from some of the dangers incident to lesser republics will expose them to the inconveniency of remaining for a longer time under the influence of those misrepresentations which the combined industry of interested men may succeed in distributing among them.

It adds no small weight to all these considerations to recollect that history informs us of no long-lived republic which had not a senate. Sparta, Rome, and Carthage are, in fact, the only states to whom that character can be applied. In each of the two first there was a senate for life. The constitution of the senate in the last is less known. Circumstantial evidence makes it probable that it was not different in this particular from the two others. It is at least certain that it had some quality or other which rendered it an anchor against popular fluctuations; and that a smaller council, drawn out of the senate, was appointed not only for life, but filled up vacancies itself. These examples, though as unfit for the imitation as they are repugnant to the genius of America, are, notwithstanding, when compared with the fugitive and turbulent existence of other ancient republics, very instructive proofs of the necessity of some institution that will blend stability with liberty. I am not unaware of the circumstances which distinguish the American from other popular governments, as well ancient as modern; and which render extreme circumspection necessary, in reasoning from one case to the other. But after allowing due weight to this consideration it may still be maintained that there are many points of similitude which render these examples not unworthy of our attention. Many of the defects, as we have seen, which can only be supplied by a senatorial institution, are common to a numerous assembly frequently elected by the people, and to the people themselves. There are others peculiar to the former which require the control of such an institution. The people can never wilfully betray their own interests; but they may possibly be betrayed by the representatives of the people; and the danger will be evidently greater where the whole legislative trust is lodged in the hands of one body of men than where the concurrence of separate and dissimilar bodies is required in every public act.

Representation: Earlier Governments Compared

The difference most relied on between the American and other republics consists in the principle of representation, which is the pivot on which the former move, and which is supposed to have been unknown to the latter, or at least to the ancient part of them. The use which has been made of this difference, in reasonings contained in former papers, will have shown that I am disposed neither to deny its existence nor to undervalue its importance. I feel the less restraint, therefore, in observing that the position concerning the ignorance of the ancient governments on the subject of representation is by no means precisely true in the latitude commonly given to it. Without entering into a disquisition which here would be misplaced, I will refer to a few known facts in support of what I advance.

In the most pure democracies of Greece, many of the executive functions were performed, not by the people themselves, but by officers elected by the people, and *representing* the people in their *executive* capacity.

Prior to the reform of Solon, Athens was governed by nine Archons, annually *elected by the people at large*. The degree of power delegated to them seems to be left in great obscurity. Subsequent to that period we find an assembly, first of four, and afterwards of six hundred members, annually *elected by the people;* and *partially* representing them in their *legislative* capacity, since they were not only associated with the people in the function of making laws, but had the exclusive right of originating legislative propositions to the people. The senate of Carthage, also, whatever might be its power or the duration of its appointment, appears to have been elective by the suffrages of the people. Similar instances might be traced in most, if not all, the popular governments of antiquity.

Lastly, in Sparta we meet with the Ephori, and in Rome with the Tribunes; two bodies, small indeed in number, but annually *elected by the whole body of the people,* and considered as the *representatives* of the people, almost in their *plenipotentiary* capacity. The Cosmi of Crete were also annually *elected by the people,* and have been considered by some authors as an institution analogous to those of Sparta and Rome, with this difference only, that in the election of that representative body the right of suffrage was communicated to a part only of the people.

From these facts, to which many others might be added, it is clear that the principle of representation was neither unknown to the ancients nor wholly overlooked in their political constitutions. The true distinction between these and the American governments lies *in the total exclusion of the people in their collective capacity,* from any share in the *latter,* and not in the *total exclusion of the representatives of the people* from the administration of the *former.* The distinction, however, thus qualified, must be admitted to leave a most advantageous superiority in favor of the United States. But to insure to this advantage its full effect, we must be careful not to separate it from the other advantage, of an extensive territory. For it cannot be believed that any form of representative government could have succeeded within the narrow limits occupied by the democracies of Greece.

In answer to all these arguments, suggested by reason, illustrated by examples, and enforced by our own experience, the jealous adversary of the Constitution will probably content himself with repeating that a senate appointed not immediately by the people, and for the term of six years, must gradually acquire a dangerous pre-eminence in the government and finally transform it into a tyrannical aristocracy.

To this general answer the general reply ought to be sufficient, that liberty may be endangered by the abuses of liberty as well as by the abuses of power; that there are numerous instances of the former as well as of the latter; and that the former, rather than the latter, is apparently most to be apprehended by the United States. But a more particular reply may be given.

Before such a revolution can be effected, the Senate, it is to be observed, must in the first place corrupt itself; must next corrupt the State legislatures, must then corrupt the House of Representatives, and must finally corrupt the people at large. It is evident that the Senate must be first corrupted before it can attempt an establishment of tyranny. Without corrupting the State legislatures it cannot prosecute the attempt because the periodical change of members would otherwise regenerate the whole body. Without exerting the means of corruption with equal success on the House of Representatives, the opposition of that co-equal branch of the government would inevitably defeat the attempt; and without corrupting the people themselves, a succession of new representatives would speedily restore all things to their pristine order. Is there any man who can seriously persuade himself that the proposed Senate can, by any possible means within the compass of human address, arrive at the object of a lawless ambition through all these obstructions?

The Maryland Example

If reason condemns the suspicion, the same sentence is pronounced by experience. The constitution of Maryland furnishes the most apposite example. The Senate of that State is elected, as the federal Senate will be, indirectly by the people, and for a term less by one year only than the federal Senate. It is distinguished, also, by the remarkable prerogative of filling up its own vacancies within the term of its appointment, and at the same time is not under the control of any such rotation as is provided for the federal Senate. There are some other lesser distinctions which would expose the former to colorable objections that do not lie against the latter. If the federal Senate, therefore, really contained the danger which has been so loudly proclaimed, some symptoms at least of a like danger ought by this time to have been betrayed by the Senate of Maryland, but no such symptoms have appeared. On the contrary, the jealousies at first entertained by men of the same description with those who view with terror the correspondent part of the federal Constitution have been gradually extinguished by the progress of the experiment; and the Maryland constitution is daily deriving, from the salutary operation of this part of it, a reputation in which it will probably not be rivaled by that of any State in the Union.

But if anything could silence the jealousies on this subject, it ought to be the British example. The Senate there, instead of being elected for a term of six years, and of being unconfined to particular families or fortunes, is an hereditary assembly of opulent nobles. The House of Representatives, instead of being elected for two years, and by the whole body of the people, is elected for seven years, and, in very great proportion, by a very small proportion of the people. Here, unquestionably, ought to be seen in full display the aristocratic usurpations and tyranny which are at some future period to be exemplified in the United States. Unfortunately, however, for the anti-federal argument, the British history informs us that this hereditary assembly has not been able to defend itself against the continual encroachments of the House of Representatives, and that it no sooner lost the support of the monarch than it was actually crushed by the weight of the popular branch.

As far as antiquity can instruct us on this subject, its examples support the reasoning which we have employed. In Sparta, the Ephori, the annual representatives of the people, were found an overmatch for the senate for life, continually gained on its authority and finally drew all power into their own hands. The Tribunes of Rome who were the representatives of the people prevailed, it is well known, in almost every contest with the senate for life, and in the end gained the most complete triumph over it. The fact is the more remarkable as unanimity was required in every act of the Tribunes, even after their number was augmented to ten. It proves the irresistible force possessed by that branch of a free government, which has the people on its side. To these examples might be added that of Carthage, whose senate, according to the testimony of Polybius, instead of drawing all power into its vortex had, at the commencement of the second Punic War, lost almost the whole of its original portion.

Besides the conclusive evidence resulting from this assemblage of facts that the federal Senate will never be able to transform itself, by gradual usurpations, into an independent and aristocratic body, we are warranted in believing that if such a revolution should ever happen from causes which the foresight of man cannot guard against, the House of Representatives, with the people on their side, will at all times be able to bring back the Constitution to its primitive form and principles. Against the force of the immediate representatives of the people nothing will be able to maintain even the constitutional authority of the Senate, but such a display of enlightened policy, and attachment to the public good, as will divide with that branch of the legislature the affections and support of the entire body of the people themselves.

No. 70

The Same View Continued in Relation to the Unity of the Executive, with an Examination of the Project of an Executive Council

Hamilton summarizes the powers of the presidency. "Energy in the executive is a leading character in the definition of good government." A strong presidency protects against foreign attacks and assures administration of justice, protection of property, and liberty "against the enterprises and assaults of ambition, of faction, and of anarchy." Conversely, "a feeble executive implies a feeble execution of government." He examines several proposals for limiting presidential powers and rejects them, including government by several leaders of equal power and government by a leader and council.

What are the ingredients of an energetic executive? Unity, duration, adequate support, and competent powers. Sound political leaders will declare "in favor of a single executive and a numerous legislature." Political unity can be destroyed by splitting powers, "vesting the power in two or more magistrates of equal dignity and authority," or by supporting a leader who is in reality controlled by a council. If the country's political leadership is "consisting of a plurality of persons, they might impede or frustrate the most important measures of the government in the most critical emergencies of the state."

Hamilton likewise observes "how often the great interests of society are sacrificed to the vanity, to the conceit, and to the obstinacy of individuals, who have credit enough to make their passions and their caprices interesting to mankind."

There is an idea, which is not without its advocates, that a vigorous executive is inconsistent with the genius of republican government. The enlightened well-wishers to this species of government must at least hope that the supposition is destitute of foundation; since they can never admit its truth, without at the same time admitting the condemnation of their own principles. Energy in the executive is a leading character in the definition of good government. It is essential to the protection of the community against foreign attacks; it is not less essential to the steady administration of the laws; to the protection of property against those irregular and high-handed combinations which sometimes interrupt the ordinary course of justice; to the security of liberty against the enterprises and assaults of ambition, of faction, and of anarchy. Every man the least conversant in Roman history knows how often that republic was obliged to take refuge in the absolute power of a single man, under the formidable title of dictator, as well against the intrigues of ambitious individuals who aspired to the tyranny, and the seditions of whole classes of the community whose conduct threatened the existence of all government, as against the invasions of external enemies who menaced the conquest and destruction of Rome.

There can be no need, however, to multiply arguments or examples on this head. A feeble executive implies a feeble execution of the government.

A feeble execution is but another phrase for a bad execution; and a government ill executed, whatever it may be in theory, must be, in practice, a bad government.

What Is an "Energetic Executive?"

Taking it for granted, therefore, that all men of sense will agree in the necessity of an energetic executive, it will only remain to inquire, what are the ingredients which constitute this energy? How far can they be combined with those other ingredients which constitute safety in the republican sense? And how far does this combination characterize the plan which has been reported by the convention? The ingredients which constitute energy in the executive are unity; duration; an adequate provision for its support; and competent powers. The ingredients which constitute safety in the republican sense are a due dependence on the people, and a due responsibility.

Those politicians and statesmen who have been the most celebrated for the soundness of their principles and for the justness of their views have declared in favor of a single executive and a numerous legislature. They have, with great propriety, considered energy as the most necessary qualification of the former, and have regarded this as most applicable to power in a single hand; while they have, with equal propriety, considered the latter as best adapted to deliberation and wisdom, and best calculated to conciliate the confidence of the people and to secure their privileges and interests.

Destroying Executive Powers by Dividing Them

That unity is conducive to energy will not be disputed. Decision, activity, secrecy, and dispatch will generally characterize the proceedings of one man in a much more eminent degree than the proceedings of any greater number; and in proportion as the number is increased, these qualities will be diminished.

This unity may be destroyed in two ways: either by vesting the power in two or more magistrates of equal dignity and authority, or by vesting it ostensibly in one man, subject in whole or in part to the control and co-operation of others, in the capacity of counselors to him. Of the first, the two consuls of Rome may serve as an example; of the last, we shall find examples in the constitutions of several of the States. New York and New Jersey, if I recollect right, are the only States which have intrusted the executive authority wholly to single men.[1] Both these methods of destroying the unity of the executive have their partisans; but the votaries of an executive council are the most numerous. They are both liable, if not to equal, to similar objections, and may in most lights be examined in conjunction.

The experience of other nations will afford little instruction on this head. As far, however, as it teaches anything, it teaches us not to be enamored of plurality in the executive. We have seen that the Achaeans, on an experiment of two Praetors, were induced to abolish one. The Roman history records many instances of mischiefs to the republic from the dissensions between the consuls, and between the military tribunes, who were at times substituted for the consuls. But it gives us no specimens of any peculiar advantages derived to the state from the circumstance of the plurality of those magistrates. That the dissensions between them were not more frequent or more fatal is matter of astonishment, until we advert to the singular position in which the republic was almost continually placed, and to the prudent policy pointed out by the circumstances of the state, and pursued by the consuls, of making a division of the government between them. The patricians engaged in a perpetual struggle with the plebeians for the preservation of their ancient authorities and dignities; the consuls, who were generally chosen out of the former body, were commonly united by the personal interest they had in the defense of the privileges of their order. In addition to this motive of union, after the arms of the republic had considerably expanded the bounds of its empire, it became an established custom with the consuls to divide the administration between themselves by lot—one of them remaining at Rome to govern the city and its environs, the other taking command in the more distant provinces. This expedient must no doubt have had great influence in preventing those collisions and rivalships which might otherwise have embroiled the peace of the republic.

A Weak Executive and the Spread of Faction

But quitting the dim light of historical research, and attaching ourselves purely to the dictates of reason and good sense, we shall discover much greater cause to reject than to approve the idea of plurality in the executive, under any modification whatever.

Whenever two or more persons are engaged in any common enterprise or pursuit, there is always danger of difference of opinion. If it be a public trust or office in which they are clothed with equal dignity and authority, there is peculiar danger of personal emulation and even animosity. From either, and especially from all these causes, the most bitter dissensions are apt to spring. Whenever these happen, they lessen the respectability, weaken the authority, and distract the plans and operations of those whom they divide. If they should unfortunately assail the supreme executive magistracy of a country, consisting of a plurality of persons, they might impede or frustrate the most important measures of the government in the most critical emergencies of the state. And what is still worse, they might split the community into the most violent and irreconcilable factions, adhering differently to the different individuals who composed the magistracy.

Rulers' Conceit and the Sacrifice
of Society's True Interests

Men often oppose a thing merely because they have had no agency in planning it, or because it may have been planned by those whom they dislike. But if they have been consulted, and have happened to disapprove, opposition then becomes, in their estimation, an indispensable duty of self-love. They seem to think themselves bound in honor, and by all the motives of personal infallibility, to defeat the success of what has been resolved upon contrary to their sentiments. Men of upright, benevolent tempers have too many opportunities of remarking, with horror, to what desperate lengths this disposition is sometimes carried, and how often the great interests of society are sacrificed to the vanity, to the conceit, and to the obstinacy of individuals, who have credit enough to make their passions and their caprices interesting to mankind. Perhaps the question now before the public may, in its consequences, afford melancholy proofs of the effects of this despicable frailty, or rather detestable vice, in the human character.

Upon the principles of a free government, inconveniences from the source just mentioned must necessarily be submitted to in the formation of the legislature; but it is unnecessary, and therefore unwise, to introduce them into the constitution of the executive. It is here too that they may be most pernicious. In the legislature, promptitude of decision is oftener an evil than a benefit. The differences of opinion, and the jarring of parties in that department of the government, though they may sometimes obstruct salutary plans, yet often promote deliberation and circumspection, and serve to check excesses in the majority. When a resolution too is once taken, the opposition must be at an end. That resolution is a law, and resistance to it punishable. But no favorable circumstances palliate or atone for the disadvantages of dissension in the executive department. Here they are pure and unmixed. There is no point at which they cease to operate. They serve to embarrass and weaken the execution of the plan or measure to which they relate, from the first step to the final conclusion of it. They constantly counteract those qualities in the executive which are the most necessary ingredients in its composition—vigor and expedition, and this without any counterbalancing good. In the conduct of war, in which the energy of the executive is the bulwark of the national security, everything would be to be apprehended from its plurality.

It must be confessed that these observations apply with principal weight to the first case supposed—that is, to a plurality of magistrates of equal dignity and authority, a scheme, the advocates for which are not likely to form a numerous sect; but they apply, though not with equal yet with considerable weight, to the project of a council, whose concurrence is made constitutionally necessary to the operations of the ostensible executive. An artful cabal in that council would be able to distract and to enervate the whole system of administration. If no such cabal should exist, the mere diversity of views and opinions would alone be sufficient to tincture the exercise of the executive authority with a spirit of habitual feebleness and dilatoriness.

But one of the weightiest objections to a plurality in the executive, and which lies as much against the last as the first plan is that it tends to conceal faults and destroy responsibility. Responsibility is of two kinds— to censure and to punishment. The first is the more important of the two, especially in an elective offlce. Men in public trust will much oftener act in such a manner as to render them unworthy of being any longer trusted, than in such a manner as to make them obnoxious to legal punishment. But the multiplication of the executive adds to the difficulty of detection in either case. It often becomes impossible, amidst mutual accusations, to determine on whom the blame or the punishment of a pernicious measure, or series of pernicious measures, ought really to fall. It is shifted from one to another with so much dexterity, and under such plausible appearances, that the public opinion is left in suspense about the real author. The circumstances which may have led to any national miscarriage or misfortune are sometimes so complicated that where there are a number of actors who may have had different degrees and kinds of agency, though we may clearly see upon the whole that there has been mismanagement, yet it may be impracticable to pronounce to whose account the evil which may have been incurred is truly chargeable.

"I was overruled by my council." "The council were so divided in their opinions that it was impossible to obtain any better resolution on the point." These and similar pretexts are constantly at hand, whether true or false. And who is there that will either take the trouble or incur the odium of a strict scrutiny into the secret springs of the transaction? Should there be found a citizen zealous enough to undertake the unpromising task, if there happened to be a collusion between the parties concerned, how easy it is to clothe the circumstances with so much ambiguity as to render it uncertain what was the precise conduct of any of those parties.

The Danger of Collusion Between Executive and Council

In the single instance in which the governor of this State is coupled with a council—that is, in the appointment to offices, we have seen the mischiefs of it in the view now under consideration. Scandalous appointments to important offices have been made. Some cases, indeed, have been so flagrant that all parties have agreed in the impropriety of the thing. When inquiry has been made, the blame has been laid by the governor on the members of the council, who, on their part, have charged it upon his nomination; while the people remain altogether at a loss to determine by whose influence their interests have been committed to hands so unqualified and so manifestly improper. In tenderness to individuals, I forbear to descend to particulars.

It is evident from these considerations that the plurality of the executive tends to deprive the people of the two greatest securities they can have for the faithful exercise of any delegated power, *first,* the restraints of public opinion, which lose their efficacy, as well on account of the division of the censure attendant on bad measures among a number as on account of the uncertainty on whom it ought to fall; and, *second,* the opportunity of discovering with facility and clearness the misconduct of the persons they trust, in order either to their removal from office or to their actual punishment in cases which admit of it.

In England, the king is a perpetual magistrate; and it is a maxim which has obtained for the sake of the public peace that he is unaccountable for his administration, and his person sacred. Nothing, therefore, can be wiser in that kingdom than to annex to the king a constitutional council, who may be responsible to the nation for the advice they give. Without this, there would be no responsibility whatever in the executive department— an idea inadmissible in a free government. But even there the king is not bound by the resolutions of his council, though they are answerable for the advice they give. He is the absolute master of his own conduct in the exercise of his office and may observe or disregard the counsel given to him at his sole discretion.

But in a republic where every magistrate ought to be personally responsible for his behavior in office, the reason which in the British Constitution dictates the propriety of a council not only ceases to apply, but turns against the institution. In the monarchy of Great Britain, it furnishes a substitute for the prohibited responsibility of the Chief Magistrate, which serves in some degree as a hostage to the national justice for his good behavior. In the American republic, it would serve to destroy, or would greatly diminish, the intended and necessary responsibility of the Chief Magistrate himself.

The idea of a council to the executive, which has so generally obtained in the State constitutions, has been derived from that maxim of republican jealousy which considers power as safer in the hands of a number of men than of a single man. If the maxim should be admitted to be applicable to the case, I should contend that the advantage on that side would not counterbalance the numerous disadvantages on the opposite side. But I do not think the rule at all applicable to the executive power. I clearly concur in opinion, in this particular, with a writer[2] whom the celebrated Junius pronounces to be "deep, solid, and ingenious," that "the executive power is more easily confined when it is one"; that it is far more safe there should be a single object for the jealousy and watchfulness of the people; and, in a word, that all multiplication of the executive is rather dangerous than friendly to liberty.

One Person More Easily Accountable than a Council of Leaders

A little consideration will satisfy us that the species of security sought for in the multiplication of the executive is unattainable. Numbers must be so great as to render combination difficult, or they are rather a source of danger than of security. The united credit and influence of several individuals must be more formidable to liberty than the credit and influence of either of them separately. When power, therefore, is placed in the hands of so small a number of men as to admit of their interests and views being easily combined in a common enterprise, by an artful leader, it becomes more liable to abuse, and more dangerous when abused, than if it be lodged in the hands of one man, who, from the very circumstance of his being alone, will be more narrowly watched and more readily suspected, and who cannot unite so great a mass of influence as when he is associated with others. The decemvirs of Rome, whose name denotes their number,[3] were more to be dreaded in their usurpation than any one of them would have been. No person would think of proposing an executive much more numerous than that body; from six to a dozen have been suggested for the number of the council. The extreme of these numbers is not too great for an easy combination; and from such a combination America would have more to fear than from the ambition of any single individual. A council to a magistrate, who is himself responsible for what he does, are generally nothing better than a clog upon his good intentions, are often the instruments and accomplices of his bad, and are almost always a cloak to his faults.

I forbear to dwell upon the subject of expense; though it be evident that if the council should be numerous enough to answer the principal end aimed at by the institution, the salaries of the members, who must be drawn from their homes to reside at the seat of government, would form an item in the catalogue of public expenditures too serious to be incurred for an object of equivocal utility.

I will only add that, prior to the appearance of the Constitution, I rarely met with an intelligent man from any of the States who did not admit, as the result of experience, that the unity of the executive of this State was one of the best of the distinguishing features of our Constitution.

No. 78

A View of the Constitution of the Judicial Department in Relation to the Tenure of Good Behavior

In this key essay, judicial appointments and the need for long-term tenure "during good behavior" are discussed, as are the powers accorded different courts. Hamilton states the need for an independent judiciary, a judiciary described as having "neither force nor will but merely judgment." An independent judiciary is an "excellent barrier to the encroachments and oppression of the representative body," and "the best expedient which can be devised in any government to secure a steady, upright, and impartial administration of the laws." He states, "The courts must declare the sense of the law; and if they should be disposed to exercise will instead of judgment the consequence would equally be the substitution of their pleasure to that of the legislative body." Any society may be affected by injustices and "ill humors." Here "the firmness of the judicial magistracy is of vast importance in mitigating the severity and confining the operation of such laws." Hamilton leaves his readers a stark reminder of the need for an independent judiciary: "No man can be sure that he may not be tomorrow the victim of a spirit of injustice, by which he may be a gainer today."

We proceed now to an examination of the judiciary department of the proposed government.

In unfolding the defects of the existing Confederation, the utility and necessity of a federal judicature have been clearly pointed out. It is the less necessary to recapitulate the considerations there urged as the propriety of the institution in the abstract is not disputed; the only questions which have been raised being relative to the manner of constituting it, and to its extent. To these points, therefore, our observations shall be confined.

The manner of constituting it seems to embrace these several objects: 1st. The mode of appointing the judges. 2nd. The tenure by which they are to hold their places. 3rd. The partition of the judiciary authority between different courts and their relations to each other.

First. As to the mode of appointing the judges: this is the same with that of appointing the officers of the Union in general and has been so fully discussed in the two last numbers that nothing can be said here which would not be useless repetition.

Second. As to the tenure by which the judges are to hold their places: this chiefly concerns their duration in office, the provisions for their support, the precautions for their responsibility.

Long-Term Judicial Tenure

According to the plan of the convention, all judges who may be appointed by the United States are to hold their offices *during good behavior;* which is conformable to the most approved of the State constitutions, and among the rest, to that of the State. Its propriety having been drawn into question by the adversaries of that plan is no light symptom of the rage for objection which disorders their imaginations and judgments. The standard of good behavior for the continuance in office of the judicial magistracy is certainly one of the most valuable of the modern improvements in the practice of government. In a monarchy it is an excellent barrier to the despotism of the prince; in a republic it is a no less excellent barrier to the encroachments and oppressions of the representative body. And it is the best expedient which can be devised in any government to secure a steady, upright, and impartial administration of the laws.

A Judiciary with "Neither Force nor Will but Merely Judgment"

Whoever attentively considers the different departments of power must perceive that, in a government in which they are separated from each other, the judiciary, from the nature of its functions, will always be the least dangerous to the political rights of the Constitution; because it will be least in a capacity to annoy or injure them. The executive not only dispenses the honors but holds the sword of the community. The legislature not only commands the purse but prescribes the rules by which the duties and rights of every citizen are to be regulated. The judiciary, on the contrary, has no influence over either the sword or the purse; no direction either of the strength or of the wealth of the society, and can take no active resolution whatever. It may truly be said to have neither force nor will but merely judgment; and must ultimately depend upon the aid of the executive arm even for the efficacy of its judgments.

This simple view of the matter suggests several important consequences. It proves incontestably that the judiciary is beyond comparison the weakest of the three departments of power;[1] that it can never attack with success either of the other two; and that all possible care is requisite to enable it to defend itself against their attacks. It equally proves that though individual oppression may now and then proceed from the courts of justice, the general liberty of the people can never be endangered from that quarter; I mean so long as the judiciary remains truly distinct from both the legislature and the executive. For I agree that "there is no liberty if the power of judging be not separated from the legislative and executive powers."[2] And it proves, in the last place, that as liberty can have nothing to fear from the judiciary alone, but would have everything to fear from its union with either of the other departments; that as all the effects of such a union must ensue from a dependence of the former on the latter, notwithstanding a nominal and apparent separation; that as, from the natural feebleness of the judiciary, it is in continual jeopardy of being overpowered, awed, or influenced by its co-ordinate branches; and that as nothing can contribute so much to its firmness and independence as permanency in office, this quality may therefore be justly regarded as an indispensable ingredient in its constitution, and, in a great measure, as the citadel of the public justice and the public security.

The Complete Independence of the Judiciary

The complete independence of the courts of justice is peculiarly essential in a limited Constitution. By a limited Constitution, I understand one which contains certain specified exceptions to the legislative authority; such, for instance, as that it shall pass no bills of attainder, no *ex post facto* laws, and the like. Limitations of this kind can be preserved in practice no other way than through the medium of courts of justice, whose duty it must be to declare all acts contrary to the manifest tenor of the Constitution void. Without this, all the reservations of particular rights or privileges would amount to nothing.

Some perplexity respecting the rights of the courts to pronounce legislative acts void, because contrary to the Constitution, has arisen from an imagination that the doctrine would imply a superiority of the judiciary to the legislative power. It is urged that the authority which can declare the acts of another void must necessarily be superior to the one whose acts may be declared void. As this doctrine is of great importance in all the American constitutions, a brief discussion of the grounds on which it rests cannot be unacceptable.

There is no position which depends on clearer principles than that every act of a delegated authority, contrary to the tenor of the commission under which it is exercised, is void. No legislative act, therefore, contrary to the Constitution, can be valid. To deny this would be to affirm that the deputy is greater than his principal; that the servant is above his master; that the representatives of the people are superior to the people themselves; that men acting by virtue of powers may do not only what their powers do not authorize, but what they forbid.

If it be said that the legislative body are themselves the constitutional judges of their own powers and that the construction they put upon them is conclusive upon the other departments it may be answered that this cannot be the natural presumption where it is not to be collected from any particular provisions in the Constitution. It is not otherwise to be supposed that the Constitution could intend to enable the representatives of the people to substitute their *will* to that of their constituents. It is far more rational to suppose that the courts were designed to be an intermediate body between the people and the legislature in order, among other things, to keep the latter within the limits assigned to their authority. The interpretation of the laws is the proper and peculiar province of the courts. A constitution is, in fact, and must be regarded by the judges as, a fundamental law. It therefore belongs to them to ascertain its meaning as well as the meaning of any particular act proceeding from the legislative body. If there should happen to be an irreconcilable variance between the two, that which has the superior obligation and validity ought, of course, to be preferred; or, in other words, the Constitution ought to be preferred to the statute, the intention of the people to the intention of their agents.

Nor does this conclusion by any means suppose a superiority of the judicial to the legislative power. It only supposes that the power of the people is superior to both, and that where the will of the legislature, declared in its statutes, stands in opposition to that of the people, declared in the Constitution, the judges ought to be governed by the latter rather than the former. They ought to regulate their decisions by the fundamental laws rather than by those which are not fundamental.

How to Resolve Conflicts of Laws

This exercise of judicial discretion in determining between two contradictory laws is exemplified in a familiar instance. It not uncommonly happens that there are two statutes existing at one time, clashing in whole or in part with each other and neither of them containing any repealing clause or expression. In such a case, it is the province of the courts to liquidate and fix their meaning and operation. So far as they can, by fair construction, be reconciled to each other, reason and law conspire to dictate that this should be done; where this is impracticable, it becomes a matter of necessity to give effect to one in exclusion of the other. The rule which has obtained in the courts for determining their relative validity is that the last in order of time shall be preferred to the first. But this is a mere rule of construction, not derived from any positive law but from the nature and reason of the thing. It is a rule not enjoined upon the courts by legislative provision but adopted by themselves, as consonant to truth and propriety, for the direction of their conduct as interpreters of the law. They thought it reasonable that between the interfering acts of an *equal* authority that which was the last indication of its will should have the preference.

But in regard to the interfering acts of a superior and subordinate authority of an original and derivative power, the nature and reason of the thing indicate the converse of that rule as proper to be followed. They teach us that the prior act of a superior ought to be preferred to the subsequent act of an inferior and subordinate authority; and that accordingly, whenever a particular statute contravenes the Constitution, it will be the duty of the judicial tribunals to adhere to the latter and disregard the former.

It can be of no weight to say that the courts, on the pretense of a repugnancy, may substitute their own pleasure to the constitutional intentions of the legislature. This might as well happen in the case of two contradictory statutes; or it might as well happen in every adjudication upon any single statute. The courts must declare the sense of the law; and if they should be disposed to exercise will instead of judgment the consequence would equally be the substitution of their pleasure for that of the legislative body. The observation, if it proved anything, would prove that there ought to be no judges distinct from that body.

If, then, the courts of justice are to be considered as the bulwarks of a limited Constitution against legislative encroachments, this consideration will afford a strong argument for the permanent tenure of judicial offices, since nothing will contribute so much as this to that independent spirit in the judges which must be essential to the faithful performance of so arduous a duty.

This independence of the judges is equally requisite to guard the Constitution and the rights of individuals from the effects of those ill humors which the arts of designing men, or the influence of particular conjunctures, sometimes disseminate among the people themselves, and which, though they speedily give place to better information, and more deliberate reflection, have a tendency, in the meantime, to occasion dangerous innovations in the government, and serious oppressions of the minor party in the community. Though I trust the friends of the proposed Constitution will never concur with its enemies[3] in questioning that fundamental principle of republican government which admits the right of the people to alter or abolish the established Constitution whenever they find it inconsistent with their happiness: yet it is not to be inferred from this principle that the representatives of the people, whenever a momentary inclination happens to lay hold of a majority of their constituents incompatible with the provisions in the existing Constitution, would, on that account, be justifiable in a violation of those provisions; or that the courts would be under a greater obligation to connive at infractions in this shape than when they had proceeded wholly from the cabals of the representative body. Until the people have, by some solemn and authoritative act, annulled or changed the established form, it is binding upon themselves collectively, as well as individually; and no presumption, or even knowledge, of their sentiment can warrant their representatives in a departure from it prior to such an act. But it is easy to see that it would require an uncommon portion of fortitude in the judges to do their duty as faithful guardians of the Constitution, where legislative invasions of it had been instigated by the major voice of the community.

To Protect Against "the Injury of the Private Rights of Particular Classes of Citizens"

But it is not with a view to infractions of the Constitution only that the independence of the judges may be an essential safeguard against the effects of occasional ill humors in the society. These sometimes extend no farther than to the injury of the private rights of particular classes of citizens, by unjust and partial laws. Here also the firmness of the judicial magistracy is of vast importance in mitigating the severity and confining the operation of such laws. It not only serves to moderate the immediate mischiefs of those which may have been passed but it operates as a check upon the legislative body in passing them; who, perceiving that obstacles to the success of an iniquitous intention are to be expected from the scruples of the courts, are in a manner compelled, by the very motives of the injustice they meditate, to qualify their attempts. This is a circumstance calculated to have more influence upon the character of our governments than but few may be aware of. The benefits of the integrity and moderation of the judiciary have already been felt in more States than one; and though they may have displeased those whose sinister expectations they may have disappointed, they must have commanded the esteem and applause of all the virtuous and disinterested. Considerate men of every description ought to prize whatever will tend to beget or fortify that temper in the courts; as no man can be sure that he may not be tomorrow the victim of a spirit of injustice, by which he may be a gainer today. And every man must now feel that the inevitable tendency of such a spirit is to sap the foundations of public and private confidence and to introduce in its stead universal distrust and distress.

That inflexible and uniform adherence to the rights of the Constitution, and of individuals, which we perceive to be indispensable in the courts of justice, can certainly not be expected from judges who hold their offices by a temporary commission. Periodical appointments, however regulated, or by whomsoever made, would, in some way or other, be fatal to their necessary independence. If the power of making them was committed either to the executive or legislature there would be danger of an improper complaisance to the branch which possessed it; if to both, there would be an unwillingness to hazard the displeasure of either; if to the people, or to persons chosen by them for the special purpose, there would be too great a disposition to consult popularity to justify a reliance that nothing would be consulted but the Constitution and the laws.

There is yet a further and weighty reason for the permanency of the judicial offices which is deducible from the nature of the qualifications they require. It has been frequently remarked with great propriety that a voluminous code of laws is one of the inconveniences necessarily connected with the advantages of a free government. To avoid an arbitrary discretion in the courts, it is indispensable that they should be bound down by strict rules and precedents which serve to define and point out their duty in every particular case that comes before them; and it will readily be conceived from the variety of controversies which grow out of the folly and wickedness of mankind that the records of those precedents must unavoidably swell to a very considerable bulk and must demand long and laborious study to acquire a competent knowledge of them. Hence it is that there can be but few men in the society who will have sufficient skill in the laws to qualify them for the stations of judges. And making the proper deductions for the ordinary depravity of human nature, the number must be still smaller of those who unite the requisite integrity with the requisite knowledge. These considerations apprise us that the government can have no great option between fit characters; and that a temporary duration in office which would naturally discourage such characters from quitting a lucrative line of practice to accept a seat on the bench would have a tendency to throw the administration of justice into hands less able and less well qualified to conduct it with utility and dignity. In the present circumstances of this country and in those in which it is likely to be for a long time to come, the disadvantages on this score would be greater than they may at first sight appear; but it must be confessed that they are far inferior to those which present themselves under the other aspects of the subject.

Upon the whole, there can be no room to doubt that the convention acted wisely in copying from the models of those constitutions which have established *good behavior* as the tenure of their judicial offices, in the point of duration; and that so far from being blamable on this account, their plan would have been inexcusably defective if it had wanted this important feature of good government. The experience of Great Britain affords an illustrious comment on the excellence of the institution.

No. 79

A Further View of the Judicial Department in Relation to the Provisions for the Support and Responsibility of the Judges

"A power over a man's subsistence amounts to a power over his will," Hamilton observes, in stressing the importance of adequate judicial salaries. The conditions under which judges can be removed are also enumerated.

Next to permanency in office, nothing can contribute more to the independence of the judges than a fixed provision for their support. The remark made in relation to the President is equally applicable here. In the general course of human nature, *a power over a man's subsistence amounts to a power over his will.* And we can never hope to see realized in practice the complete separation of the judicial from the legislative power, in any system which leaves the former dependent for pecuniary resources on the occasional grants of the latter. The enlightened friends to good government in every State have seen cause to lament the want of precise and explicit precautions in the State constitutions on this head. Some of these indeed have declared that *permanent*[1] salaries should be established for the judges; but the experiment has in some instances shown that such expressions are not sufficiently definite to preclude legislative evasions. Something still more positive and unequivocal has been evinced to be requisite. The plan of the convention accordingly has provided that the judges of the United States "shall at *stated times* receive for their services a compensation which shall not be *diminished* during their continuance in office."

This, all circumstances considered, is the most eligible provision that could have been devised. It will readily be understood that the fluctuations in the value of money and in the state of society rendered a fixed rate of compensation in the Constitution inadmissible. What might be extravagant today might in half a century become penurious and inadequate. It was therefore necessary to leave it to the discretion of the legislature to vary its provisions in conformity to the variations in circumstances, yet under such restrictions as to put it out of the power of that body to change the condition of the individual for the worse. A man may then be sure of the ground upon which he stands, and can never be deterred from his duty by the apprehension of being placed in a less eligible situation. The clause which has been quoted combines both advantages. The salaries of judicial offices may from time to time be altered, as occasion shall require, yet so as never to lessen the allowance with which any particular judge comes into office, in respect to him. It will be observed that a difference has been made by the convention between the compensation of the President and of the judges. That of the former can neither be increased nor diminished; that of the latter can only not be diminished. This probably arose from the difference in the duration of the respective offices. As the President is to be elected for no more than four years, it can rarely happen that an adequate salary, fixed at the commencement of that period, will not continue to be such to the end of it. But with regard to the judges who, if they behave properly, will be secured in their places for life. It may well happen, especially in the early stages of the government, that a stipend which would be very sufficient at their first appointment would become too small in the progress of their service.

Adequate Judicial Salaries

This provision for the support of the judges bears every mark of prudence and efficacy; and it may be safely affirmed that, together with the permanent tenure of their offices, it affords a better prospect of their independence than is discoverable in the constitutions of any of the States in regard to their own judges.

The precautions for their responsibility are comprised in the article respecting impeachments. They are liable to be impeached for malconduct by the House of Representatives and tried by the Senate; and, if convicted, may be dismissed from office and disqualified from holding any other. This is the only provision on the point which is consistent with the necessary independence of the judicial character, and is the only one which we find in our own Constitution in respect to our own judges.

Removing Judges

The want of a provision for removing the judges on account of inability has been a subject of complaint. But all considerate men will be sensible that such a provision would either not be practiced upon or would be more liable to abuse than calculated to answer any good purpose. The mensuration of the faculties of the mind has, I believe, no place in the catalogue of known arts. An attempt to fix the boundary between the regions of ability and inability would much oftener give scope to personal and party attachments and enmities than advance the interests of justice or the public good. The result, except in the case of insanity, must for the most part be arbitrary; and insanity, without any formal or express provision, may be safely pronounced to be a virtual disqualification.

The constitution of New York, to avoid investigations that must forever be vague and dangerous, has taken a particular age as the criterion of inability. No man can be a judge beyond sixty. I believe there are few at present who do not disapprove of this provision. There is no station in relation to which it is less proper than to that of a judge. The deliberating and comparing faculties generally preserve their strength much beyond that period in men who survive it; and when, in addition to this circumstance we consider how few there are who outlive the season of intellectual vigor and how improbable it is that any considerable portion of the bench, whether more or less numerous, should be in such a situation at the same time, we shall be ready to conclude that limitations of this sort have little to recommend them. In a republic where fortunes are not affluent and pensions not expedient, the dismission of men from stations in which they have served their country long and usefully, on which they depend for subsistence, and from which it will be too late to resort to any other occupation for a livelihood, ought to have some better apology to humanity than is to be found in the imaginary danger of a superannuated bench.

No. 84

Concerning Several Miscellaneous Objections

Federalist Paper No. 84 is a catchall for some concluding arguments and the least enduring of the essays. Hamilton argues a bill of rights is not needed, since rights are protected throughout the Constitution and in the state constitutions. In fact, at the moment Hamilton was writing, momentum for a bill of rights was gaining support throughout the states. Likewise, he says the Constitution does not discuss what will later be a thorny constitutional issue, press freedom, because "who can give it any definition which would not leave the utmost latitude for evasion?" Finally, he tries to quell fears that the new government will be expensive to operate. "Whence is the dreaded augmentation of expense to spring?" he asks, and gives a hasty answer. The modest increase in the federal government's size will be offset by short sessions for Congress, and "a great part of the business which now keeps Congress sitting through the year will be transacted by the President."

In this course of the foregoing review of the Constitution, I have taken notice of, and endeavoured to answer, most of the objections which have appeared against it. There however remain a few which either did not fall naturally under any particular head or were forgotten in their proper places. These shall now be discussed; but as the subject has been drawn into great length, I shall so far consult brevity as to comprise all my observations on these miscellaneous points in a single paper.

A Bill of Rights Not Needed

The most considerable of these remaining objections is that the plan of the convention contains no bill of rights. Among other answers given to this, it has been upon different occasions remarked that the constitutions of several of the States are in a similar predicament. I add that New York is of this number. And yet the opposers of the new system in this State, who profess an unlimited admiration for its constitution, are among the most intemperate partisans of a bill of rights. To justify their zeal in this matter they allege two things: one is that, though the constitution of New York has no bill of rights prefixed to it, yet it contains, in the body of it, various provisions in favor of particular privileges and rights which, in substance, amount to the same thing; the other is that the Constitution adopts, in their full extent, the common and statute laws of Great Britain, by which many other rights not expressed in it are equally secured.

To the first I answer that the Constitution proposed by the convention contains, as well as the constitution of this State, a number of such provisions.

Independent of those which relate to the structure of the government, we find the following: Article I, section 3, clause 7—"Judgment in cases of impeachment shall not extend further than to removal from office and disqualification to hold and enjoy any office of honor, trust, or profit under the United States; but the party convicted shall, nevertheless, be liable and subject to indictment, trial, judgment, and punishment according to law." Section 9, of the same article, clause 2—"The privilege of the writ of *habeas corpus* shall not be suspended, unless when in cases of rebellion or invasion the public safety may require it." Clause 3—"No bill of attainder or *ex post facto* law shall be passed." Clause 7—"No title of nobility shall be granted by the United States; and no person holding any office of profit or trust under them shall, without the consent of the Congress, accept of any present emolument, office, or title of any kind whatever, from any king, prince, or foreign State." Article 3, section 2, clause 3—"The trial of all crimes, except in cases of impeachment, shall be by jury; and such trial shall be held in the State where the said crimes shall have been committed; but when not committed within any State, the trial shall be at such place or places as the Congress may by law have directed." Section 3, of the same article—"Treason against the United States shall consist only in levying war against them, or in adhering to their enemies, giving them aid and comfort. No person shall be convicted of treason, unless on the testimony of two witnesses to the same overt act, or on confession in open court." And clause 3, of the same section—"The Congress shall have the power to declare the punishment of treason but no attainder of treason shall work corruption of blood, or forfeiture except during the life of the person attainted."

It may well be a question whether these are not, upon the whole, of equal importance with any which are to be found in the constitution of this State. The establishment of the writ of *habeas corpus,* the prohibition of *ex post facto* laws, and of titles of nobility, *to which we have no corresponding provision in our Constitution,* are perhaps greater securities to liberty and republicanism than any it contains. The creation of crimes after the commission of the fact, or in other words, the subjecting of men to punishment for things which, when they were done, were breaches of no law, and the practice of arbitrary imprisonments, have been, in all ages, the favorite and most formidable instruments of tyranny. The observations of the judicious Blackstone,[1] in reference to the latter, are well worthy of recital: "To bereave a man of life [says he] or by violence to confiscate his estate, without accusation or trial, would be so gross and notorious an act of despotism as must at once convey the alarm of tyranny throughout the whole nation; but confinement of the person, by secretly hurrying him to jail; where his sufferings are unknown or forgotten, is a less public, a less striking, and therefore a *more dangerous engine* of arbitrary government."[2] And as a remedy for this fatal evil he is everywhere peculiarly emphatical in his encomiums on the *habeas corpus* act, which in one place he calls "the bulwark of the British Constitution."[3]

Titles of Nobility Excluded

Nothing need be said to illustrate the importance of the prohibition of titles of nobility. This may truly be denominated the cornerstone of republican government; for so long as they are excluded there can never be serious danger that the government will be any other than that of the people.

To the second, that is, to the pretended establishment of the common and statute law by the Constitution, I answer that they are expressly made subject "to such alterations and provisions as the legislature shall from time to time make concerning the same." They are therefore at any moment liable to repeal by the ordinary legislative power, and of course have no constitutional sanction. The only use of the declaration was to recognize the ancient law and to remove doubts which might have been occasioned by the Revolution. This consequently can be considered as no part of a declaration of rights, which under our constitutions must be intended as limitations of the power of the government itself.

It has been several times truly remarked that bills of rights are, in their origin, stipulations between kings and their subjects, abridgments of prerogative in favour of privilege, reservations of rights not surrendered to the prince. Such was Magna Carta obtained by the barons, sword in hand, from King John. Such were the subsequent confirmations of that charter by subsequent princes. Such was the *Petition of Right* assented to by Charles the First in the beginning of his reign. Such, also, was the Declaration of Right presented by the Lords and Commons to the Prince of Orange in 1688, and afterwards thrown into the form of an act of Parliament called the Bill of Rights. It is evident, therefore, that, according to their primitive signification, they have no application to constitutions, professedly founded upon the power of the people and executed by their immediate representatives and servants. Here, in strictness, the people surrender nothing; and as they retain everything they have no need of particular reservations, "WE, THE PEOPLE of the United States, to secure the blessings of liberty to ourselves and our posterity, do *ordain* and *establish* this Constitution for the United States of America." Here is a better recognition of popular rights than volumes of those aphorisms which make the principal figure in several of our State bills of rights and which would sound much better in a treatise of ethics than in a constitution of government.

But a minute detail of particular rights is certainly far less applicable to a Constitution like that under consideration, which is merely intended to regulate the general political interests of the nation, than to a constitution which has the regulation of every species of personal and private concerns. If, therefore, the loud clamors against the plan of the convention, on this score, are well founded, no epithets of reprobation will be too strong for the constitution of this State. But the truth is that both of them contain all which, in relation to their objects, is reasonably to be desired.

I go further and affirm that bills of rights, in the sense and to the extent in which they are contended for, are not only unnecessary in the proposed Constitution but would even be dangerous. They would contain various exceptions to powers which are not granted; and, on this very account, would afford a colorable pretext to claim more than were granted. For why declare that things shall not be done which there is no power to do? Why, for instance, should it be said that the liberty of the press shall not be restrained, when no power is given by which restrictions may be imposed? I will not contend that such a provision would confer a regulating power; but it is evident that it would furnish, to men disposed to usurp, a plausible pretense for claiming that power. They might urge with a semblance of reason that the Constitution ought not to be charged with the absurdity of providing against the abuse of an authority which was not given, and that the provision against restraining the liberty of the press afforded a clear implication that a power to prescribe proper regulations concerning it was intended to be vested in the national government. This may serve as a specimen of the numerous handles which would be given to the doctrine of constructive powers, by the indulgence of an injudicious zeal for bills of rights.

Liberty of the Press

On the subject of the liberty of the press, as much as has been said, I cannot forbear adding a remark or two: in the first place, I observe that there is not a syllable concerning it in the constitution of this State; in the next, I contend that whatever has been said about it in that of any other State amounts to nothing. What signifies a declaration that "the liberty of the press shall be inviolably preserved"? What is the liberty of the press? Who can give it any definition which would not leave the utmost latitude for evasion? I hold it to be impracticable; and from this I infer that its security, whatever fine declarations may be inserted in any constitution respecting it, must altogether depend on public opinion, and on the general spirit of the people and of the government.[4] And here, after all, as is intimated upon another occasion, must we seek for the only solid basis of all our rights.

There remains but one other view of this matter to conclude the point . The truth is, after all the declamations we have heard, that the Constitution is itself, in every rational sense, and to every useful purpose, a bill of rights. The several bills of rights in Great Britain form its Constitution, and conversely the constitution of each State is its bill of rights. And the proposed Constitution, if adopted, will be the bill of rights of the Union. Is it one object of a bill of rights to declare and specify the political privileges of the citizens in the structure and administration of the government? This is done in the most ample and precise manner in the plan of the convention; comprehending various precautions for the public security which are not to be found in any of the State constitutions. Is another object of a bill of rights to define certain immunities and modes of proceeding, which are relative to personal and private concerns? This we have seen has also been attended to in a variety of cases in the same plan. Adverting therefore to the substantial meaning of a bill of rights, it is absurd to allege that it is not to be found in the work of the convention. It may be said that it does not go far enough though it will not be easy to make this appear; but it can with no propriety be contended that there is no such thing. It certainly must be immaterial what mode is observed as to the order of declaring the rights of the citizens if they are to be found in any part of the instrument which establishes the government. And hence it must be apparent that much of what has been said on this subject rests merely on verbal and nominal distinctions, entirely foreign from the substance of the thing.

Another objection which has been made, and which, from the frequency of its repetition, it is to be presumed is relied on, is of this nature: "It is improper [say the objectors] to confer such large powers as are proposed upon the national government, because the seat of that government must of necessity be too remote from many of the States to admit of a proper knowledge on the part of the constituent of the conduct of the representative body." This argument, if it proves anything, proves that there ought to be no general government whatever. For the powers which, it seems to be agreed on all hands, ought to be vested in the Union, cannot be safely intrusted to a body which is not under every requisite control. But there are satisfactory reasons to show that the objection is in reality not well founded. There is in most of the arguments which relate to distance a palpable illusion of the imagination. What are the sources of information by which the people in Montgomery County must regulate their judgment of the conduct of their representatives in the State legislature? Of personal observation they can have no benefit. This is confined to the citizens on the spot. They must therefore depend on the information of intelligent men, in whom they confide; and how must these men obtain their information? Evidently from the complexion of public measures, from the public prints, from the correspondences with their representatives, and with other persons who reside at the place of their deliberations. This does not apply to Montgomery County only, but to all the counties at any considerable distance from the seat of government.

It is equally evident that the same sources of information would be open to the people in relation to the conduct of their representatives in the general government and the impediments to a prompt communication which distance may be supposed to create will be overbalanced by the effects of the vigilance of the State governments. The executive and legislative bodies of each State will be so many sentinels over the persons employed in every department of the national administration; and as it will be in their power to adopt and pursue a regular and effectual system of intelligence, they can never be at a loss to know the behavior of those who represent their constituents in the national councils, and can readily communicate the same knowledge to the people. Their disposition to apprise the community of whatever may prejudice its interests from another quarter may be relied upon, if it were only from the rivalship of power. And we may conclude with the fullest assurance that the people, through that channel, will be better informed of the conduct of their national representatives than they can be by any means they now possess, of that of their State representatives.

It ought also to be remembered that the citizens who inhabit the country at and near the seat of government will, in all questions that affect the general liberty and prosperity, have the same interest with those who are at a distance, and that they will stand ready to sound the alarm when necessary, and to point out the actors in any pernicious project. The public papers will be expeditious messengers of intelligence to the most remote inhabitants of the Union.

Among the many extraordinary objections which have appeared against the proposed Constitution, the most extraordinary and the least colorable one is derived from the want of some provision respecting the debts due *to* the United States. This has been represented as a tacit relinquishment of those debts, and as a wicked contrivance to screen public defaulters. The newspapers have teemed with the most inflammatory railings on this head; and yet there is nothing clearer than that the suggestion is entirely void of foundation, and is the offspring of extreme ignorance or extreme dishonesty. In addition to the remarks I have made upon the subject in another place, I shall only observe that as it is a plain dictate of common sense, so it is also an established doctrine of political law, that *"States neither lose any of their rights, nor are discharged from any of their obligations, by a change in the form of their civil government."*[5]

The last objection of any consequence, which I at present recollect, turns upon the article of expense. If it were even true that the adoption of the proposed government would occasion a considerable increase of expense, it would be an objection that ought to have no weight against the plan.

The great bulk of the citizens of America are with reason convinced that Union is the basis of their political happiness. Men of sense of all parties now with few exceptions agree that it cannot be preserved under the present system, nor without radical alterations; that new and extensive powers ought to be granted to the national head, and that these require a different organization of the federal government—a single body being an unsafe depositary of such ample authorities. In conceding all this, the question of expense must be given up; for it is impossible, with any degree of safety, to narrow the foundation upon which the system is to stand. The two branches of the legislature are, in the first instance, to consist of only sixty-five persons, which is the same number of which Congress, under the existing Confederation, may be composed. It is true that this number is intended to be increased; but this is to keep pace with the increase of the population and resources of the country. It is evident that a less number would, even in the first instance, have been unsafe, and that a continuance of the present number would, in a more advanced stage of population, be a very inadequate representation of the people.

"Whence Is the Dreaded Augmentation of Expense to Spring?"

Whence is the dreaded augmentation of expense to spring? One source pointed out is the multiplication of offices under the new government. Let us examine this a little.

It is evident that the principal departments of the administration under the present government are the same which will be required under the new. There are now a Secretary at War, a Secretary for Foreign Affairs, a Secretary for Domestic Affairs, a Board of Treasury, consisting of three persons, a treasurer, assistants, clerks, etc. These offices are indispensable under any system and will suffice under the new as well as under the old. As to ambassadors and other ministers and agents in foreign countries, the proposed Constitution can make no other difference than to render their characters, where they reside, more respectable, and their services more useful. As to persons to be employed in the collection of the revenues, it is unquestionably true that these will form a very considerable addition to the number of federal officers; but it will not follow that this will occasion an increase of public expense. It will be in most cases nothing more than an exchange of State officers for national officers. In the collection of all duties, for instance, the persons employed will be wholly of the latter description. The States individually will stand in no need of any for this purpose. What difference can it make in point of expense to pay officers of the customs appointed by the State or those appointed by the United States?

There is no good reason to suppose that either the number or the salaries of the latter will be greater than those of the former.

Where then are we to seek for those additional articles of expense which are to swell the account to the enormous size that has been represented to us? The chief item which occurs to me respects the support of the judges of the United States. I do not add the President, because there is now a president of Congress, whose expenses may not be far, if anything, short of those which will be incurred on account of the President of the United States. The support of the judges will clearly be an extra expense, but to what extent will depend on the particular plan which may be adopted in practice in regard to this matter. But it can upon no reasonable plan amount to a sum which will be an object of material consequence.

Let us now see what there is to counterbalance any extra expense that may attend the establishment of the proposed government. The first thing that presents itself is that a great part of the business which now keeps Congress sitting through the year will be transacted by the President. Even the management of foreign negotiations will naturally devolve upon him, according to general principles concerted with the Senate, and subject to their final concurrence. Hence it is evident that a portion of the year will suffice for the session of both the Senate and the House of Representatives; we may suppose about a fourth for the latter and a third, or perhaps a half, for the former. The extra business of treaties and appointments may give this extra occupation to the Senate. From this circumstance we may infer that, until the House of Representatives shall be increased greatly beyond its present number, there will be a considerable saving of expense from the difference between the constant session of the present and the temporary session of the future Congress.

But there is another circumstance of great importance in the view of economy. The business of the United States has hitherto occupied the State legislatures, as well as Congress. The latter has made requisitions which the former have had to provide for. Hence it has happened that the sessions of the State legislatures have been protracted greatly beyond what was necessary for the execution of the mere local business of the States. More than half their time has been frequently employed in matters which related to the United States. Now the members who compose the legislatures of the several States amount to two thousand and upwards, which number has hitherto performed what under the new system will be done in the first instance by sixty-five persons, and probably at no future period by above a fourth or a fifth of that number. The Congress under the proposed government will do all the business of the United States themselves, without the intervention of the State legislatures, who thenceforth will have only to attend to the affairs of their particular States, and will not have to sit in any proportion as long as they have heretofore done. This difference in the time of the sessions of the State legislatures will be all clear gain, and will alone form an article of saving, which may be regarded as an equivalent for any additional objects of expense that may be occasioned by the adoption of the new system.

The result from these observations is that the sources of additional expense from the establishment of the proposed Constitution are much fewer than may have been imagined; that they are counterbalanced by considerable objects of saving; and that while it is questionable on which side the scale will preponderate, it is certain that a government less expensive would be incompetent to the purpose of the Union.

No. 85

Conclusion

"Let us now pause and ask ourselves whether, in the course of these papers, the proposed Constitution has not been satisfactorily vindicated from the aspersions thrown upon it; and whether it has not been shown to be worthy of the public approbation and necessary to the public safety and prosperity," Hamilton writes, knowing full well that his response is a satisfactory "Yes." Next he argues that, for the question to be answered honestly, the reader must hold "no partial motive, no particular interest, no pride of opinion, no temporary passion or prejudice." "Let him beware of an obstinate adherence to party; let him reflect that the object upon which he is to decide is not a particular interest of the community, but the very existence of the nation," Hamilton concludes, adding, in case the reader is wavering, "and let him remember that a majority of America had already given its sanction to the plan which he is to approve or reject." In this summing up, Hamilton says, "I am persuaded that it is the best which our political situation, habits, and opinions will admit." In language as enthusiastic as that contained in the opening Federalist Papers, *he looks "forward with trembling anxiety" to establishing a constitution "in time of profound peace, by the voluntary consent of a whole people."*

According to the formal division of the subject of these papers announced in my first number, there would appear still to remain for discussion two points: "the analogy of the proposed government to your own State constitution," and "the additional security which its adoption will afford to republican government, to liberty, and to property." But these heads have been so fully anticipated and exhausted in the progress of the work that it would now scarcely be possible to do anything more than repeat, in a more dilated form, what has been heretofore said, which the advanced stage of the question and the time already spent upon it conspire to forbid.

It is remarkable that the resemblance of the plan of the convention to the act which organizes the government of this State holds, not less with regard to many of the supposed defects than to the real excellences of the former. Among the pretended defects are the re-eligibility of the executive, the want of a council, the omission of a formal bill of rights, the omission of a provision respecting the liberty of the press. These and several others which have been noted in the course of our inquiries are as much chargeable on the existing constitution of this State as on the one proposed for the Union; and a man must have slender pretensions to consistency who can rail at the latter for imperfections which he finds no difficulty in excusing in the former. Nor indeed can there be a better proof of the insincerity and affectation of some of the zealous adversaries of the plan of the convention among us who profess to be the devoted admirers of the government under which they live than the fury with which they have attacked that plan, for matters in regard to which our own constitution is equally or perhaps more vulnerable.

The additional securities to republican government, to liberty, and to property, to be derived from the adoption of the plan under consideration, consist chiefly in the restraints which the preservation of the Union will impose on local factions and insurrections, and on the ambition of powerful individuals in single States who might acquire credit and influence enough from leaders and favorites to become the despots of the people; in the diminution of the opportunities to foreign intrigue, which the dissolution of the Confederacy would invite and facilitate; in the prevention of extensive military establishments, which could not fail to grow out of wars between the States in a disunited situation; in the express guaranty of a republican form of government to each; in the absolute and universal exclusion of titles of nobility; and in the precautions against the repetition of those practices on the part of the State governments which have undermined the foundations of property and credit, have planted mutual distrust in the breasts of all classes of citizens, and have occasioned an almost universal prostration of morals.

Thus have I, fellow-citizens, executed the task I had assigned to myself; with what success your conduct must determine. I trust at least you will admit that I have not failed in the assurance I gave you respecting the spirit with which my endeavors should be conducted. I have addressed myself purely to your judgments, and have studiously avoided those asperities which are too apt to disgrace political disputants of all parties and which have been not a little provoked by the language and conduct of the opponents of the Constitution. The charge of a conspiracy against the liberties of the people which has been indiscriminately brought against the advocates of the plan has something in it too wanton and too malignant not to excite the indignation of every man who feels in his own bosom a refutation of the calumny. The perpetual changes which have been rung upon the wealthy, the well-born, and the great have been such as to inspire the disgust of all sensible men. And the unwarrantable concealments and misrepresentations which have been in various ways practiced to keep the truth from the public eye have been of a nature to demand the reprobation of all honest men. It is not impossible that these circumstances may have occasionally betrayed me into intemperances of expression which I did not intend; it is certain that I have frequently felt a struggle between sensibility and moderation; and if the former has in some instances prevailed, it must be my excuse that it has been neither often nor much.

The Constitution Vindicated

Let us now pause and ask ourselves whether, in the course of these papers, the proposed Constitution has not been satisfactorily vindicated from the aspersions thrown upon it; and whether it has not been shown to be worthy of the public approbation and necessary to the public safety and prosperity. Every man is bound to answer these questions to himself, according to the best of his conscience and understanding, and to act agreeably to the genuine and sober dictates of his judgment. This is a duty from which nothing can give him a dispensation. 'Tis one that he is called upon, nay, constrained by all the obligations that form the bonds of society, to discharge sincerely and honestly. No partial motive, no particular interest, no pride of opinion, no temporary passion or prejudice, will justify to himself, to his country, or to his posterity, an improper election of the part he is to act. Let him beware of an obstinate adherence to party; let him reflect that the object upon which he is to decide is not a particular interest of the community, but the very existence of the nation; and let him remember that a majority of America has already given its sanction to the plan which he is to approve or reject.

I shall not dissemble that I feel an entire confidence in the arguments which recommend the proposed system to your adoption, and that I am unable to discern any real force in those by which it has been opposed. I am persuaded that it is the best which our political situation, habits, and opinions will admit, and superior to any the revolution has produced.

The Constitution: "The Best That the Present Views and Circumstances of the Country Would Permit"

Concessions on the part of the friends of the plan that it has not a claim to absolute perfection have afforded matter of no small triumph to its enemies. "Why," say they, "should we adopt an imperfect thing? Why not amend it and make it perfect before it is irrevocably established?" This may be plausible enough, but it is only plausible. In the first place I remark that the extent of these concessions has been greatly exaggerated. They have been stated as amounting to an admission that the plan is radically defective and that without material alterations the rights and the interests of the community cannot be safely confided to it. This, as far as I have understood the meaning of those who make the concessions, is an entire perversion of their sense. No advocate of the measure can be found who will not declare as his sentiment that the system, though it may not be perfect in every part, is, upon the whole, a good one; is the best that the present views and circumstances of the country will permit; and is such a one as promises every species of security which a reasonable people can desire.

I answer in the next place that I should esteem it the extreme of imprudence to prolong the precarious state of our national affairs and to expose the Union to the jeopardy of successive experiments in the chimerical pursuit of a perfect plan. I never expect to see a perfect work from imperfect man. The result of the deliberations of all collective bodies must necessarily be a compound, as well of the errors and prejudices as of the good sense and wisdom of the individuals of whom they are composed. The compacts which are to embrace thirteen distinct States in a common bond of amity and union must as necessarily be a compromise of as many dissimilar interests and inclinations. How can perfection spring from such materials?

The reasons assigned in an excellent little pamphlet lately published in this city[1] are unanswerable to show the utter improbability of assembling a new convention under circumstances in any degree so favorable to a happy issue as those in which the late convention met, deliberated, and concluded. I will not repeat the arguments there used, as I presume the production itself has had an extensive circulation. It is certainly well worth the perusal of every friend to his country. There is, however, one point of light in which the subject of amendments still remains to be considered, and in which it has not yet been exhibited to public view. I cannot resolve to conclude without first taking a survey of it in this aspect.

It appears to me susceptible of absolute demonstration that it will be far more easy to obtain subsequent than previous amendments to the Constitution. The moment an alteration is made in the present plan it becomes, to the purpose of adoption, a new one, and must undergo a new decision of each State. To its complete establishment throughout the Union it will therefore require the concurrence of thirteen States. If, on the contrary, the Constitution proposed should once be ratified by all the States as it stands, alterations in it may at any time be effected by nine States. Here, then, the chances are as thirteen to nine[2] in favor of subsequent amendment, rather than of the original adoption of an entire system.

This is not all. Every Constitution for the United States must inevitably consist of a great variety of particulars in which thirteen independent States are to be accommodated in their interests or opinions of interest. We may of course expect to see, in any body of men charged with its original formation, very different combinations of the parts upon different points. Many of those who form a majority on one question may become the minority on a second, and an association dissimilar to either may constitute the majority on a third. Hence the necessity of moulding and arranging all the particulars which are to compose the whole in such a manner as to satisfy all the parties to the compact; and hence, also, an immense multiplication of difficulties and casualties in obtaining the collective assent to a final act. The degree of that multiplication must evidently be in a ratio to the number of particulars and the number of parties.

But every amendment to the Constitution, if once established, would be a single proposition, and might be brought forward singly. There would then be no necessity for management or compromise in relation to any other point—no giving nor taking. The will of the requisite number would at once bring the matter to a decisive issue. And consequently, whenever nine, or rather ten States, were united in the desire of a particular amendment, that amendment must infallibly take place. There can, therefore, be no comparison between the facility of effecting an amendment and that of establishing, in the first instance, a complete Constitution.

In opposition to the probability of subsequent amendments, it has been urged that the persons delegated to the administration of the national government will always be disinclined to yield up any portion of the authority of which they were once possessed. For my own part, I acknowledge a thorough conviction that any amendments which may, upon mature consideration, be thought useful, will be applicable to the organization of the government, not to the mass of its powers; and on this account alone I think there is no weight in the observation just stated. I also think there is little weight in it on another account. The intrinsic difficulty of governing thirteen states at any rate, independent of calculations upon an ordinary degree of public spirit and integrity will, in my opinion, constantly *impose* on the national rulers the *necessity* of a spirit of accommodation to the reasonable expectations of their constituents. But there is yet a further consideration, which proves beyond the possibility of doubt that the observation is futile. It is this: that the national rulers, whenever nine States concur, will have no option upon the subject. By the fifth article of the plan, the Congress will be *obliged* "on the application of the legislatures of two thirds of the States [which at present amount to nine], to call a convention for proposing amendments which *shall be valid,* to all intents and purposes, as part of the Constitution, when ratified by the legislatures of three fourths of the states, or by conventions in three fourths thereof." The words of this article are peremptory. The Congress *"shall* call a convention." Nothing in this particular is left to the discretion of that body. And of consequence all the declamation about the disinclination to a change vanishes in air. Nor however difficult it may be supposed to unite two thirds or three fourths of the State legislatures in amendments which may affect local interests can there be any room to apprehend any such difficulty in a union on points which are merely relative to the general liberty or security of the people. We may safely rely on the disposition of the State legislatures to erect barriers against the encroachments of the national authority.

If the foregoing argument is a fallacy, certain it is that I am myself deceived by it for it is, in my conception, one of those rare instances in which a political truth can be brought to the test of mathematical demonstration. Those who see the matter in the same light with me, however zealous they may be for amendments, must agree in the propriety of a previous adoption as the most direct road to their own object. The zeal for attempts to amend, prior to the establishment of the Constitution, must abate in every man who is ready to accede to the truth of the following observations of a writer equally solid and ingenious: "To balance a large state or society [says he], whether monarchical or republican, on general laws, is a work of so great difficulty that no human genius, however comprehensive, is able, by the mere dint of reason and reflection, to effect it. The judgments of many must unite in the work; experience must guide their labor; time must bring it to perfection, and the feeling of inconveniences must correct the mistakes which they *inevitably* fall into in their first trials and experiments."[3] These judicious reflections contain a lesson of moderation to all the sincere lovers of the Union, and ought to put them upon their guard against hazarding anarchy, civil war, a perpetual alienation of the States from each other, and perhaps the military despotism of a victorious demagogue, in the pursuit of what they are not likely to obtain, but from time and experience. It may be in me a defect of political fortitude but I acknowledge that I cannot entertain an equal tranquillity with those who affect to treat the dangers of a longer continuance in our present situation as imaginary. A nation without a national government is, in my view, an awful spectacle. The establishment of a Constitution, in time of profound peace, by the voluntary consent of a whole people, is a prodigy, to the completion of which I look forward with trembling anxiety. I can reconcile it to no rules of prudence to let go the hold we now have, in so arduous an enterprise, upon seven out of the thirteen States, and after having passed over so considerable a part of the ground, to recommence the course. I dread the more the consequences of new attempts because I know that powerful individuals in this and other States, are enemies to a general national government in every possible shape.

The Constitution
of the
United States of America

We the People of the United States, in Order to form a more perfect Union, establish Justice, insure domestic Tranquility, provide for the common defence, promote the general Welfare, and secure the Blessings of Liberty to ourselves and our Posterity, do ordain and establish this Constitution for the United States of America.

Article. I.

Section. 1. All legislative Powers herein granted shall be vested in a Congress of the United States, which shall consist of a Senate and House of Representatives.

Section. 2. The House of Representatives shall be composed of Members chosen every second Year by the People of the several States, and the Electors in each State shall have the Qualifications requisite for Electors of the most numerous Branch of the State Legislature.

No Person shall be a Representative who shall not have attained to the Age of twenty five Years, and been seven Years a Citizen of the United States, and who shall not, when elected, be an Inhabitant of that State in which he shall be chosen.

[Representatives and direct Taxes shall be apportioned among the several States which may be included within this Union, according to their respective Numbers, which shall be determined by adding to the whole Number of free Persons, including those bound to Service for a Term of Years, and excluding Indians not taxed, three fifths of all other Persons.]* The actual Enumeration shall be made within three Years after the first Meeting of the Congress of the United States, and within every subsequent Term of ten Years, in such Manner as they shall by Law direct. The number of Representatives shall not exceed one for every thirty Thousand, but each State shall have at Least one Representative; and until such enumeration shall be made, the State of New Hampshire shall be entitled to chuse three, Massachusetts eight, Rhode-Island and Providence Plantations one, Connecticut five, New-York six, New Jersey four, Pennsylvania eight, Delaware one, Maryland six, Virginia ten, North Carolina five, South Carolina five, and Georgia three.

When vacancies happen in the Representation from any State, the Executive Authority thereof shall issue Writs of Election to fill such Vacancies.

The House of Representatives shall chuse their Speaker and other Officers; and shall have the sole Power of Impeachment.

Section. 3. The Senate of the United States shall be composed of two Senators from each State, [chosen by the Legislature thereof,]** for six Years; and each Senator shall have one Vote.

Immediately after they shall be assembled in Consequence of the first Election, they shall be divided as equally as may be into three Classes. The Seats of the Senators of the first Class shall be vacated at the Expiration of the second Year, of the second Class at the Expiration of the fourth Year, and of the third Class at the Expiration of the sixth Year, so that one third may be chosen every second Year; [and if Vacancies happen by Resignation, or otherwise, during the Recess of the Legislature of any State, the Executive thereof may make temporary Appointments until the next Meeting of the Legislature, which shall then fill such Vacancies.]**

No person shall be a Senator who shall not have attained to the Age of thirty Years, and been nine Years a Citizen of the United States, and who shall not, when elected, be an Inhabitant of that State for which he shall be chosen.

The Vice President of the United States shall be President of the Senate, but shall have no Vote, unless they be equally divided.

The Senate shall chuse their other Officers, and also a President pro

---

* Changed by section 2 of the Fourteenth Amendment.
** Changed by the Seventeenth Amendment.

tempore, in the absence of the Vice President, or when he shall exercise the Office of President of the United States.

The Senate shall have the sole Power to try all Impeachments. When sitting for that Purpose, they shall be on Oath or Affirmation. When the President of the United States is tried, the Chief Justice shall preside: And no Person shall be convicted without the Concurrence of two thirds of the Members present.

Judgment in Cases of Impeachment shall not extend further than to removal from Office, and disqualification to hold and enjoy any Office of honor, Trust or Profit under the United States: but the Party convicted shall nevertheless be liable and subject to Indictment, Trial, Judgment and Punishment, according to Law.

Section. 4. The Times, Places and Manner of holding Elections for Senators and Representatives, shall be prescribed in each State by the Legislature thereof; but the Congress may at any time by Law make or alter such Regulations, except as to the Places of Chusing Senators.

The Congress shall assemble at least once in every Year, and such Meeting shall be [on the first Monday in December,]* unless they shall by Law appoint a different Day.

Section. 5. Each House shall be the Judge of the Elections, Returns and Qualifications of its own Members, and a Majority of each shall constitute a Quorum to do Business; but a smaller Number may adjourn from day to day, and may be authorized to compel the Attendance of absent Members, in such Manner, and under such Penalties as each House may provide.

Each House may determine the Rules of its Proceedings, punish its Members for disorderly Behaviour, and, with the Concurrence of two thirds, expel a Member.

Each House shall keep a Journal of its Proceedings, and from time to time publish the same, excepting such Parts as may in their Judgment require Secrecy; and the Yeas and Nays of the Members of either House on any question shall, at the Desire of one fifth of those Present, be entered on the Journal.

Neither House, during the Session of Congress, shall, without the Consent of the other, adjourn for more than three days, nor to any other Place than that in which the two Houses shall be sitting.

* Changed by section 2 of the Twentieth Amendment.

Section. 6. The Senators and Representatives shall receive a Compensation for their Services, to be ascertained by Law, and paid out of the Treasury of the United States. They shall in all Cases, except Treason, Felony and Breach of the Peace, be privileged from Arrest during their Attendance at the Session of their respective Houses, and in going to and returning from the same; and for any Speech or Debate in either House, they shall not be questioned in any other Place.

No Senator or Representative shall, during the Time for which he was elected, be appointed to any civil Office under the Authority of the United States, which shall have been created, or the Emoluments whereof shall have been encreased during such time; and no Person holding any Office under the United States, shall be Member of either House during his Continuance in Office.

Section. 7. All Bills for raising Revenue shall originate in the House of Representatives; but the Senate may propose or concur with Amendments as on other Bills.

Every Bill which shall have passed the House of Representatives and the Senate, shall, before it becomes a Law, be presented to the President of the United States; If he approve he shall sign it, but if not he shall return it, with his Objections to that House in which it shall have originated, who shall enter the Objections at large on their Journal, and proceed to reconsider it. If after such Reconsideration two thirds of that House shall agree to pass the Bill, it shall be sent, together with the Objections, to the other House, by which it shall likewise be reconsidered, and if approved by two thirds of that House, it shall become a Law. But in all such Cases the Votes of both Houses shall be determined by yeas and Nays, and the Names of the Persons voting for and against the Bill shall be entered on the Journal of each House respectively. If any Bill shall not be returned by the President within ten Days (Sundays excepted) after it shall have been presented to him, the Same shall be a Law, in like Manner as if he had signed it, unless the Congress by their Adjournment prevent its Return, in which Case it shall not be a Law.

Every Order, Resolution, or Vote to which the Concurrence of the Senate and House of Representatives may be necessary (except on a question of Adjournment) shall be presented to the President of the United States; and before the Same shall take Effect, shall be approved by him, or being disapproved by him, shall be repassed by two thirds of the Senate and

House of Representatives, according to the Rules and Limitations prescribed in the Case of a Bill.

Section. 8. The Congress shall have Power To lay and collect Taxes, Duties, Imposts and Excises, to pay the Debts and provide for the common Defence and general Welfare of the United States; but all Duties, Imposts and Excises shall be uniform throughout the United States;

To borrow money on the credit of the United States;

To regulate Commerce with foreign Nations, and among the several States, and with the Indian Tribes;

To establish an uniform Rule of Naturalization, and uniform Laws on the subject of Bankruptcies throughout the United States;

To coin Money, regulate the Value thereof, and of foreign Coin, and fix the Standard of Weights and Measures;

To provide for the Punishment of counterfeiting the Securities and current Coin of the United States;

To establish Post Offices and post Roads;

To promote the Progress of Science and useful Arts, by securing for limited Times to Authors and Inventors the exclusive Right to their respective Writings and Discoveries;

To constitute Tribunals inferior to the supreme Court;

To define and punish Piracies and Felonies committed on the high Seas, and Offenses against the Law of Nations;

To declare War, grant Letters of Marque and Reprisal, and make Rules concerning Captures on Land and Water;

To raise and support Armies, but no Appropriation of Money to that Use shall be for a longer Term than two Years;

To provide and maintain a Navy;

To make Rules for the Government and Regulation of the land and naval Forces;

To provide for calling forth the Militia to execute the Laws of the Union, suppress Insurrections and repel Invasions;

To provide for organizing, arming, and disciplining the Militia, and for governing such Part of them as may be employed in the Service of the United States, reserving to the States respectively, the Appointment of the Officers, and the Authority of training the Militia according to the discipline prescribed by Congress;

To exercise exclusive Legislation in all Cases whatsoever, over such District (not exceeding ten Miles square) as may, by Cession of particular

States, and the Acceptance of Congress, become the Seat of the Government of the United States, and to exercise like Authority over all Places purchased by the Consent of the Legislature of the State in which the Same shall be, for the Erection of Forts, Magazines, Arsenals, dock-Yards, and other needful Buildings;—And

To make all Laws which shall be necessary and proper for carrying into Execution the foregoing Powers, and all other Powers vested by this Constitution in the Government of the United States, or in any Department or Officer thereof.

Section. 9. The Migration or Importation of such Persons as any of the States now existing shall think proper to admit, shall not be prohibited by the Congress prior to the Year one thousand eight hundred and eight, but a tax or duty may be imposed on such Importation, not exceeding ten dollars for each Person.

The privilege of the Writ of Habeas Corpus shall not be suspended, unless when in Cases of Rebellion or Invasion the public Safety may require it.

No Bill of Attainder or ex post facto Law shall be passed.

No Capitation, or other direct, Tax shall be laid, unless in Proportion to the Census or Enumeration herein before directed to be taken.*

No Tax or Duty shall be laid on Articles exported from any State.

No Preference shall be given by any Regulation of Commerce or Revenue to the Ports of one State over those of another; nor shall Vessels bound to, or from, one State, be obliged to enter, clear, or pay Duties in another.

No Money shall be drawn from the Treasury, but in Consequence of Appropriations made by Law; and a regular Statement and Account of the Receipts and Expenditures of all public Money shall be published from time to time.

No Title of Nobility shall be granted by the United States; And no Person holding any Office of Profit or Trust under them, shall, without the Consent of the Congress, accept of any present, Emolument, Office, or Title, of any kind whatever, from any King, Prince, or foreign State.

Section. 10. No State shall enter into any Treaty, Alliance, or Confederation; grant Letters of Marque and Reprisal; coin Money; emit Bills of

---

* See the Sixteenth Amendment.

Credit; make any Thing but gold and silver Coin a Tender in Payment of Debts; pass any Bill of Attainder, ex post facto Law, or Law impairing the Obligation of Contracts, or grant any Title of Nobility.

No State shall, without the Consent of the Congress, lay any Imposts or Duties on Imports or Exports, except what may be absolutely necessary for executing its inspection Laws: and the net Produce of all Duties and Imposts, laid by any State on Imports or Exports, shall be for the Use of the Treasury of the United States; and all such Laws shall be subject to the Revision and Controul of the Congress.

No State shall, without the Consent of Congress, lay any duty of Tonnage, keep Troops, or Ships of War in time of Peace, enter into any Agreement or Compact with another State, or with a foreign Power, or engage in War, unless actually invaded, or in such imminent Danger as will not admit of delay.

Article. II.

Section. 1. The executive Power shall be vested in a President of the United States of America. He shall hold his Office during the Term of four Years, and, together with the Vice President, chosen for the same Term, be elected, as follows:

Each State shall appoint, in such Manner as the Legislature thereof may direct, a Number of Electors, equal to the whole Number of Senators and Representatives to which the State may be entitled in the Congress: but no Senator or Representative, or Person holding an Office of Trust or Profit under the United States, shall be appointed an Elector.

[The Electors shall meet in their respective States, and vote by Ballot for two Persons, of whom one at least shall not be an Inhabitant of the same State with themselves. And they shall make a List of all the Persons voted for, and of the Number of Votes for each; which List they shall sign and certify, and transmit sealed to the Seat of the Government of the United States, directed to the President of the Senate. The President of the Senate shall, in the Presence of the Senate and House of Representatives, open all the Certificates, and the Votes shall then be counted. The Person having the greatest Number of Votes shall be the President, if such Number be a Majority of the whole Number of Electors appointed; and if there be more than one who have such Majority, and have an equal Number of Votes, then the House of Representatives shall immediately chuse by Ballot one of them for President; and if no Person have a Majority, then from the five highest on the List the said House shall in like Manner chuse the President. But in chusing the President, the Votes shall be taken by States, the Representation from each State having one Vote; a quorum for this Purpose shall consist of a Member or Members from two thirds of the States, and a Majority of all the States shall be necessary to a Choice. In every Case, after the Choice of the President, the Person having the greatest Number of Votes of the Electors shall be the Vice President. But if there should remain two or more who have equal Votes, the Senate shall chuse from them by Ballot the Vice President.]*

The Congress may determine the Time of chusing the Electors, and the Day on which they shall give their Votes; which Day shall be the same throughout the United States.

No person except a natural born Citizen, or a Citizen of the United States, at the time of the Adoption of this Constitution, shall be eligible to the Office of President; neither shall any Person be eligible to that Office who shall not have attained to the Age of thirty five Years, and been fourteen Years a Resident within the United States.

[In Case of the Removal of the President from Office, or of his Death, Resignation, or Inability to discharge the Powers and Duties of the said Office, the same shall devolve on the Vice President, and the Congress may by Law provide for the Case of Removal, Death, Resignation or Inability, both of the President and Vice President, declaring what Officer shall then act as President, and such Officer shall act accordingly, until the Disability be removed, or a President shall be elected.]**

The President shall, at stated Times, receive for his Services, a Compensation, which shall neither be increased nor diminished during the Period for which he shall have been elected, and he shall not receive within that Period any other Emolument from the United States, or any of them.

Before he enter on the execution of his Office, he shall take the following Oath or Affirmation:—"I do solemnly swear (or affirm) that I will faithfully execute the Office of President of the United States, and will to the best of my Ability, preserve, protect and defend the Constitution of the United States."

Section. 2. The President shall be Commander in Chief of the Army and Navy of the United States, and of the Militia of the several States, when called into the actual Service of the United States; he may require the

* Changed by the Twelfth Amendment.
** Changed by the Twenty-fifth Amendment.

Opinion, in writing, of the principal Officer in each of the executive Departments, upon any subject relating to the Duties of their respective Offices, and he shall have Power to Grant Reprieves and Pardons for Offenses against the United States, except in Cases of Impeachment.

He shall have Power, by and with the Advice and Consent of the Senate, to make Treaties, provided two thirds of the Senators present concur; and he shall nominate, and by and with the Advice and Consent of the Senate, shall appoint Ambassadors, other public Ministers and Consuls, Judges of the supreme Court, and all other Officers of the United States, whose Appointments are not herein otherwise provided for, and which shall be established by Law: but the Congress may by Law vest the Appointment of such inferior Officers, as they think proper, in the President alone, in the Courts of Law, or in the Heads of Departments.

The President shall have Power to fill up all Vacancies that may happen during the Recess of the Senate, by granting Commissions which shall expire at the end of their next Session.

Section. 3. He shall from time to time give to the Congress Information of the State of the Union, and recommend to their Consideration such Measures as he shall judge necessary and expedient; he may, on extraordinary Occasions, convene both Houses, or either of them, and in Case of Disagreement between them, with Respect to the Time of Adjournment, he may adjourn them to such Time as he shall think proper; he shall receive Ambassadors and other public Ministers; he shall take Care that the Laws be faithfully executed, and shall Commission all the Officers of the United States.

Section. 4. The President, Vice President and all civil Officers of the United States, shall be removed from Office on Impeachment for, and Conviction of, Treason, Bribery, or other high Crimes and Misdemeanors.

Article. III.

Section. 1. The judicial Power of the United States, shall be vested in one supreme Court, and in such inferior Courts as the Congress may from time to time ordain and establish. The Judges, both of the supreme and inferior Courts, shall hold their Offices during good Behaviour, and shall, at stated Times, receive for their Services, a Compensation, which shall not be diminished during their Continuance in Office.

Section. 2. The judicial Power shall extend to all Cases, in Law and Equity, arising under this Constitution, the Laws of the United States, and Treaties made, or which shall be made, under their Authority;—to all Cases affecting Ambassadors, other public Ministers and Consuls;—to all Cases of admiralty and maritime Jurisdiction;—to Controversies to which the United States shall be a Party;—to Controversies between two or more States;—[between a State and Citizens of another State;—]* between Citizens of different States;—between Citizens of the same State claiming Lands under Grants of different States, [and between a State, or the Citizens thereof, and foreign States, Citizens or Subjects.]*

In all Cases affecting Ambassadors, other public Ministers and Consuls, and those in which a State shall be Party, the supreme Court shall have original Jurisdiction. In all the other Cases before mentioned, the supreme Court shall have appellate Jurisdiction, both as to Law and Fact, with such Exceptions, and under such Regulations as the Congress shall make.

The Trial of all Crimes, except in Cases of Impeachment, shall be by Jury; and such Trial shall be held in the State where the said Crimes shall have been committed; but when not committed within any State, the Trial shall be at such Place or Places as the Congress may by Law have directed.

Section. 3. Treason against the United States, shall consist only in levying War against them, or in adhering to their enemies, giving them Aid and Comfort. No Person shall be convicted of Treason unless on the Testimony of two Witnesses to the same overt Act, or on Confession in open Court.

The Congress shall have power to declare the Punishment of Treason, but no Attainder of Treason shall work Corruption of Blood, or Forfeiture except during the Life of the Person attainted.

Article. IV.

Section. 1. Full Faith and Credit shall be given in each State to the public Acts, Records, and judicial Proceedings of every other State. And the Congress may by general Laws prescribe the Manner in which such Acts, Records and Proceedings shall be proved, and the effect thereof.

* Changed by the Eleventh Amendment.

Section. 2. The Citizens of each State shall be entitled to all Privileges and Immunities of Citizens in the several States.

A Person charged in any State with Treason, Felony, or other Crime, who shall flee from Justice, and be found in another State, shall on Demand of the executive Authority of the State from which he fled, be delivered up, to be removed to the State having Jurisdiction of the Crime.

[No Person held to Service or Labour in one State, under the Laws thereof, escaping into another, shall, in Consequence of any Law or Regulation therein, be discharged from such Service or Labour, but shall be delivered up on Claim of the Party to whom such Service or Labour may be due.]*

Section. 3. New States may be admitted by the Congress into this Union; but no new State shall be formed or erected within the Jurisdiction of any other State; nor any State be formed by the Junction of two or more States, or parts of States, without the Consent of the Legislatures of the States concerned as well as of the Congress.

The Congress shall have Power to dispose of and make all needful Rules and Regulations respecting the Territory or other Property belonging to the United States; and nothing in this Constitution shall be so construed as to Prejudice any Claims of the United States, or of any particular State.

Section. 4. The United States shall guarantee to every State in this Union a Republican Form of Government, and shall protect each of them against Invasion; and on Application of the Legislature, or of the Executive (when the Legislature cannot be convened) against domestic Violence.

Article. V.

The Congress, whenever two thirds of both Houses shall deem it necessary, shall propose Amendments to this Constitution, or, on the Application of the Legislatures of two thirds of the several States, shall call a Convention for proposing Amendments, which, in either Case, shall be valid to all Intents and Purposes, as Part of this Constitution, when ratified by the Legislatures of three fourths of the several States, or by Conventions in three fourths thereof, as the one or the other Mode of Ratification may be proposed by the Congress; Provided that no Amendment which may be

* Changed by the Thirteenth Amendment.

made prior to the Year One thousand eight hundred and eight shall in any Manner affect the first and fourth Clauses in the Ninth Section of the first Article; and that no State, without its Consent, shall be deprived of its equal Suffrage in the Senate.

Article. VI.

All Debts contracted and Engagements entered into, before the Adoption of this Constitution, shall be as valid against the United States under this Constitution, as under the Confederation.

This Constitution, and the Laws of the United States which shall be made in Pursuance thereof; and all Treaties made, or which shall be made, under the Authority of the United States, shall be the supreme Law of the Land; and the Judges in every State shall be bound thereby, any Thing in the Constitution or Laws of any State to the Contrary notwithstanding.

The Senators and Representatives before mentioned, and the Members of the several State Legislatures, and all executive and judicial Officers, both of the United States and of the several States, shall be bound by Oath or Affirmation, to support this Constitution; but no religious Test shall ever be required as a Qualification to any Office or public Trust under the United States.

Article. VII.

The Ratification of the Conventions of nine States, shall be sufficient for the Establishment of this Constitution between the States so ratifying the Same.

Done in Convention by the unanimous Consent of the States present the Seventeenth Day of September in the Year of our Lord one thousand seven hundred and Eighty seven and of the Independence of the United States of America the Twelfth In Witness whereof We have hereunto subscribed our Names,

G.° Washington—Presid.ᵗ
and deputy from Virginia

New Hampshire *John Langdon*
Nicholas Gilman

Massachusetts *Nathaniel Gorham*
Rufus King

Connecticut *Wm. Saml. Johnson*
            Roger Sherman

New York *Alexander Hamilton*

New Jersey *Wil: Livingston*
            David Brearley
            Wm. Patterson
            Jona: Dayton

Pennsylvania *B Franklin*
              Thomas Mifflin
              Robt Morris
              Geo. Clymer
              Thos. FitzSimons
              Jared Ingersoll
              James Wilson
              Gouv Morris

Delaware *Geo: Read*
          Gunning Bedford jun
          John Dickinson
          Richard Bassett
          Jaco: Broom

Maryland *James McHenry*
          Dan of St Thos. Jenifer
          Danl Carroll

Virginia *John Blair—*
          James Madison Jr.

North Carolina *Wm. Blount*
                Richd. Dobbs Spaight
                Hu Williamson

South Carolina *J. Rutledge*
                Charles Cotesworth Pinckney
                Charles Pinckney
                Pierce Butler

Georgia *William Few*
         Abr Baldwin

Attest *William Jackson* Secretary

Amendments to the Constitution of the United States of America

Amendment I.*

Congress shall make no law respecting an establishment of religion, or prohibiting the free exercise thereof; or abridging the freedom of speech, or of the press, or the right of the people peaceably to assemble, and to petition the Government for a redress of grievances.

Amendment II.

A well regulated Militia, being necessary to the security of a free State, the right of the people to keep and bear Arms, shall not be infringed.

Amendment III.

No Soldier shall, in time of peace be quartered in any house, without the consent of the Owner, nor in time of war, but in a manner to be prescribed by law.

Amendment IV.

The right of the people to be secure in their persons, houses, papers, and effects, against unreasonable searches and seizures, shall not be violated, and no Warrants shall issue, but upon probable cause, supported by Oath or affirmation, and particularly describing the place to be searched, and the persons or things to be seized.

* The first ten Amendments (Bill of Rights) were ratified effective December 15, 1791.

Amendment V.

No person shall be held to answer for a capital, or otherwise infamous crime, unless on a presentment or indictment of a Grand Jury, except in cases arising in the land or naval forces, or in the Militia, when in actual service in time of War or public danger; nor shall any person be subject for the same offence to be twice put in jeopardy of life or limb, nor shall be compelled in any criminal case to be a witness against himself, nor be deprived of life, liberty, or property, without due process of law; nor shall private property be taken for public use without just compensation.

Amendment VI.

In all criminal prosecutions, the accused shall enjoy the right to a speedy and public trial, by an impartial jury of the State and district wherein the crime shall have been committed; which district shall have been previously ascertained by law, and to be informed of the nature and cause of the accusation; to be confronted with the witnesses against him; to have compulsory process for obtaining witnesses in his favor, and to have the assistance of counsel for his defence.

Amendment VII.

In Suits at common law, where the value in controversy shall exceed twenty dollars, the right of trial by jury shall be preserved, and no fact tried by a jury shall be otherwise re-examined in any Court of the United States, than according to the rules of the common law.

Amendment VIII.

Excessive bail shall not be required, nor excessive fines imposed, nor cruel and unusual punishments inflicted.

Amendment IX.

The enumeration in the Constitution of certain rights shall not be construed to deny or disparage others retained by the people.

Amendment X.

The powers not delegated to the United States by the Constitution, nor prohibited by it to the States, are reserved to the States respectively, or to the people.

Amendment XI.*

The Judicial power of the United States shall not be construed to extend to any suit in law or equity, commenced or prosecuted against one of the United States by Citizens of another State, or by Citizens or Subjects of any Foreign State.

Amendment XII.**

The Electors shall meet in their respective states, and vote by ballot for President and Vice President, one of whom, at least, shall not be an inhabitant of the same state with themselves; they shall name in their ballots the person voted for as President, and in distinct ballots the person voted for as Vice-President, and they shall make distinct lists of all persons voted for as President, and of all persons voted for as Vice-President, and of the number of votes for each, which lists they shall sign and certify, and transmit sealed to the seat of the government of the United States, directed to the President of the Senate;—The President of the Senate shall, in the presence of the Senate and House of Representatives, open all the certificates and the votes shall then be counted;—The person having the greatest number of votes for President, shall be the President, if such number be a majority of the whole number of Electors appointed; and if no person have such majority, then from the persons having the highest numbers not exceeding three on the list of those voted for as President, the House of Representatives shall choose immediately, by ballot, the President. But in choosing the President, the votes shall be taken by states, the representation from each state having one vote; a quorum for this purpose shall consist of a member or members from two-thirds of the states, and a majority of all the states shall be necessary to a choice. [And if the House of Representatives shall not choose a President whenever the right of choice shall devolve upon them, before the fourth day of March next following, then the Vice-President shall act as President, as in the case of the death or other constitutional disability of the President—]*** The person having the greatest number of votes as Vice-President, shall be the Vice-President, if such number be a majority of the whole number of Electors appointed, and if no person have a majority, then from the two highest numbers on the list,

---

* The Eleventh Amendment was ratified February 7, 1795.
** The Twelfth Amendment was ratified June 15, 1804.
*** Superseded by section 3 of the Twentieth Amendment.

the Senate shall choose the Vice-President; a quorum for the purpose shall consist of two-thirds of the whole number of Senators, and a majority of the whole number shall be necessary to a choice. But no person constitutionally ineligible to the office of President shall be eligible to that of Vice-President of the United States.

Amendment XIII.*

Section 1. Neither slavery nor involuntary servitude, except as a punishment for crime whereof the party shall have been duly convicted, shall exist within the United States, or any place subject to their jurisdiction.

Section 2. Congress shall have power to enforce this article by appropriate legislation.

Amendment XIV.**

Section 1. All persons born or naturalized in the United States and subject to the jurisdiction thereof, are citizens of the United States and of the State wherein they reside. No State shall make or enforce any law which shall abridge the privileges or immunities of citizens of the United States; nor shall any State deprive any person of life, liberty, or property, without due process of law; nor deny to any person within its jurisdiction the equal protection of the laws.

Section 2. Representatives shall be apportioned among the several States according to their respective numbers, counting the whole number of persons in each State, excluding Indians not taxed. But when the right to vote at any election for the choice of electors for President and Vice President of the United States, Representatives in Congress, the Executive and Judicial officers of a State, or the members of the Legislature thereof, is denied to any of the male inhabitants of such State, being twenty-one years of age, and citizens of the United States, or in any way abridged, except for participation in rebellion, or other crime, the basis of representation therein shall be reduced in the proportion which the number of such male citizens shall bear to the whole number of male citizens twenty-one years of age in such State.

---

* The Thirteenth Amendment was ratified December 6, 1865.
** The Fourteenth Amendment was ratified July 9, 1868.

Section 3. No person shall be a Senator or Representative in Congress, or elector of President and Vice President, or hold any office, civil or military, under the United States, or under any State, who, having previously taken an oath, as a member of Congress, or as an officer of the United States, or as a member of any State legislature, or as an executive or judicial officer of any State, to support the Constitution of the United States, shall have engaged in insurrection or rebellion against the same, or given aid or comfort to the enemies thereof. But Congress may by a vote of two-thirds of each House, remove such disability.

Section 4. The validity of the public debt of the United States, authorized by law, including debts incurred for payment of pensions and bounties for services in suppressing insurrection or rebellion, shall not be questioned. But neither the United States nor any State shall assume or pay any debt or obligation incurred in aid of insurrection or rebellion against the United States, or any claim for the loss or emancipation of any slave; but all such debts, obligations and claims shall be held illegal and void.

Section 5. The Congress shall have power to enforce, by appropriate legislation, the provisions of this article.

Amendment XV.*

Section 1. The right of citizens of the United States to vote shall not be denied or abridged by the United States or by any State on account of race, color, or previous conditions of servitude.
Section 2. The Congress shall have power to enforce this article by appropriate legislation.

Amendment XVI.**

The Congress shall have power to lay and collect taxes on incomes, from whatever source derived, without apportionment among the several States, and without regard to any census or enumeration.

Amendment XVII.***

The Senate of the United States shall be composed of two Senators from each State, elected by the people thereof, for six years; and each

---

* The Fifteenth Amendment was ratified February 3, 1870.
** The Sixteenth Amendment was ratified February 3, 1913.
*** The Seventeenth Amendment was ratified April 8, 1913.

Senator shall have one vote. The electors in each State shall have the qualifications requisite for electors of the most numerous branch of the State legislatures.

When vacancies happen in the representation of any State in the Senate, the executive authority of such State shall issue writs of election to fill such vacancies: *Provided,* That the legislature of any State may empower the executive thereof to make temporary appointments until the people fill the vacancies by election as the legislature may direct.

This amendment shall not be so construed as to affect the election or term of any Senator chosen before it becomes valid as part of the Constitution.

Amendment XVIII.*

[**Section 1.** After one year from the ratification of this article the manufacture, sale, or transportation of intoxicating liquors within, the importation thereof into, or the exportation thereof from the United States and all territory subject to the jurisdiction thereof for beverage purposes is hereby prohibited.

Section 2. The Congress and the several States shall have concurrent power to enforce this article by appropriate legislation.

Section 3. This article shall be inoperative unless it shall have been ratified as an amendment to the Constitution by the legislatures of the several States, as provided in the Constitution, within seven years from the date of the submission hereof to the States by the Congress.]

Amendment XIX.**

The right of citizens of the United States to vote shall not be denied or abridged by the United States or by any State on account of sex.

Congress shall have power to enforce this article by appropriate legislation.

Amendment XX.***

Section 1. The terms of the President and the Vice President shall end at noon on the 20th day of January, and the terms of Senators and

---

* The Eighteenth Amendment was ratified January 16, 1919. It was repealed by the Twenty-first Amendment, December 5, 1933.
** The Nineteenth Amendment was ratified August 18, 1920.
*** The Twentieth Amendment was ratified January 23, 1933.

Representatives at noon on the 3rd day of January, of the years in which such terms would have ended if this article had not been ratified; and the terms of their successors shall then begin.

Section 2. The Congress shall assemble at least once in every year, and such meeting shall begin at noon on the 3rd day of January, unless they shall by law appoint a different day.

Section 3. If, at the time fixed for the beginning of the term of the President, the President elect shall have died, the Vice President elect shall become President. If a President shall not have been chosen before the time fixed for the beginning of his term, or if the President elect shall have failed to qualify, then the Vice President elect shall act as President until a President shall have qualified; and the Congress may by law provide for the case wherein neither a President elect nor a Vice President elect shall have qualified, declaring who shall then act as President, or the manner in which one who is to act shall be selected, and such person shall act accordingly until a President or Vice President shall have qualified.

Section 4. The Congress may by law provide for the case of the death of any of the persons from whom the House of Representatives may choose a President whenever the right of choice shall have devolved upon them, and for the case of the death of any of the persons from whom the Senate may choose a Vice President whenever the right of choice shall have devolved upon them.

Section 5. Sections 1 and 2 shall take effect on the 15th day of October following the ratification of this article.

Section 6. This article shall be inoperative unless it shall have been ratified as an amendment to the Constitution by the legislatures of three-fourths of the several States within seven years from the date of its submission.

Amendment XXI.*

Section 1. The eighteenth article of amendment to the Constitution of the United States is hereby repealed.

* The Twenty-first Amendment was ratified December 5, 1933.

Section 2. The transportation or importation into any State, Territory, or possession of the United States for delivery or use therein of intoxicating liquors, in violation of the laws thereof, is hereby prohibited.

Section 3. The article shall be inoperative unless it shall have been ratified as an amendment to the Constitution by conventions in the several States, as provided in the Constitution, within seven years from the date of the submission hereof to the States by the Congress.

Amendment XXII.*

Section 1. No person shall be elected to the office of the President more than twice, and no person who has held the office of President, or acted as President, for more than two years of a term to which some other person was elected President shall be elected to the office of the President more than once. But this Article shall not apply to any person holding the office of President when this Article was proposed by the Congress, and shall not prevent any person who may be holding the office of President, or acting as President, during the term within which this Article becomes operative from holding the office of President or acting as President during the remainder of such term.

Section 2. This article shall be inoperative unless it shall have been ratified as an amendment to the Constitution by the legislatures of three-fourths of the several States within seven years from the date of its submission to the States by the Congress.

Amendment XXIII.**

Section 1. The District constituting the seat of Government of the United States shall appoint in such manner as the Congress may direct:

A number of electors of President and Vice President equal to the whole number of Senators and Representatives in Congress to which the District would be entitled if it were a State, but in no event more than the least populous State; they shall be in addition to those appointed by the States, but they shall be considered, for the purposes of the election of President and Vice President, to be electors appointed by a State; and they shall meet

* The Twenty-second Amendment was ratified February 27, 1951.
** The Twenty-third Amendment was ratified March 29, 1961.

in the District and perform such duties as provided by the twelfth article of amendment.

Section 2. The Congress shall have power to enforce this article by appropriate legislation.

Amendment XXIV.*

Section 1. The right of citizens of the United States to vote in any primary or other election for President or Vice President, for electors for President or Vice President, or for Senator or Representative in Congress, shall not be denied or abridged by the United States or any State by reason of failure to pay any poll tax or other tax.

Section 2. The Congress shall have the power to enforce this article by appropriate legislation.

Amendment XXV.**

Section 1. In case of the removal of the President from office or of his death or resignation, the Vice President shall become President.

Section 2. Whenever there is a vacancy in the office of the Vice President, the President shall nominate a Vice President who shall take office upon confirmation by a majority vote of both Houses of Congress.

Section 3. Whenever the President transmits to the President pro tempore of the Senate and the Speaker of the House of Representatives his written declaration that he is unable to discharge the powers and duties of his office, and until he transmits to them a written declaration to the contrary, such powers and duties shall be discharged by the Vice President as Acting President.

Section 4. Whenever the Vice President and a majority of either the principal officers of the executive departments or of such other body as Congress may by law provide, transmit to the President pro tempore of the Senate and the Speaker of the House of Representatives their written declaration that the President is unable to discharge the powers and duties of his office, the Vice President shall immediately assume the powers and duties of the office as Acting President.

Thereafter, when the President transmits to the President pro tempore of the Senate and the Speaker of the House of Representatives his written

* The Twenty-fourth Amendment was ratified January 23, 1964.
** The Twenty-fifth Amendment was ratified February 10, 1967.

declaration that no inability exists, he shall resume the powers and duties of his office unless the Vice President and a majority of either the principal officers of the executive department or of such other body as Congress may by law provide, transmit within four days to the President pro tempore of the Senate and the Speaker of the House of Representatives their written declaration that the President is unable to discharge the powers and duties of his office. Thereupon Congress shall decide the issue, assembling within forty-eight hours for that purpose if not in session. If the Congress, within twenty-one days after receipt of the latter written declaration, or, if Congress is not in session, within twenty-one days after Congress is required to assemble, determines by two-thirds vote of both Houses that the President is unable to discharge the powers and duties of his office, the Vice President shall continue to discharge the same as Acting President; otherwise, the President shall resume the powers and duties of his office.

Amendment XXVI*

Section 1. The right of citizens of the United States, who are eighteen years of age or older, to vote shall not be denied or abridged by the United States or by any State on account of age.

Section 2. The Congress shall have power to enforce this article by appropriate legislation.

---

* The Twenty-sixth Amendment was ratified July 1, 1971.

Notes

Preface

1. Martin Diamond, *The Federalist*, in Leo Strauss et al., *History of Political Philosophy*, 553 (1963).
2. 228 U.S. 118 (1912).
3. 312 U.S. 52 (1941).
4. 453 U.S. 654 (1981).
5. Joseph Story, *Commentaries on the Constitution of the United States*, vol. I (Cambridge, Mass.: Hilliard Gray and Company, 1883), v.

Editor's Preface

1. Alexander Hamilton, James Madison, and John Jay, *The Federalist Papers,* ed. Clinton Rossiter (New York: New American Library, 1961), vii.
2. Page Smith, *The Shaping of America: A People's History of the Young Republic,* vol. III (New York: McGraw-Hill Book Company, 1980), 105.

Introduction

1. Page Smith describes this transition as the demise of Classical-Christian and the rise of Secular-Democratic thought in American life. Page Smith, *The Shaping of America: A People's History of the Young Republic,* vol. III (New York: McGraw-Hill Book Company, 1980), xxiii.
2. The extensive debates, ample political literature, and intellectual ferment of this period are chronicled in Gordon S. Wood, *The Creation of the American Republic, 1776–1787* (New York: W. W. Norton & Company, 1972).
3. Robert A. Ferguson, "'We Do Ordain and Establish': The Constitution as Literary Text" (unpublished ms., Williamsburg, Va., 1987), 26.
4. For a discussion of pamphlet literature and intellectual ferment in this period, see

Bernard Bailyn, *The Ideological Origins of the American Revolution* (Cambridge: The Belknap Press of Harvard University Press, 1992).

5. Julien P. Boyd, ed., *The Papers of Thomas Jefferson*, vol. 12 (Princeton, N.J.: Princeton University Press, 1955), 276.

6. Quoted in Catherine Drinker Bowen, *Miracle at Philadelphia: The Story of the Constitutional Convention May to September 1787* (Boston: Little, Brown and Company, 1986), 263.

7. Quoted in Samuel Eliot Morison, *The Oxford History of the American People* (New York: Oxford University Press, 1965), 308.

8. The literature on the Anti-Federalists is voluminous; for example, see Jackson Turner Main, *The AntiFederalists, Critics of the Constitution, 1781–1788* (New York: W. W. Norton & Company, 1974).

9. Quoted in James Madison, Alexander Hamilton, and John Jay, *The Federalist Papers*, ed. Isaac Kramnick (London: Penguin Books, 1987), 75.

10. Ralph Ketchum, *James Madison, A Biography* (Charlottesville: University of Virginia Press, 1990), ix.

11. I am grateful to Professor William F. Harris of the University of Pennsylvania's political science department for calling my attention to this image. Ketchum, in *James Madison,* also writes: "Madison saw at Princeton David Rittenhouse's intricate orrery, demonstrating the clock-like precision of the heavenly bodies as they moved in their perfectly predictable orbits. Its patterned motion was always the metaphor for Madison's concept of the way his world operated" (p. 50).

12. Morris to J. Penn, May 20, 1774, in U.S. Congress, *American Archives*, comp. Peter Force, vol. I (Washington, D.C.: 1837–53), 342–343.

13. *Miracle at Philadelphia,* 232.

14. *The Debate of the State Conventions on the Adoption of the Federal Constitution, as Recommended by the General Convention at Philadelphia in 1787,* ed. J. Elliot, vol. II (Philadelphia: 1886), 301.

15. Julien P. Boyd, ed., *The Papers of Thomas Jefferson*, vol. 12 (Princeton, N.J.: Princeton University Press, 1955), 278.

16. Max Farrand, ed., *The Records of the Federal Convention of 1787,* vol. I (New Haven: Yale University Press, 1966), 136.

17. "Philadelphiansis: A Critic of the Constitution," in *The Declaration of Independence and the Constitution,* ed. E. Latham (Lexington, Mass.: Heath, 1976), 176–177.

18. Quoted in William Lee Miller, *The Business of May Next, James Madison and the Founding* (Charlottesville: University of Virginia Press, 1992), 228.

19. Henry quoted in *Oxford History,* 315.

20. Warren E. Burger, foreword to *Miracle at Philadelphia,* ix.

21. Forrest McDonald, *Novus Ordo Seclorum: The Intellectual Origins of the Constitution* (Lawrence: University Press of Kansas, 1985).

22. Richard Hofstadter, *The American Political Tradition and the Men Who Made It* (New York: Vintage Books, 1955), 7.

23. Ibid., 3.

24. *James Madison, A Biography,* 50.

25. John C. Fitzpatrick, ed., *The Writings of George Washington,* vol. 30, June 20, 1788–January 21, 1790 (Washington, D.C.: United States Government Printing Office, 1939), 66.

Federalist Paper No. 6

1. The League of Cambry, comprehending the Emperor, the King of France, the King of Aragon, and most of the Italian princes and states.
2. The Duke of Marlborough.
3. *Vide Principes des Négociations* par l'Abbé de Mably.

Federalist Paper No. 8

1. This objection will be fully examined in its proper place, and it will be shown that the only rational precaution which could have been taken on this subject has been taken; and a much better one than is to be found in any constitution that has been heretofore framed in America, most of which contain no guard at all on this subject.

Federalist Paper No. 9

1. *Spirit of Laws,* Vol. I, Book IX, Chap. I.

Federalist Paper No. 15

1. "I mean for the Union."

Federalist Paper No. 70

1. New York has no council except for the single purpose of appointing to offices; New Jersey has a council whom the governor may consult. But I think, from the terms of the Constitution, their resolutions do not bind him.
2. Delolme.
3. Ten.

Federalist Paper No. 78

1. The celebrated Montesquieu, speaking of them, says: "Of the three powers above mentioned, the judiciary is next to nothing."—*Spirit of Laws,* Vol. I, page 186.
2. *Idem,* page 181.
3. *Vide Protest of the Minority of the Convention of Pennsylvania,* Martin's speech, etc.

Federalist Paper No. 79

1. *Vide Constitution of Massachusetts,* Chapter 2, Section I, Article 13.

Federalist Paper No. 84

1. *Vide* Blackstone's *Commentaries,* Vol. I, page 136.
2. Sir William Blackstone (1723–80) published the most widely cited text in Anglo-

American constitutional law, his *Commentaries on the Laws of England,* between 1765 and 1769. By 1787 ten editions of this standard work had appeared in print.—Ed.

3. *Idem,* Vol. 4, page 438.

4. To show that there is a power in the Constitution by which the liberty of the press may be affected, recourse has been had to the power of taxation. It is said that duties may be laid upon the publications so high as to amount to a prohibition. I know not by what logic it could be maintained that the declarations in the State constitutions, in favor of the freedom of the press, would be a constitutional impediment of the imposition of duties upon publications by the state legislatures. It cannot certainly be pretended that any degree of duties, however low, would be an abridgment of the liberty of the press. We know that newspapers are taxed in Great Britain, and yet it is notorious that the press nowhere enjoys greater liberty than in that country. And if duties of any kind may be laid without a violation of that liberty, it is evident that the extent must depend on legislative discretion, regulated by public opinion; so that, after all, general declarations respecting the liberty of the press will give it no greater security than it will have without them. The same invasions of it may be effected under the State constitutions which contain those declarations through the means of taxation, as under the proposed Constituiton, which has nothing of the kind. It would be quite as significant to declare that government ought to be free, that taxes ought not to be excessive, etc., as that the liberty of the press ought not to be restrained.

5. *Vide* Rutherford's *Institutes,* Vol. 2, Book 11, Chapter X, Sections XIV and XV. *Vide* also Grotius, Book 11, Chapter IX, Sections VIII and IX.

Federalist Paper No. 85

1. Entitled "An Address to the People of the State of New York."
2. It may rather be said ten, for though two thirds may set on foot the measure, three fourths must ratify.
3. Hume's *Essays,* Vol. 1, page 128: "The Rise of Arts and Sciences."

Index

Page numbers in **boldface** refer to the text of the *Federalist Papers*.

About the Editor

Frederick Quinn, like the authors of *The Federalist Papers* themselves, has a strong interest in the Constitution, and he approaches the papers with broad and varied experience as a historian and a career foreign service officer. Quinn, working closely with former Chief Justice Warren E. Burger, served as International Coordinator for the Bicentennial of the U.S. Constitution, promoting an exchange of ideas among constitutionalists around the world.

As a foreign service officer, Quinn has engaged in discussions of the issues of democratic governance in Czechoslovakia and in various nations of Asia, Africa, and Latin America. He has lectured widely on the Constitution at universities and colleges in the United States as well.

Quinn received his Ph.D. in history from the University of California at Los Angeles. He also has master's degrees from UCLA in modern European history and African history, anthropology, and literature. His B.A. is from Allegheny College. He has published extensively in scholarly and popular journals.